The Best Of *The Mailbox*®—Book 3
Intermediate Edition

W9-BGG-112

Our favorite ideas from the 1993–1997 issues of the Intermediate edition
of *The Mailbox*® magazine

Editor in Chief
Margaret Michel

Product Director
Kathy Wolf

Editor
Becky Andrews

Copy Editors
Lynn Bemer Coble, Karen L. Huffman,
Jennifer Rudisill, Debbie Shoffner, Gina Sutphin

Artists
Jennifer Tipton Bennett, Cathy Spangler Bruce, Pam Crane, Clevell Harris, Susan Hodnett, Sheila
Krill, Mary Lester, Rob Mayworth, Kimberly Richard, Rebecca Saunders, Barry Slate, Donna K. Teal

Cover Artist
Jeannine Lorenz

Typographers
Scott Lyons
Lynette Maxwell

About This Book

Since its publication in 1988, the first *Best Of* The Mailbox®—*Intermediate* book has become one of the most popular titles available to teachers of grades 4–6 today. In 1994 we presented the second in the series, *The Best Of* The Mailbox®—*Book 2* (Intermediate edition), which proved to be another favorite with teachers. Now we're proud to present the newest *Best Of* The Mailbox® book for intermediate teachers. Inside these covers, you'll find many of the best teacher-tested ideas published in *The* Intermediate *Mailbox*® since 1993. Our editors selected these practical ideas from those sent to us by teachers across the United States. We've included many of our regularly featured sections of the magazine plus special teaching units and reproducibles.

www.themailbox.com

Table Of Contents

BULLETIN BOARDS

Bulletin Boards ....

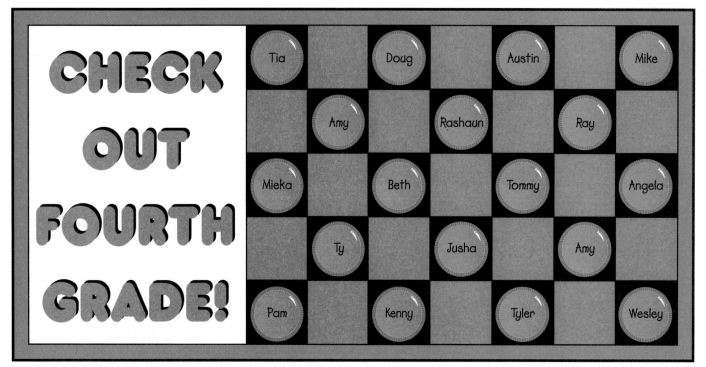

Check out the ease and eye-catching appeal of this simple back-to-school display! Cover a board with red and black sheets of construction paper to make a giant checkerboard. Use a black permanent marker to label red, plastic picnic plates with student names. Add the plates to the checkerboard background.

Ronda Pek—Gr. 4, North Muskegon Public Schools, North Muskegon, MI

This bulletin board is the centerpiece of my back-to-school classroom decor based on a theater theme. I also display book posters around the classroom instead of movie posters. When students arrive on the first day, I greet them at the door and give each one a ticket. These tickets are redeemed later in the day for popcorn. What a fun way to give students a sneak preview of the great year ahead!

Susan Barnett—Gr. 6, Northwest Elementary, Fort Wayne, IN

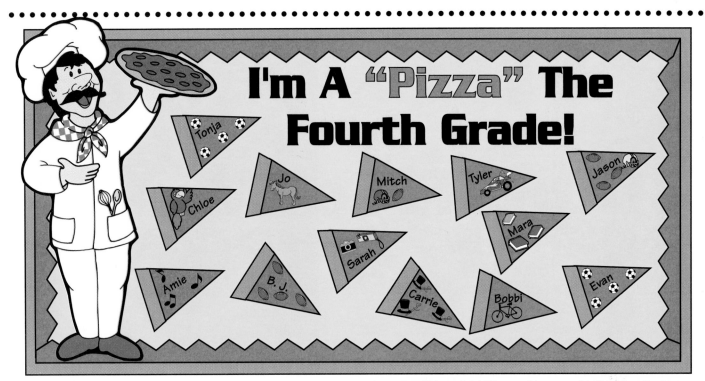

I'm A "Pizza" The Fourth Grade!

No matter how you slice it, this student-created bulletin board will be a hit! First enlarge and color the chef pattern on page 19. Next provide each student with a wedge-shaped sheet of art paper. Instruct each student to write his name on the wedge in large black letters, then add small symbols on the wedge as pizza ingredients. These symbols should represent interests of the student: hobbies, sports, favorite books, etc. After outlining the ingredients with a black marker, have each student color his pizza slice bright red. (For a related art activity, see page 49.)

Perry Stio—Gr. 4, M. L. King School, Piscataway, NJ

What A Match!

On the first day of school, provide each student with one white and one pastel sheet of construction paper. Instruct students to fold each sheet in half; then have each child attach a school photo of himself to the inside bottom of the colored sheet. (If a photo is unavailable, have the student draw a self-portrait.) Inside the white sheet, have each student write descriptive words and phrases about himself. Collect the completed sheets. Number the colored ones and letter the white ones; then post them on a bulletin board as shown. After a week of getting to know one another, play the Match Game. Have students take turns calling numbers and letters from the papers until each photo and description are matched.

The best part of this good-work display is preparing the background paper! Cover a bulletin board with white (or any light-colored) paper. Pour several colors of fluorescent paints in pie pans. Have each student gently place his hand, palm down, in a pan of paint, then make a handprint on the bulletin-board paper. When the paint has dried, use the board for highlighting students' outstanding work.

Shannon Berry—Gr. 4, Heritage Christian School, Brookfield, WI

Combine reading and geography with an easy-to-make display. Mount a world map on a bulletin board. Each time your class reads a book, discuss the book's setting and locate it on the map. Label a construction-paper suitcase (pattern on page 20) with the book's title, author, and setting; then use yarn and a pushpin to connect the suitcase to the location on the map.

adapted from an idea by Marta Johnson—Gr. 4, Haw Creek School, Asheville, NC

You can bank on improving vocabularies with this interactive display! Use the pattern on page 21 to make a large piggy bank for the board. Label 24 green index cards with alphabet letters as shown. Punch a hole in the upper right corner of each card; then place the card on a metal ring. Mount the 24 rings on the board with pushpins. Punch holes in more blank cards. Store the cards in a basket labeled "Deposit Slips." When a student finds a new word in his reading, he writes it on a blank card; then he writes the definition and his name on the back of the card. The student adds, or deposits, the card into the word bank by placing it on the correct ring (behind the letter card). When you have a few extra minutes, take a ring from the board and review the words with students.

Marilyn Crenshaw—Gr. 4
David Elementary
The Woodlands, TX

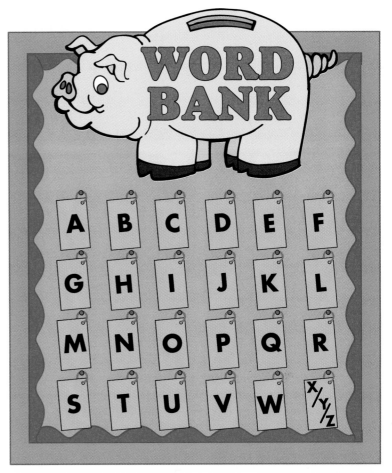

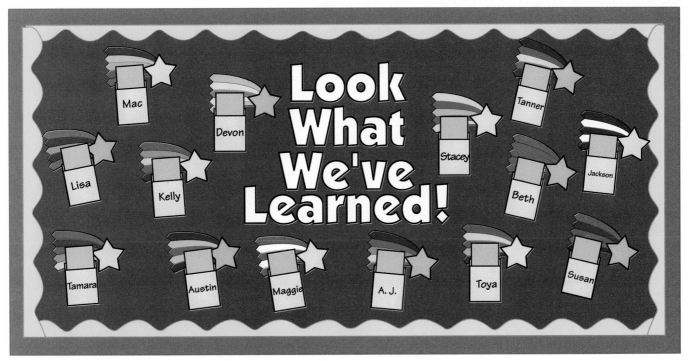

This simple display invites students to share what they've learned. Write the name of each student on a library card pocket; then attach the pockets to the board. Provide each student with a copy of the star pattern on page 22 to decorate and mount near his pocket. Each week place a colored strip of paper inside every pocket. During that week, each child labels his strip with something he has learned; then he places the strip back in his pocket. At the end of the grading term, staple each student's strips together and send them home to his parents.

Lisa Curry—Gr. 4, River Oaks Baptist School, Houston, TX

Here's a group assignment display that doubles as a class photo gallery. Cut out one artist palette for each group. Label a construction-paper circle for each student. To assign students to groups, place the circles on the palettes. To reassign groups, simply move the circles. Display photos of group activities on the board also.

Cathy Ogg—Gr. 4, Happy Valley Elementary, Johnson City, TN

Motivate your class to consider the qualities of good character with this display. Pin two lengths of cord across a board. Have students brainstorm a list of positive character traits; then have each child write one trait on a clothing cutout to clip on the clotheslines. Each morning choose several traits for students to discuss and write about in their journals.

Beverly Langland, Trinity Christian Academy, Jacksonville, FL

LOOK "WHOOO'S" WORKED HARD!

To make a good work display for all seasons, duplicate the owl on page 23 for each child. After students color, cut out, and label the owls with their names, mount the birds on a paper tree. Have students use the patterns on page 23 to make fall leaves for the scene. In the winter, remove the leaves and add student-made snowflakes. For spring, have students add green leaves and tissue-paper blossoms.

Courtney Lemmons—Gr. 5, Pioneer Intermediate School, Noble, OK

Featuring Fall's Finest!

Create an appealing display that's perfect for showing off fall's finest student work. Staple a large orange garbage bag (the type decorated with a jack-o'-lantern's face) to the board, leaving the top unstapled. Stuff wadded-up pieces of newspaper between the board and the bag to make a three-dimensional pumpkin. Tie off the top of the bag with black ribbon. Duplicate the leaf pattern on page 25 on red, orange, and yellow construction paper. Have each student select a piece of work to display; then have him write his reasons for selecting the piece on a duplicated leaf. Staple each child's leaf and paper around the pumpkin. The Great Pumpkin never looked better!

Gena Capps, Dalewood Elementary, Nashville, TN

What pet peeve drives you batty? Have students interview family members and friends to find out their pet peeves. Give each student a bat pattern (see page 24) to trace on black paper. Then have him cut out the bat and embellish it with paper eyes and fangs. Instruct the student to cut out one white and one black cloud from paper; then have him describe a pet peeve on the white cloud. Arrange the bat and cloud shapes on a board as shown.

Julia Alarie—Gr. 6, Essex Middle School, Essex, VT

In October, my students complete a lesson on feelings—what causes them and how they are expressed on our faces. Each student draws a caricature of a feeling we discussed (see the list below) on a pumpkin pattern (page 24). We then feature our patch of portraits on a colorful fall bulletin board.

Lynn Marie Gilbertson—Gr. 4
James Sales Elementary
Tacoma, WA

exhausted	enraged
confused	ashamed
ecstatic	cautious
guilty	smug
suspicious	depressed
angry	overwhelmed
hysterical	hopeful
frustrated	lonely
sad	lovestruck
confident	jealous
embarrassed	bored
happy	surprised
mischievous	anxious
disgusted	shocked
frightened	shy

Generate a bounty of gratitude with this unique display and classroom challenge. Enlarge and color the turkey pattern on page 25 to mount on the board. Duplicate the form on page 25 on yellow construction paper. Challenge your students to complete as many forms as possible in order to reach a class total of one million items for which students are thankful! If desired, invite another class or an entire grade level to join you in the fun.

Julia Alarie—Gr. 6, Essex Middle School, Essex, VT

Colorful word birds flock to this seasonal display! Duplicate the patterns on page 26. Have each child write a tired word such as *said* or *get* on the turkey; then have him use a thesaurus and a black marker to label his bird's feathers with synonyms. For a 3-D effect, accordion-fold a small strip of paper. Glue one end of the strip to the turkey and the other end to the feathers before attaching the bird to the board.

Deborah Marik and Ruth Lees—Gr. 5, Southeast Middle School, Ravenna, OH

"How would you promote world peace?" Encourage students to think about this question; then have each child write his idea on a half sheet of paper. Duplicate the dove pattern (page 27) for each student. Instruct each student to cut out the pattern and place its dotted edge on the fold of a folded piece of white paper; then have him trace the pattern and cut it out. After unfolding the cutout, have the student glue it and his writing on a sheet of dark blue paper as shown. Have him label his dove cutout with one of the peace words listed on page 27.

adapted from an idea by Pamela J. Fox—Gr. 4, Bixby Public Schools, Bixby, OK

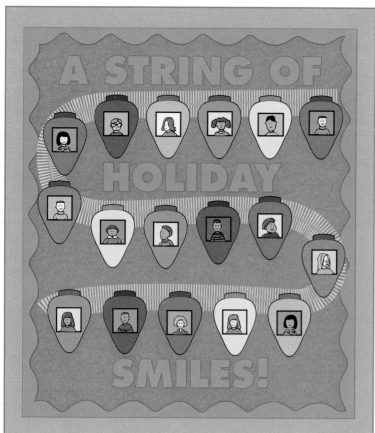

To make this cheery holiday display, duplicate a tree-light pattern (page 28) on several different colors of construction paper. Have each student cut out a pattern and glue a photo of himself onto it. Mount the lights on a garland that has been attached to a board as shown.

A few days before students head home for the holidays, give each child his light and another light pattern that has been cut from tagboard. Have the student glue the colored light onto the tagboard pattern and write a message to his parents on the back. Laminate the lights; then punch a hole in the top of each one and insert an inexpensive key ring. How's that for turning a bulletin board into wonderful holiday gifts?

Jan Drehmel—Gr. 4
Korger Chestnut School
Chippewa Falls, WI

Make your classroom more cozy with a holiday display full of warm wishes. First have each student create a construction-paper quilt square similar to the examples shown. Then have him use paper, yarn, and bits of cloth to create a face that resembles his own. Arrange the quilt squares on a white background and add a scalloped dust ruffle across the bottom. Mount several of the faces in a row across the top. Replace the faces every few days until each student has displayed his creation.

Julia Alarie—Gr. 6, Essex Middle School, Essex, VT

Wrap up the year with a display of your students' favorite books. Give each student a white, paper rectangle to decorate as a gift box. Have the student top her "box" with the bow and tag patterns on page 27. After each student decorates her package and bow, have her label the tag with the title and author of her favorite book. Add a festive touch by mounting ribbon, wrapping paper rolls, scissors, and tape on the bulletin board.

Catha Stroupe and Beth White—Media Center, Central Middle School, Dobson, NC

What's a new year without some super goals? Instruct each student to brainstorm a list of New Year's resolutions. Duplicate the football and helmet patterns on page 29. Have each student write his resolutions on a football. Display each football with a helmet that has been decorated with a student's photo and his favorite team colors. Write a list of class resolutions on a football pattern; then post it with a class picture as shown.

Michelle Calcaterra—Gr. 5, Rock Springs Elementary, Apopka, FL

After discussing the goals Dr. Martin Luther King, Jr., had for solving problems peacefully, have each student think of someone in his own life with whom he needs to make peace. Have the student write a peace treaty naming that person, explaining why he wants peace with him or her, and stating the terms of the peace. Instruct the student to copy his treaty onto a dove pattern (page 30); then have him trace and cut out another pattern from black paper. Staple each white dove over a black dove to create a shadow effect.

Kelly L. Simpson—Gr. 4, Newbury Elementary, Howell, NJ

The weather outside may be frightful, but the reading incentive of this display is delightful! Duplicate copies of the snowflake book-report form on page 28. Have students cut out, color, and complete these forms when they want to recommend cool books they've read. Add a large snowman and small student-made snowflakes to the display for a wintry touch.

Gloria Twohig—Librarian, St. Matthew's School, Campbellsport, WI

Piece together facts about famous African-Americans during Afro-American History Month with this eye-catching display. Duplicate a class supply of the pattern on page 31. Have each student write the name of a famous African-American in the center square; then have him color the rest of the pattern. Mount the patterns to make a giant quilt. Choose one square from the quilt each morning during February; then have the student who researched that famous figure share facts about him or her. Use this same idea to introduce students to one another at the beginning of a new school year. Title that board "Piecing Together A New Class."

Colleen Dabney—Gr. 5
Williamsburg Christian Academy
Williamsburg, VA

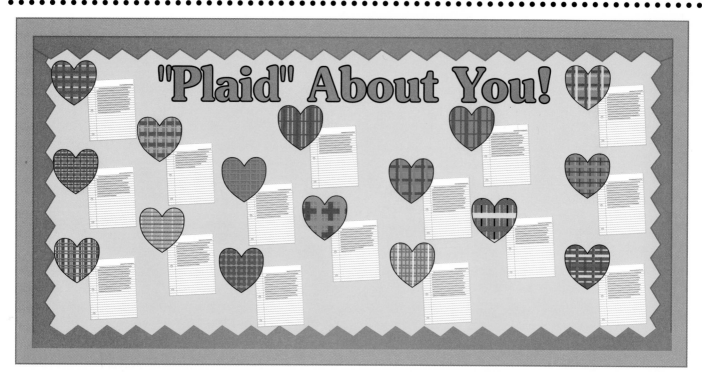

For a bright Valentine's Day display, have each student create her own heart-shaped tartan. Explain to students that a *tartan* is a plaid pattern consisting of stripes of various widths and colors. The stripes cross at right angles against a solid background. Have each student fill a sheet of white construction paper with her tartan, using colored pencils, crayons, or markers; then have her cut a heart shape from the paper. Ask each student to write a paragraph about someone she is mad about. Post the paragraphs among the hearts.

Lisa Borgo—Gr. 4, East Hanover, NJ

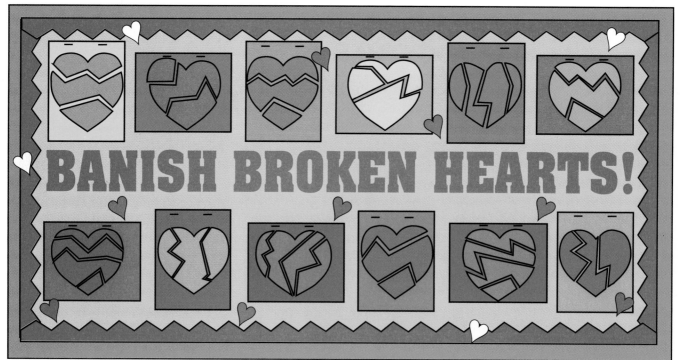

Have each student lightly draw two or more horizontal, diagonal, or vertical zigzag lines on a cut-out heart. After cutting along the lines, the student glues the pieces as shown on a contrasting color of paper. As a class, brainstorm conflicts that often arise between friends, family members, classmates, etc. Have each student write a solution to one of the problems on another sheet of paper. Place each child's heart project atop his solution; then staple the two papers at the top and mount them on the board.

Jackie M. Matthys—Gr. 4, Jackson-Keller Elementary, San Antonio, TX

Mount a label for each cooperative team as shown. Duplicate the book-report form on page 32; then place copies in a pocket attached to the pot of gold. Each time a team member completes one of the book-report forms, staple a $1 bill of play money above her team's label. (If the resulting bar graph begins to creep too high up the board, replace each set of $1 bills with a $5 bill.) The challenge to add another greenback to the board will spur students on to READ!

Marge McClintock—Gr. 5, Allen W. Roberts School, New Providence, NJ

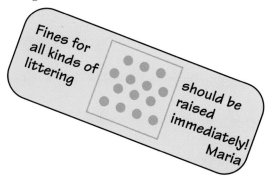

Culminate an environmental unit or celebrate Earth Day in April with a display that challenges everyone to pamper our planet. Paint a large earth on butcher paper and cut it out; then add facial features, a thermometer, and several real Band-Aids® bandages as shown. Have each student trace and cut out a bandage pattern from manila paper. Have the student label the cutout with his ideas for healing the earth's environmental woes. Mount the cutouts around the globe for a thought-provoking display.

Karen Krumanocker—Gr. 5
Rockland Elementary
Fleetwood, PA

For an end-of-the-year display that's a flock of fun to make, have each of several groups make a birdhouse from a paper grocery bag. Mount the houses as shown. On the display, have each student add a cut-out bird labeled with a sentence describing her favorite activity of the year. At the start of next year, post the houses and birds again with the title "Fifth Grade's Going To Be A Flock Of Fun!"

Colleen Dabney—Grs. 6–7
Williamsburg Christian Academy
Williamsburg, VA

Say good-bye to the school year with this simple display. Cover a bulletin board with paper. Add the title, "We're Signing Off!", and an enlarged copy of the sign painter character on page 32. Have each student record his most memorable moment directly on the board. As students enjoy the freedom of "writing on the board," you'll gain insight into the school-year events that left an impact.

Julie Plowman—Gr. 6, Adair-Casey Elementary, Adair, IA

Pattern

Use with the bulletin board on page 6.

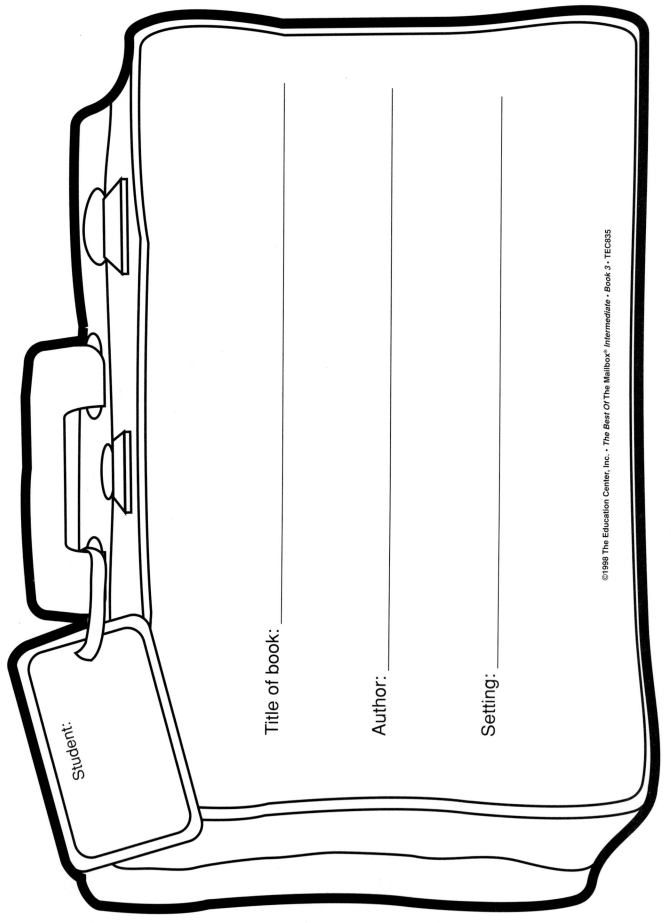

Title of book: _____

Author: _____

Setting: _____

Student:

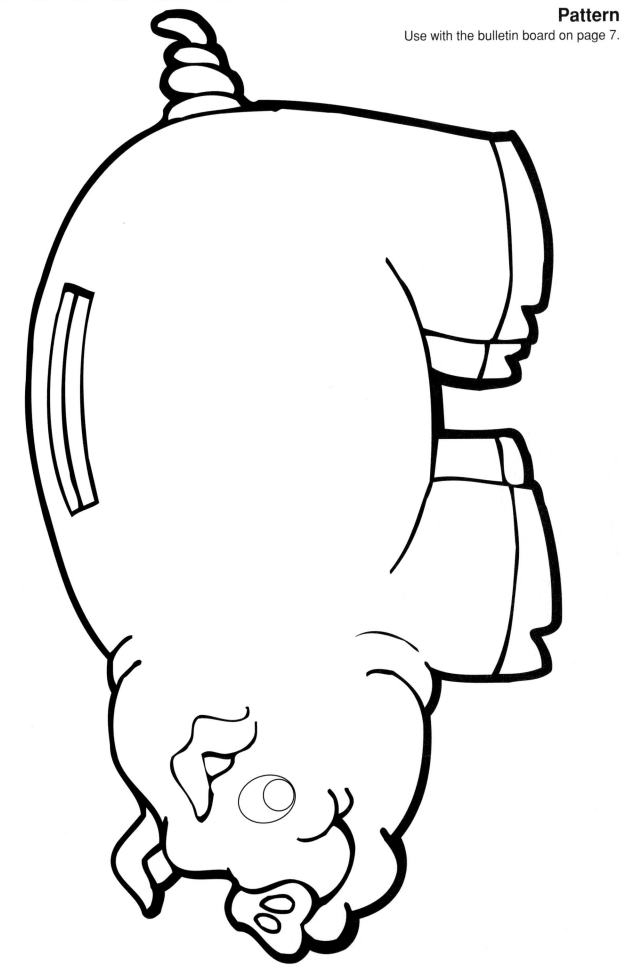

Pattern

Use with the bulletin board on page 7.

Patterns

Use with the bulletin boards on page 10.

THANKS A MILLION!

I am thankful for my

_____
number

_____ !
items

Illustrate what you're thankful for below.

Name _____

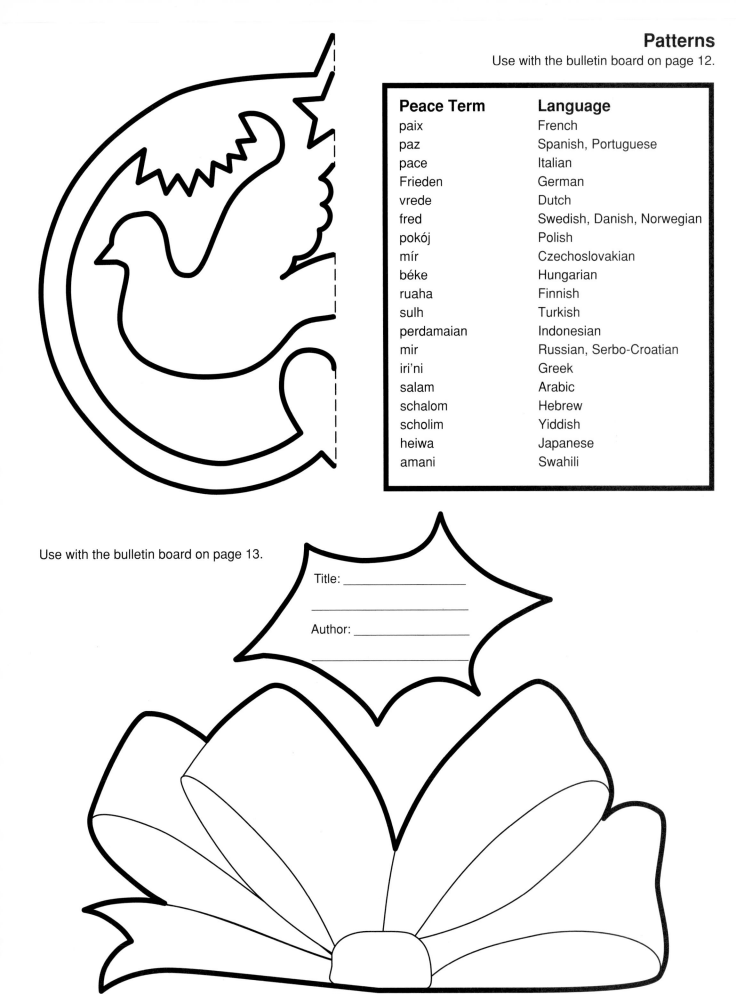

Peace Term	Language
paix	French
paz	Spanish, Portuguese
pace	Italian
Frieden	German
vrede	Dutch
fred	Swedish, Danish, Norwegian
pokój	Polish
mír	Czechoslovakian
béke	Hungarian
ruaha	Finnish
sulh	Turkish
perdamaian	Indonesian
mir	Russian, Serbo-Croatian
iri'ni	Greek
salam	Arabic
schalom	Hebrew
scholim	Yiddish
heiwa	Japanese
amani	Swahili

Use with the bulletin board on page 13.

Title: _____

_____

Author: _____

_____

Patterns

Use with the bulletin board on page 15.

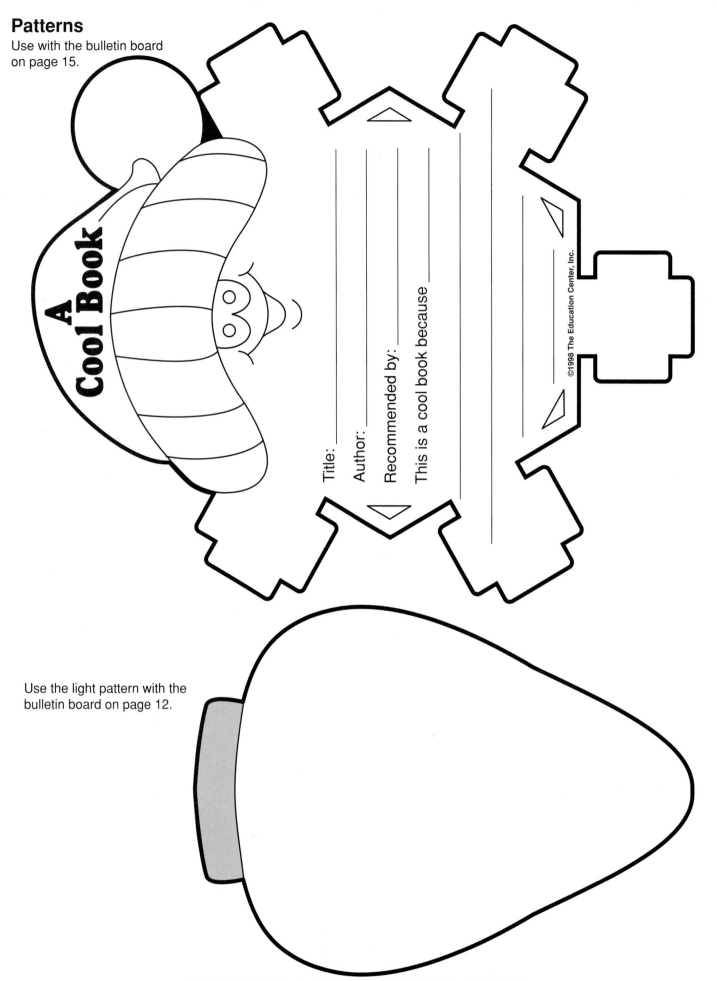

A Cool Book

Title: _____

Author: _____

Recommended by: _____

This is a cool book because _____

©1998 The Education Center, Inc.

Use the light pattern with the bulletin board on page 12.

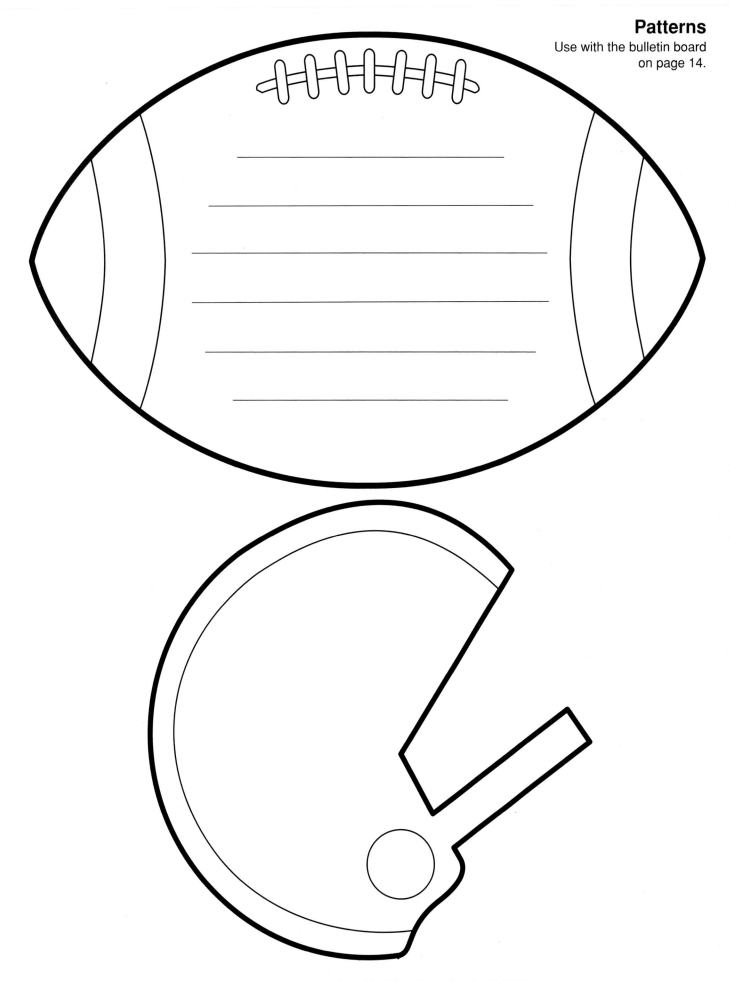

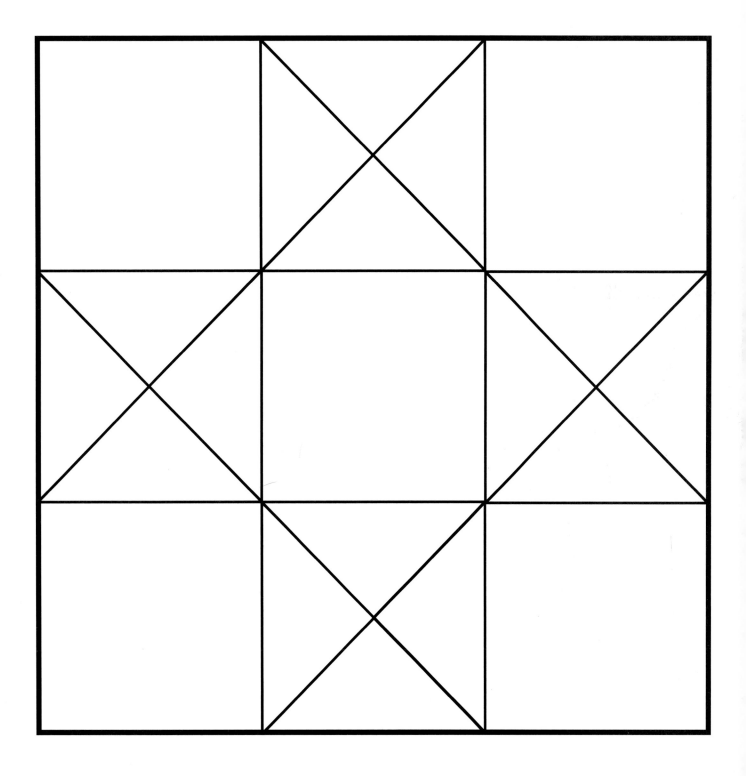

Patterns

Use with the bulletin board on page 17.

Reading 'N' Riches

Book-Report Form

Name: _____

Team: _____

Title of book: _____

Author: _____

Type of book: _____

Write a brief summary of the book:

No. of pages: _____

What would you like to change about this book?

Rank the book from 1–10 by drawing gold coins in the space below.
One coin indicates that you wouldn't recommend the book; 10 coins
means it's one of the best books you've ever read.

Use with the bulletin board on page 18.

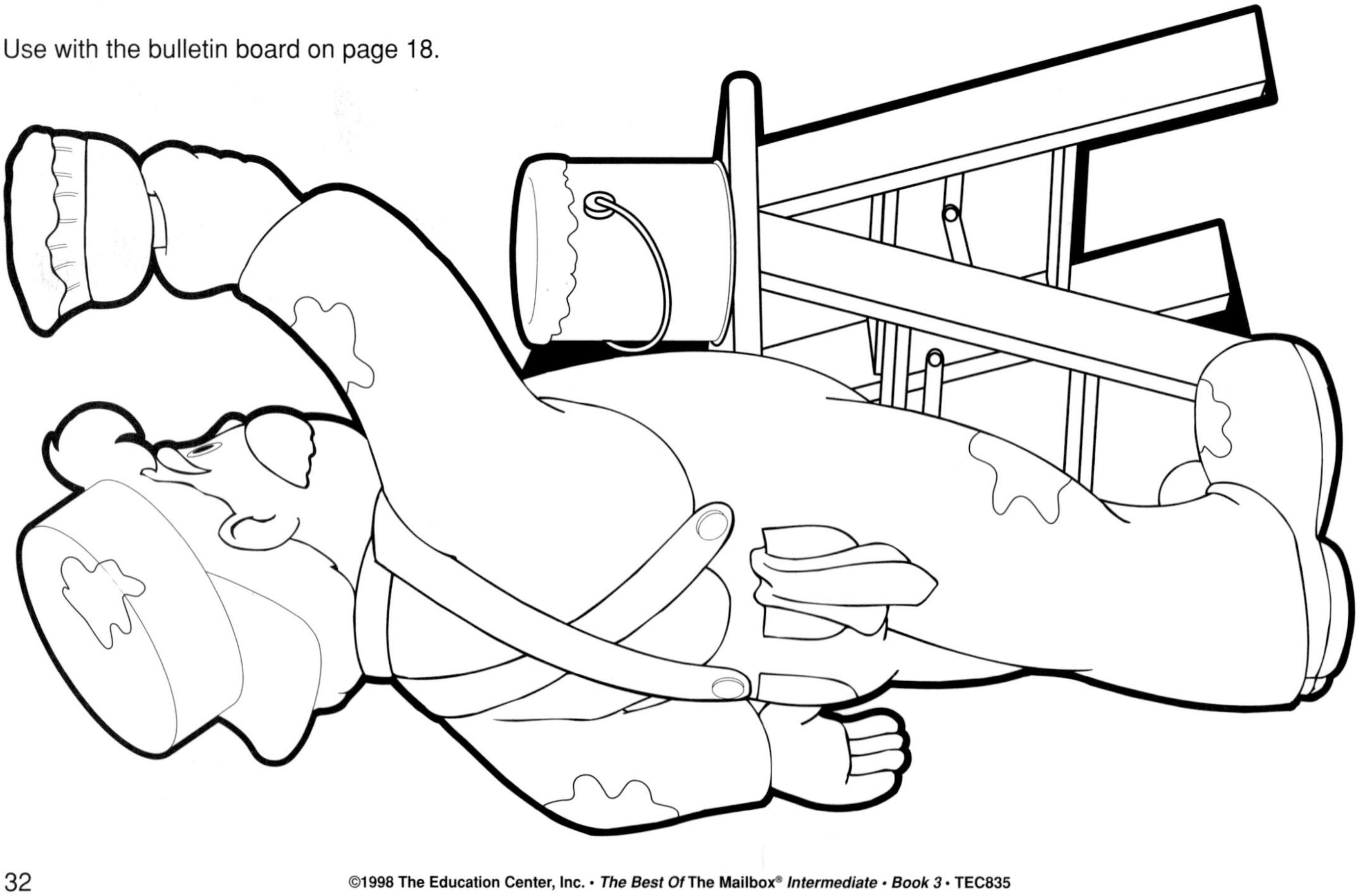

Stained-Glass Names

Decorate your windows for Open House or for any occasion with this eye-catching, stained-glass project.

Materials for one project:
    clear plastic wrap
    piece of tagboard or other stiff paper (about 10" x 10")
    paper clips
    permanent markers—assorted bright colors and black

Directions:
1. Provide each student with a piece of plastic wrap large enough to extend over the piece of tagboard. Have students secure the plastic wrap to the tagboard with paper clips.
2. Have each student use permanent markers to write his name (in fat, bubbly letters) on the plastic, using a different color for each letter.
3. Have the student outline his name with a black permanent marker.
4. To complete the project, instruct each student to carefully cut around the black outline, then remove the paper clips and lift his name from the tagboard.
5. Adhere these stained-glass names to your classroom windows. You may need to add a few drops of water to make the plastic wrap adhere to the glass.

Elizabeth Bourassa—Gr. 6
Olson School
Minneapolis, MN

We're In This Together!

Encourage class unity with the following photographic mural. Tell your students that they will be creating a class mural to commemorate the new school year. However, instead of having students draw pictures of themselves in typical back-to-school poses, tell the class that you will be taking an individual photograph of each student that will then be cut out and pasted onto the mural. Students will be responsible for coming to school the next day dressed in appropriate back-to-school garb, complete with ideas on poses and props. While you take individual snapshots of each child, have the rest of the class work on drawing and coloring a background on the mural. Have students include all or part of the school building and grounds in their drawing. Remind them that the photographic figures will be about five inches tall. Once the photographs have been developed, cut out each figure from its picture and have students work cooperatively to decide where each should be placed. Whimsical and creative arrangements are welcome! Post your mural on the wall outside your classroom and entitle it "We're In This Together!"

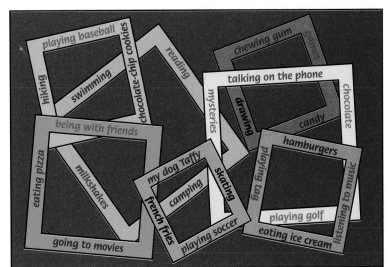

Letter Perfect!

Welcome parents and other visitors to Open House with these bright, colorful projects.

Materials:

9" x 12" white construction paper	pencils
markers and crayons	scissors
glue	
black fine-tipped marker	
assorted decorations such as glitter, sequins, and yarn	

Directions:

1. Have each student sketch the first letter of her first name on a 9" x 12" sheet of white construction paper. Instruct students to make big block letters that fill their sheets.
2. Instruct each student to write the remainder of her name somewhere on the letter, making sure that it is readable; then have the student outline her letter with a black fine-tipped marker.
3. Have the student cut out her letter.
4. Instruct the student to personalize her letter with symbols that represent her hobbies and interests. In addition, suggest that she use glitter, markers, crayons, sequins, yarn, and other available items for decoration.
5. Display all of the completed letters on a bulletin board or your classroom door.

Frame Pictures

Here's a terrific art project to use as a getting-to-know-you activity at the beginning of the year. Have students make colorful frame pictures by completing the steps below. Then post the completed pictures on a bulletin board titled "We've Been Framed!"

Materials for each student:

one 12" x 18" sheet of colorful background paper
two 7-inch paper squares—each a different color—that contrast with the background paper
scissors
glue stick
fine-tipped markers

Directions for each student:

1. Hold the two different-colored squares of paper together. Fold them in half.
2. Cut into the folded edges as shown, making as many cuts as possible until all the paper is used.
3. Open the cut pieces (which will resemble picture frames). Select any two frames—each a different color—and lay them aside.
4. Trade the remaining frames with classmates to collect as many different-colored frames as possible. While trading, introduce yourself and share about your favorite subject, food, free-time activity, etc.
5. Arrange the different-colored frames in an attractive, overlapping pattern on your background paper.
6. Glue the frames to the background.
7. Use colorful markers to write your favorite things on the edges of the frames.

Arts & Crafts

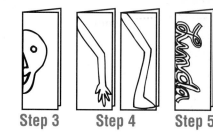

Step 3   **Step 4**   **Step 5**

Name That Skeleton!

Materials:

one 8 1/2" x 11" sheet of white duplicating paper   scissors
hole punch   pencil
one 12" x 18" sheet of black construction paper   rubber cement

Directions:

1. Fold the white paper in half twice; then unfold. Open the paper and cut on the creases to make four equal rectangles.
2. Fold each rectangle in half vertically.
3. Draw one-half of a skull along the fold of one rectangle. Punch a hole for the eyes.
4. Draw a leg on one rectangle. Draw an arm on another rectangle. (Arms and legs should be the same length.)
5. Write your name in cursive on a rectangle, about one-eighth inch from the fold. Outline your name as shown.
6. With the rectangles still folded, carefully cut out the parts of the skeleton.
7. Unfold the name and mount it on the black paper. Mount the arms, legs, and skull as shown.
8. Post the skeletons on a bulletin board titled "Who Are We? Look Carefully And Our Names You'll See!"

Linda Paul—Grs. 3-5 Gifted
Central Noble Community Schools
Albion, IN

Thanksgiving Wreath

When it comes to thanks, this holiday wreath says it all! Provide each student with a wire coat hanger, construction paper in a variety of autumn colors, scissors, markers, a length of ribbon, glue, a length of yarn, and other craft materials. Hang each wreath from the ceiling for everyone to read and enjoy.

Directions:

1. Pull and shape the coat hanger to create a circle.
2. Trace your hand 12 times on different-colored sheets of paper. Cut out each tracing.
3. On one side of each hand cutout, write a word or phrase that expresses something for which you are grateful.
4. Glue the hands around both sides of the wire, making sure that the writing on each hand shows. Also make sure to position the hand cutouts so that the hanger will be completely covered.
5. Complete the wreath by adding a ribbon bow, glitter, streamers, or other decorative items.
6. Tie a length of yarn from the top of your hanger for hanging.

Arts & Crafts

Caught In A Web!

Combine this simple art project with a research session on fall's most famous creepy crawlers—spiders! After cooperative groups have researched spiders and shared their information with the rest of the class, have each child paint the inside of a box lid with black paint. Dip a marble in white paint; then have the child roll the marble in the box to make a web design. While the lid is drying, have the student paint half of a Styrofoam® ball with black paint; then have her add yellow or orange eyes. When the project is completely dry, have the student add pipe-cleaner legs to her spider, then glue it inside the box lid to look as if it's on the web. Pin the lids on a bulletin board for a creepy, crawly, wonderful Halloween display.

Paula Kear—Gr. 4
St. Mary's School
Ellis, KS

Terrifying Towers

Here's a frighteningly good way to bring out your students' creativity during the Halloween season! Gather a supply of different-sized boxes (one per student). Provide students with colorful paper, markers, paints, and other craft supplies. Distribute one box to each child. After the student has covered the box with paper, instruct him to decorate the front and two sides to create a terrifying creature. Next have the student write a description of the origin, dangers, and habits of his creature; then have him attach this description to the back of his box. When all of the boxes are done, stack groups of four or five of them as shown to build several terrifying towers. Display the towers in the school lobby so that others can read and enjoy your students' monstrous creations.

Thanks For The Treats!

Involve students in a community service project that is filled with the spirit of giving. Collect a lid from a spray can (such as those used on cans of spray starch or furniture polish) for each student. Have students follow the steps below to make Thanksgiving tray favors for residents of a convalescent center, homeless shelter, or children's hospital ward.

Steps:
1. Cover the outside of a spray-can lid with aluminum foil.
2. Trace your hand several times on bright colors of construction paper; then cut out each tracing.
3. Glue the hand tracings in a fan shape to the lid as shown.
4. Use construction paper, glue, and other art materials to make turkey features to add to the lid.
5. Fill the resulting treat cup with trail mix, candy, or another snack.

Lightbulb Ornaments

Recycle a used lightbulb into a lovely Christmas ornament! Use a hot glue gun to place a large drop of glue on the base of the bulb. Affix an ornament hanger in the glue. Tie a colorful ribbon bow around the neck of the lightbulb. For the final, most important step, apply glitter paint in various designs on the bulb. Hang the bulb to dry. Decorate a class or school tree with these "shining" examples of how beautiful recycling can be!

Kathleen G. Lange—Gr. 5
Norman Smith Elementary
Clarksville, TN

Pudding Cup Bells

Here's another recycling idea that was just made for this festive season! Several weeks before the holidays, ask students to donate empty, cleaned pudding cups.

Materials for one ornament:

pudding cup (white or clear)   small jingle bell
glitter and glue, or glitter pens   nine-inch length of ribbon
nail   or yarn

Steps:

1. Use the nail to gently punch a hole in the bottom of the pudding cup.
2. Thread the jingle bell onto the ribbon so that the bell is midway between the two ends.
3. Tie a knot about an inch away from the bell as shown.
4. Pull the ends of the ribbon through the top of the cup so that the bell is left hanging inside; then knot the ends of the ribbon to make a hanger.
5. Decorate the outside of the pudding cup with glitter pens or glitter and glue.
6. Hang the ornament to dry.

Sonya Franklin—Gr. 5, Ladonia Elementary, Phenix City, AL

Drink Box Ornaments

If you're thirstin' for an easy-to-make holiday ornament, here it is! Have each child bring in an empty, cleaned disposable drink box. Provide a variety of gift wrap scraps; then have each child wrap his box in a selected wrap. Next have students tie colorful fabric or paper ribbons around their gifts. Tape an ornament hanger to the back of each tiny gift box; then hang your adorable ornaments on the nearest tree!

Sonya Franklin—Gr. 5

Arts & Crafts

Pasta Wreath Ornaments

For keepsake ornaments that will stand out on any tree, have students bring in a variety of pasta in different shapes (the smaller and more varied, the better). Give each child a tagboard copy of the pattern shown. Have the student glue the pasta all over the circular portion of the pattern, leaving the top uncovered. When the glue has thoroughly dried, spray the wreaths with gold spray paint. Use a hot-glue gun to attach a red ribbon hanger to the top of each wreath. For the finishing touch, have each student glue a small photo of himself behind the center hole on the back of the wreath.

Pattern

Diane Hecker—Gr. 4
Campo Bello School
Phoenix, AZ

Cinnamon-Stick Santa Pin

Make an adorable holiday pin that's a perfect gift for Mom, Grandma, or any friend!

Materials for one pin:

cinnamon stick
red acrylic paint
white iridescent craft paint
white Tulip® Puffy® fabric paint
fine-tipped permanent black marker

pin back
hot glue gun
small paintbrush
glitter glue (optional)

Steps (Allow paint to dry thoroughly between steps.):
1. Paint the cinnamon stick with red acrylic paint.
2. Paint a face with white iridescent craft paint as shown.
3. Use fabric paint to add a hat brim and moustache/beard to Santa's face.
4. Use a fine-tipped black marker to add a face and belt to Santa.
5. Embellish the hat and Santa suit with glitter glue if desired.
6. Attach a pin back to the back of Santa with a hot-glue gun.

Christine Kitzmiller—Art, Sycamore Middle School, Pleasant View, TN

German Christmas Ornaments

Bring the holiday spirit of Old World Germany into your classroom by having students decorate a tree with the following handmade ornaments:

Bavarian Pretzel Ornaments: Coat pretzels with spray adhesive; then sprinkle with glitter. After drying, string a red or green ribbon through the pretzel and hang it on the tree.

Holiday Candle Ornaments: Spray pinch clothespins with gold paint; then glue small candles (a little wider than a pencil) onto the clothespins as shown, making sure that when the clothespins are clipped onto the tree's branches, the candles stand straight up. If desired, decorate the base of each candle with lace, gold braid, or other decorative items.

Carolyn R. Fletcher—Gr. 5
Everett Elementary
Paris, TX

Arts & Crafts

Holiday Foils

Students will love these beautiful foil decorations that look difficult to make but are simple to do. Display the eye-catching projects on a bulletin board titled "Holiday Foils." Decorate the title's letters with silver glitter.

Materials for each student:

one 4 1/2" x 5" piece of tagboard
one 5" x 6 1/2" piece of aluminum foil
one 6" x 7" piece of plastic wrap
a holiday pattern
black permanent marker

colored permanent markers
tape
stapler
one 5" x 6" piece of colored paper

Directions for each student:

1. Crinkle the aluminum foil slightly; then gently smooth it out.
2. Wrap the foil around one side of the tagboard; then set the foil-covered tagboard aside.
3. Spread the plastic wrap smoothly over the pattern. Trace the pattern on the plastic wrap with the black permanent marker.
4. Color the traced shape with colored permanent markers.
5. Lift the plastic wrap from the pattern; then center the plastic wrap on the foil-wrapped tagboard.
6. Gently pull the plastic wrap until it's smooth, wrapping it around the tagboard. Tape the plastic wrap securely to the back of the tagboard.
7. Mount the foil on the colored paper by stapling each corner.

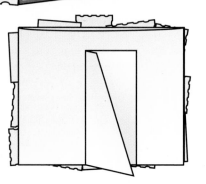

Postage-Stamp Picture Frame

Materials for each student:

12 used stamps
  (cut from their envelopes)
three 3 1/2" x 5" tagboard cards
glue

scissors
ruler
laminating film
hot glue gun

Directions for each student:

1. Cut away the interior from one tagboard card to make a frame with a one-inch border.
2. Glue the used postage stamps around the border's perimeter.
3. After the glue has dried, have an adult laminate the frame.
4. Use scissors to trim the laminating film from around the stamps, including the inside of the frame.
5. Have an adult hot-glue a second tagboard card to the laminated frame at the bottom and sides only, leaving the top open for inserting a photo.
6. Make a stand for the frame by cutting away a corner from the remaining tagboard card. Fold the card in half; then glue the uncut half to the back of the frame.
7. Insert one of your favorite photographs, cutting it to fit if necessary.

Christine Kitzmiller—Art
Sycamore Middle School
Pleasant View, TN

Magazine Wreaths

Spread a little team spirit during the holidays with a cooperative group art project. Have students bring in old magazines with lots of color pictures. Give each group a stack of magazines and scissors. Have students work together to clip out pictures of different fruits and vegetables. Also have them cut out pictures which have large areas showing different shades of green. Have each group store its clippings in a file folder with sides that have been stapled together to form a pocket.

After plenty of pictures have been clipped, give each group a 12-inch square of green construction paper. Show students how to fold the square in half, cut off the open corners to make a circle, and cut out the center section to make a ring. Instruct students to glue their fruit and vegetable cutouts onto the ring, adding "leaves" and "holly" cut from the green clippings. For the finishing touch, have each group glue a loop of yarn to the back of its project so that the wreath can be hung.

Snowy Salt Scenes

It's a cold, blustery Friday and the kids are restless. What do you pull out of your teacher's bag of tricks? This simple art project, that's what! For every four students, mix a salt solution by dissolving one teaspoon of salt in two tablespoons of water. Give each student (or have them share) a medicine dropper and a small square of black construction paper. Have each child use a pencil to draw a snow scene on his paper; then have him use the dropper to outline his drawing with the salt solution. The students will see only water at first. But when evaporation takes place (an instant science lesson!), a glistening snow scene will appear. Mount the finished scenes on a bulletin board or on your classroom windows.

Dana Peck—Gr. 4
South Clinton Elementary
Clinton, TN

Hanukkah Candles

Usher in the Festival Of Lights with a shimmering art project!

Materials for one candle:

baby food jar
small votive candle
white glue
glitter paint

colored tissue paper
paintbrush
hole puncher
water

Steps:

1. Tear the tissue paper into pieces; then punch holes in each piece.
2. Thin the glue with water; then use it and the paintbrush to cover the outside of the jar with the tissue pieces. Overlap the pieces as you work.
3. When the jar is completely covered with paper, add a final coat of glue; then let the jar dry overnight.
4. Use the glitter paint to draw Hanukkah designs on the outside of the jar. Let the jar dry.
5. Insert the small candle into the jar.

Recyclable, Romantic Robots

Say good-bye to humdrum valentine holders and hello to the most unique valentine mail carriers ever! Divide your class into several cooperative groups. Give groups a couple of weeks to collect boxes, cardboard tubes, and other recyclable items. While groups are collecting their items, gather a supply of art materials such as paint, aluminum foil, and scrap construction paper.

About two weeks before Valentine's Day, challenge each group to use its recyclables to create a romantic robot that will serve as a valentine holder for the group's members. Give each group scissors, glue, rubber cement, and a roll of masking tape. Explain that the first step will be to make the robot's body, making sure it is designed with some type of receptacle for holding group members' valentines. Use a box cutter as needed to assist students with cutting that can't be done with regular scissors. After all of the robots have been assembled, let students decorate them with paint, aluminum foil, or other items. Have each group present its completed robot to the class and demonstrate where to put group members' valentines. During the week of Valentine's Day, have students write stories about their robots, explaining their origins, special abilities, and personalities. Post the robots and stories outside your classroom for a Valentine's display that isn't likely to be forgotten!

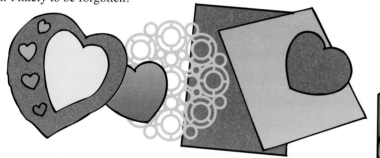

Valentine Roses

Here's a simple and sweet idea for Valentine's Day, Mother's Day, or any time you want to surprise a special someone with a one-of-a-kind gift.

Materials for one rose:
one Hershey's® Kiss®
5" x 5" square of red cellophane
one 10" floral stem (from a floral shop)
two green silk leaves (each with a wire stem)
one 12" length of stretchy green floral tape

Steps:
1. Place the cellophane on the top point of the candy kiss; then gently gather the cellophane under the bottom of the kiss.
2. Bend the top two inches of the floral stem and wrap it snugly around the gathered cellophane, making a rosebud shape.
3. Beginning at the top of the stem, stretch and wrap the green floral tape snugly around the stem (covering the excess cellophane gathered under the rosebud). Add a leaf about two inches below the bud and continue to wrap for another inch. Then add the second leaf and continue wrapping.
4. Deliver the rose to your special valentine!

Valerie Hornbaker—Gr. 6
Elreka Grade School
Hutchinson, KS

St. Patrick's Serpents

Share the legend of St. Patrick driving the snakes out of Ireland as cooperative groups make their own colorful serpents.

Materials for each group of five or six students:

one or two empty toilet-tissue tubes per student	sealing tape
one 7-foot length of rope	scrap paper
one pair of wiggle eyes	glue
tempera paints	paintbrushes

Directions:

1. Have each student paint designs and patterns on one or two toilet-tissue tubes.
2. After all the tubes have dried, have group members thread their tissue tubes onto the length of rope.
3. Have students loop and knot the end of the rope around the last tissue tube as shown.
4. Have group members extend the rope outside the first tissue tube and use sealing tape to hold it in place. Have students glue wiggle eyes and other details made from scrap paper to the snake's "head."
5. Display the snakes as a border around a bulletin board or chalkboard; or position them as a welcoming committee at your classroom door!

An Irish Quilt

Add a touch o' art to your curriculum this March! Divide students into four cooperative groups. Have each group research a particular aspect of Ireland: its people, geography, industries, history, government, arts, recreation, etc. After the research has been completed, give each group four 7" squares of white art paper. Have the group decorate its squares with drawings and captions that illustrate its topic. Glue the completed squares in rows to resemble a quilt on a large sheet of green butcher paper (or a green paper tablecloth). Add stitches with a black marker as shown. Hang your paper quilt in a hallway so that others can learn about the Emerald Isle. For a whimsical touch, have each group create the head of a slumbering leprechaun to peek out from the top of the quilt.

Paper Pysanky

Don't wait until Easter to introduce students to the rich tradition found in Ukrainian Easter eggs, called *pysanky*. Admired all over the world for their unique beauty, these eggs are usually based on a geometrical design that contains symbols and colors of meaning to the artist. Pysanky are given to family and friends to convey one's love and best wishes during the Easter season. Though the process of making pysanky is based on the batik method of applying wax in several stages and dipping the eggs in dye, your students will love making paper versions of this lovely art form.

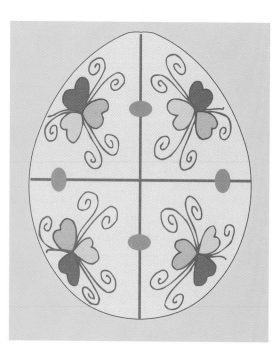

Materials:

student copies of page 45
rulers and pencils
scissors and glue

white art paper
markers or crayons
construction paper

egg-shaped templates for tracing
fine-tipped markers

Steps:

1. Use a template to trace a large egg shape in the middle of a sheet of white art paper.
2. Use a pencil and ruler to divide the egg into geometric parts (see the examples on the reproducible).
3. In real pysanky, symbols that mean something to the artist and to the person for whom the egg is being made are drawn in each section of the egg. Symbols are often repeated in a section to create a design. Think about who you would like to receive your *pysanka* (the name for a single egg); then look at the reproducible for symbols you can use (or create your own). Use a pencil to draw symbols inside the different egg sections.
4. Colors are an important part of your egg's message. Use the chart on the reproducible to help you decide how to color your pysanka so that it's suited for the person who will receive it.
5. Use fine-tipped markers to add details to your symbols.
6. Cut out your pysanka and glue it to a contrasting sheet of construction paper. Then give it to your special friend.

Simone Lepine—Gr. 5
Syracuse, NY

Finger-Painted Lilacs

In the spring when lilacs bloom, bring a fragrant bouquet to class as a model for a still-life painting project.

Materials needed for each child:

12" x 18" sheet of black construction paper
9" x 12" sheet of light-gray construction paper
pencil
scissors

fine-tipped paintbrush
glue
scrap paper

In addition to the above materials, provide each small group of students with green, white, and purple tempera paints. If desired, provide lavender and pink paints as well. First have each student make a flower vase by folding and cutting a pattern from scrap paper. Have the student trace the pattern onto the gray paper. After he has cut out his tracing, have the child glue it to the black paper. Now the fun begins! Using his fingers, have the student dab paint on the black paper to form lilac shapes. Show students how to make leaves by placing side-by-side dabs of green paint on the paper and using a paintbrush to spread the paint into a heart shape. After the paintings have dried, mount them on a bulletin board covered with pink paper. Tiptoe through the lilacs, anyone?

Ruth Green—Gr. 5, West Elementary, Slayton, MN

Pysanky Project

Have you ever dyed Easter eggs? In one special area of our globe, called the Ukraine, people have been dyeing eggs for hundreds of years. These special eggs are called *pysanky.* They are decorated with very fancy, intricate designs. In fact, no two pysanky are alike! Pysanky contain symbols and colors that have special meanings. Each is designed to communicate special wishes for the person who will receive the egg. Pysanky are given to family and friends as gifts.

Dividing The Egg: One of the first steps in making a pysanka is to divide the egg into geometric parts. Here are examples of some traditional patterns:

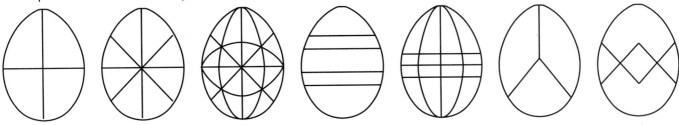

Drawing The Symbols: Once the egg is divided into geometric parts, the next step is to draw pictures and symbols inside each section. In traditional pysanky, symbols are repeated in each section to create a design. Also, nature is used to represent different messages. Use some of these traditional symbols, or create some of your own.

Flowers: beauty, children, wisdom, love, charity, goodwill

Fruits: knowledge, health, a good life, wisdom

Trees: long life, good health, strength, youthfulness

Animals: prosperity, wealth

ram's horns

Birds: fulfillment of wishes, spring, good harvest, protection

Other:

star = success

sun = growth, good fortune

spider = good fortune

water = wealth

bee = hard work, pleasantness

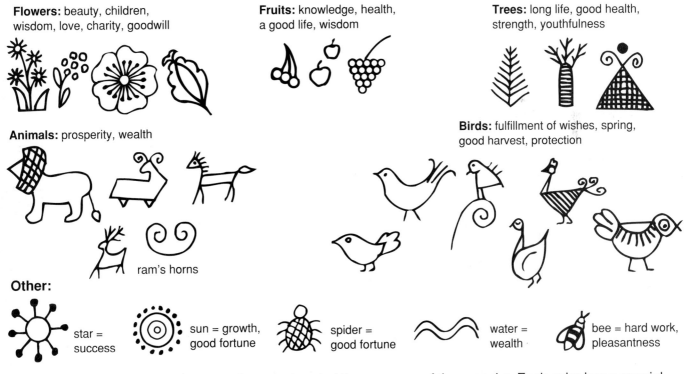

Coloring The Egg: Colors are a very important part of the message of the pysanka. Each color has a special meaning:

white = purity
green = hope, wealth, happiness
orange = power, endurance
brown = prosperity

yellow = success, wisdom
blue = sky, air, good health
red = happiness, hope, life
purple = faith, trust

Laundry Scoop Art

Turn those new laundry-box measuring scoops into attractive art creations! First spray-paint each scoop with acrylic paint. (For best results, complete this step outside.) Next use a hammer and nail to punch a hole near the top of each handle. Decorate the scoops for the season:

- As a Mother's Day gift, fit a photo inside the scoop to create a pretty picture frame.
- Place a small seasonal figurine inside the scoop to create a holiday ornament.
- For any special day or special someone, fill the scoop with sachet or potpourri. Then hot-glue netting around the edge.

To complete the scoop, add trimming—lace, eyelet, ribbon, or thick yarn—around its edge. Tie a length of colorful yarn through the hole in the handle for hanging the scoop.

Nancy Mohn—Gr. 5
Johnston Elementary
Woodstock, GA

Father's Day Letter Holder

Here it is—a letter-perfect gift for Father's Day! Have each student trace and cut out two cardboard circles that are each 3 1/2" in diameter—a cake-frosting lid works well as a pattern. Direct the student to glue the circles on either side of a 1" x 4" block of wood. Then have her write her name on the bottom of her letter holder and allow it to dry. Take the letter holders outside and spray-paint them. After the paint dries, have each student use craft paint or paint pens to decorate her letter holder. The result will be a gift any student will be proud to give her dad or a special friend!

We've Been Framed!

Looking for a fun and easy end-of-the-year art activity? Cut three 4" x 6" pieces of cardboard for each student. Direct each student to frame each of his three sections with small strips of wallpaper or Con-Tact® paper. Have the student tape the edges of his three pieces of cardboard together on the back to make a tri-frame as shown. Then have him glue a picture of himself in the center frame and add his grade, class, and school. Instruct the student to use the other two sections to record memories/accomplishments and autographs of classmates. What a great way to highlight another extraordinary year!

Fun Flowers For Favorite Folks

Let your students say "thanks for a great year" to the school secretary, cafeteria workers, guidance counselor, and other staff members with this easy gift idea. Purchase a supply of small, inexpensive potted plants (one for each person you want to thank). Then have each student or pair of students complete the following steps:

1. Cut two 5-inch circles, two 4 1/2-inch circles, and two 3-inch circles from colored newspaper ads. Group the cutouts into two sets of concentric circles.
2. Make rounded cuts along the outer edge of each circle to create flower petals.
3. Roll each petal around a toothpick to create edges that are slightly curled.
4. Stack each set of three flowers in order according to size, with the largest circle on the bottom; then glue the set of three flowers together.
5. Position a straw between the two sets of flowers to serve as a stem; then glue the flowers to the straw back-to-back.
6. Cut two small circles from a laminated paper scrap. Glue one circle to the front center and one to the back center of the flower.
7. Insert the completed flower in the soil of a potted plant.

Gerrie Gutowski—Gr. 4
Sombra Del Monte School
Albuquerque, NM

Time In A Bottle

"If I could save this year in a bottle…." What *would* be in that bottle if you could fill it with memories of the school year that's about to come to an end? Pose that question to your students; then set them loose to create these memory-filled projects.

Steps for each student:
1. Cut out a bottle shape from a large piece of white construction paper. Include a lid.
2. Write your name on your bottle's lid.
3. Use a black marker or crayon to divide the bottle into four sections.
4. Decorate the sections so that they illustrate the following topics:
   • The funniest thing that happened this year
   • Five words that describe this year
   • The most important thing I learned this year
   • An area in which I improved this year
5. Optional: Trace your bottle on a clear acetate sheet. Cut out the tracing; then tape or staple it on top of your bottle.

Post the bottles on a bulletin board titled "If We Could Save Time In A Bottle…."

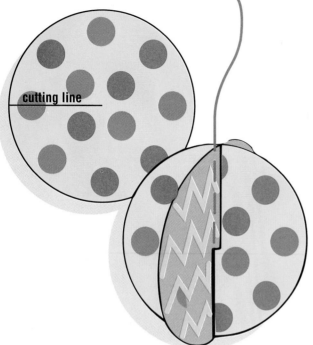

cutting line

Pattern Projects

They're everywhere: patterns on clothing, in nature, on buildings, even on your desktop. Encourage students to notice the patterns around them; then follow up your pattern search with a simple art activity.

Materials:
two same-size circles cut from plain, white index cards
four circles (the same size as the white circles), each
   cut from a different color of paper
glue   fine-tipped markers
scissors   needle and thread

Steps:
1. Glue a colored circle to each side of the two white circles.
2. Use fine-tipped markers to decorate each side of the two circles with a different pattern.
3. Use the needle to make a small hole in the center of each circle. Cut a slit from the outer edge to the center as shown.
4. Fit the two circles together at the slits as shown.
5. Stitch a length of thread into one side of the three-dimensional, spherelike shape and hang the shape from the ceiling. Or make several shapes and hang them from a coat hanger to make an interesting mobile.

A New Twist On Trash

After completing a unit on recycling, each of my students brought several cleaned throwaway items to school. Then they worked together to transform the trash into some out-of-the-ordinary creatures. Crazy critters filled our room—we even transformed a toothpaste box, a toilet-paper tube, a tuna fish can, and a few other items into the most unusual bride and groom to ever walk down the aisle! To extend the project further, students named their creations and wrote descriptions of their habitats, foods, defenses against enemies, etc. It was one time when I was happy to see my kids "trash" our classroom!

Julie Ford—Gr. 6, Molalla Grade School, Molalla, OR

Your Number's Up!

Include a bit of art and practice with patterns in this nifty numeration project. Pull the aces through nines from a deck of playing cards and place them in a bag. Have each child draw a card from the bag. Each student sketches a giant, fat shape of his numeral on a large piece of butcher paper; then he uses a pencil to fill the numeral with distinctive patterns and designs. After the designs are completed, provide students with bright tempera paints and brushes of various thicknesses (be sure to supply some small, fine-tipped brushes so students can paint the smaller details with ease). Cut out the numerals after the paint has dried; then post them in a hallway for an eye-catching display that's sure to attract a large number of admirers!

Foil Collages

For a little razzle-dazzle, get creative with food coloring, glue, and foil. To make this dazzling project, crumple a piece of aluminum foil; then flatten it, leaving it somewhat crinkled. Add a few drops of food coloring to each of several small containers of white glue. Brush a thin, even coat of several colors of tinted glue onto the foil, occasionally allowing the colors to mix. Allow the glue to dry overnight.

Cut the foil into small bits and separate the bits by color. Glue the bits to a black construction-paper background in a collage of a distinctive shape. How's that for sparkle?

Cheryl Braida
St. Joseph/St. Mary School
Kingston, Ontario, Canada

Build A Bug

After completing a unit on insects, turn your students loose to create their own one-of-a-kind bugs. Provide students with colored construction paper, scissors, glue, tape, a hole punch, glitter, and other art materials. Demonstrate the following simple techniques before beginning the project:

- *paper curling*: using scissors to curl a strip of paper
- *paper fanning*: accordion-folding a one-inch-wide strip of paper
- *cylinder making*: rolling a piece of paper into a cylinder, securing it with tape

Have students practice these techniques with notebook paper.

Next encourage students to build their own bugs with construction paper and other art materials. Remind students to examine their bugs to make sure they are interesting from all angles. Encourage the use of different patterns, textures, and shapes. Holes can be punched and glitter added for dramatic effects.

Hang the completed bugs from the ceiling. Or group them on a table; then ask each student to write the name and a brief description of his bug on an index card.

Pat Green
Allen Middle School
Greensboro, NC

Kid-Lover's Pizzas

You've heard of "cheese-lover's" and "meat-lover's" pizzas. Take this idea a step further by having your students create their own Kid-Lover's pizzas to showcase special hobbies or interests. Instruct each student to draw and cut out a large circle from a sheet of poster board. After he decides on the type of pizza he'll make ("Baseball-Lover's," "Dog-Lover's," "Art-Lover's," etc.), instruct each student to boldly color in the pizza ingredients and crust using crayons. For example, a "Dog-Lover's" pizza might include dog biscuits, a collar, a leash, a food bowl, and a grooming brush. After coloring in the ingredients, the student paints a red tempera "sauce" over the entire pizza. The wax crayon will resist this wash. Display the completed pizzas in and around pizza boxes (donated by a local pizzeria) mounted on a bulletin board.

Pat Green

Cereal-Box Covered Wagons

Feature cereal-box covered wagons as a unique display during a unit on the westward movement. To make a covered-wagon's bed, have each student cut away the front panel from an empty cereal box and save it for making the wheels. After taping the box's top flaps closed, direct the student to cover the outside of his wagon's bed with brown paper. Have the student trace four circles on the front panel he cut off earlier and then cut them out. Next have him color each of these circles to resemble a wagon wheel. Help the student staple the wheels to the bottom of the wagon bed; then have him staple two 1 1/2" x 17" poster-board "bows" across the bed from one side to the other.

Next direct the student to look at illustrations in books about the westward movement (see the booklist). Have him draw a scene from this historical period on each half of a 12" x 18" sheet of manila paper (the wagon's cover) so that a scene can be viewed from either side of the wagon. Then have him glue this cover to the bows and wagon's bed. Let the student make other additions, such as a bench for the front of the wagon, horses or oxen to pull it, and people to ride in or run alongside it.

Nancy Oglevie Jaeger—Gr. 5
Sangre Ridge Elementary
Stillwater, OK

Suggested Books:

If You Traveled West In A Covered Wagon
by Ellen Levine
(Scholastic Inc., 1992)

Little House On The Prairie
by Laura Ingalls Wilder
(HarperCollins Children's Books, 1961)

Wagon Train: A Family Goes West In 1865
by Courtni C. Wright
(Holiday House, Inc.; 1995)

Wagon Train: A Journey On The Oregon Trail
by Dorothy H. Patent
(Walker & Co., 1995)

Native American Sand Paintings

Celebrate our country's rich Native American heritage by making colorful sand paintings.

Materials:

white sand (obtained from a hardware or farm supply store)
powdered tempera in three bright colors
three small bowls
white glue (diluted with an equal amount of water)
bottom of a gift box (large enough for the cardboard to fit inside)
measuring cup
paintbrush
9" square of cardboard
three plastic spoons
pencil and scrap paper
tablespoon

Steps:

1. Use a pencil to draw a sketch of your design on a scrap piece of paper.
2. Paint the entire surface of the cardboard with diluted glue.
3. Place the cardboard in a box or plastic tub; then pour white sand carefully over the cardboard until it is completely covered. Let it dry.
4. In each bowl, mix three tablespoons of one color of tempera paint with one cup of white sand. Place a plastic spoon in each bowl.
5. Pour the glue (from its squeeze bottle) onto the cardboard to "draw" your picture. Then, working quickly and with only one color at a time, spoon colored sand over the glue.
6. When one color is dry (which will take several hours), repeat step 5 twice with the other colors.

LIFESAVERS...

Student Supplies

Substitute Teachers · Starting The Day · Classroom Materials

Management
Tips

LIFESAVERS...
management tips for teachers

Traveling Researchers

My students often go to the media center to research and compile reports. To avoid frequent trips back to the classroom for supplies, I purchased a three-tier basket cart on wheels. I filled the cart with scissors, crayons, a hole puncher, extra paper, and other necessary resources for the current project. Now this traveling resource center goes wherever my researchers go—saving us time and energy!

Marta Johnson—Gr. 4, Haw Creek School, Asheville, NC

Lead Beds

Dull pencils don't slow my cooperative-learning groups down! Students begin each day with two sharp pencils. When a student's pencil point breaks or gets dull, he simply places his pencil in the "lead bed" located on his cooperative group's table. These "beds" are actually soup cans decorated with Con-Tact® paper. A class helper sharpens the pencils at lunchtime and at the end of the day. Classwork stays neat and time is used effectively!

Shelly Zennon
Casa Grande, AZ

Novel Solution

Need a source of teaching ideas for your next novel? Create your own teacher's edition. Purchase a personal copy of the novel. As you preview the book, underline important vocabulary words and significant phrases or figures of speech. Make notations in the margins next to sections that illustrate predictions, character personalities, cause and effect, and other skills. At the end of each chapter, jot down any writing activities that occur to you. This handy tool will prove useful year after year.

Laura Vazquez—Gr. 5
Charles R. Hadley Elementary
Miami Springs, FL

Teacher Mail Basket

The most hectic time of the school day is when students first arrive. There's attendance to take, lunch forms to complete, coat zippers to unstick, and parent notes to read. To relieve some of the stress of this busy time, create a teacher mail basket. Students place any notes to the teacher inside the basket in the morning. Then at the first available moment, you can check the basket for any mail. Morning confusion is lessened and your sanity is preserved for another day!

Michelle Kasmiske—Gr. 4
Monroe Elementary
Janesville, WI

Handy Red Pens

What one tool has made more corrections than any other? The red pen, of course! Provide each student with his own pen for making corrections. Attach the rough side of sticky-back Velcro® to the front of each student's desk; then attach the soft side to a red pen. When it's time to correct papers, students will always have marking pens right at their fingertips.

Lorri Burton—Gr. 5
Huddleston Elementary
Huddleston, VA

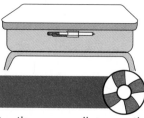

Timer Tip

I use a great little device to get my students' attention: a small magnetic timer attached to my chalkboard. When students get a little too noisy, I simply turn on the timer. The time it takes students to settle down is the amount of time they have to wait before going out to recess or playing a game. It's amazing that students can hear that timer begin—no matter how noisy it is in the classroom! Substitute teachers find this timer especially helpful.

Debbie Patrick—Gr. 5, Park Forest Elementary, State College, PA

Classroom Library

Do you have trouble keeping track of the ever-growing number of books in your class library? Simplify your record keeping by assigning each book a number. Hold the book closed and write the number across the page edges at the top of the book. Arrange the books in numerical order. Record the title, author, publisher, cost, and assigned number for each book on an individual Rolodex® card. Now the class librarian has only to scan the book tops to notice a missing book.

Virginia Hernandez-Gage, Kealing Junior High, Austin, TX

Extra Copy Binder

As any experienced teacher knows, students often lose ditto copies. (Maybe the desk gremlin eats them!) Since our paper is rationed, I try to save duplicating paper by running off only one extra copy and placing it in the Extra Copy Binder. Students who lose their original copies must use the Extra Copy Binder to complete the assignment on their own paper. Because students know that using the binder means more work for them, it's a great incentive for them to be more responsible.

Nancy L. Mohn—Gr. 5
Johnston Elementary
Woodstock, GA

Report-Card Relief

Don't be left hanging during report-card time! Put a labeled hanging file folder for each student in one of your desk or filing-cabinet drawers. Use the folders to store notes on student behavior, work samples, classroom observations, and other valuable documentation. When you are ready to begin working on report cards, take home a few student files at a time and use the helpful information to complete the evaluations in no time at all. These folders also serve as a great reference at conference time!

Wendy Bousquet—Substitute Grs. K–6
Scarborough, Ontario
Canada

Supporting Your Substitute

Get your substitute teacher off to a great start with this helpful organizational tip. Use several 4" x 6" index cards to outline your classroom routines. Some sample card headings could include *Before School, Opening Routines, Time Fillers, Emergency Procedures,* and *End Of The Day.* On each of the cards, record the appropriate information about your classroom routines. Laminate the cards and bind them together with a metal ring. The cards save you time because you do not have to rewrite the same information each day you are absent. They are also an invaluable reference for your substitute.

Leslie Jackson—Substitute Teacher
Aschaffenburg Elementary
Aschaffenburg, Germany

Collateral Connection

I have found an easy, fun, and effective way to encourage students to be responsible about returning things that they borrow. I write the word *collateral* on a sentence strip, paste the sentence strip onto a sheet of colored construction paper, laminate it, and tape it to the side of a sturdy dishpan. When one of my fourth graders borrows something, he must leave as collateral some item of equal value in the dishpan. When he returns the borrowed item to its owner, he gets back his collateral. This activity teaches responsibility and prepares students for the real world.

Ann Irwin—Gr. 4
Gilmer Intermediate
Gilmer, TX

"I'm Finished" Packet

For those times when my students have completed classwork and need a break before beginning their homework, I prepare "I'm Finished" packets. For each student, I fill a large manila envelope with a variety of fun, independent activities—most of which I have found in back issues of *The Mailbox®* magazine and in *The Best Of The Mailbox®* book. The packets are kept at my desk when not in use. Students receive extra credit for every two completed activities. They enjoy working at their own pace and appreciate knowing that they have nothing to lose from their efforts.

Lynn Aydlett, Virginia Beach, VA

Color-Coded File Cabinet

Has your file cabinet become more of a dumping ground than a valuable organizational tool? If so, try this simple filing system. Purchase hanging file folders in different colors. Label each colored set with a subject such as Literature, Science, Seasonal Activities, and Administrative Information. Next purchase pocket folders in the same colors as the hanging folders. Label the front of each folder with a specific topic such as Myths, Rocks And Minerals, and Valentine's Day. Use the right side of each folder to store information, reproducibles, forms, patterns, etc. As you use an item from the right pocket, transfer it to the left pocket. At a glance, you'll know what you've already used. And filing becomes a much easier, less bothersome task!

Lea Holton, Audubon Elementary, Louisville, KY

The Fix And Finish File

Free time is a great time to teach students to finish incomplete assignments and correct their own mistakes. Cover a box with colorful paper and label it "Fix And Finish File." Place a labeled file folder for each of your students in the box. If a student turns in work that needs to be finished or corrected, lightly highlight the area needing work and place the paper in the student's file. When a student has free time, he can take out his folder and get to work. What a great way to keep on top of things and eliminate idle time!

Karyn Tritelli—Gr. 4, St. Catherine of Siena School, Wilmington, DE

Student-Finder Chart

It's a challenge to remember all the different places in our school where my students may be. To help me out, I write all of my students' names down the left column of an incentive chart. In each blank across the top, I write a different place or job: restroom, office, errand, nurse, Chapter I, etc. I post the chart on a bulletin board near the door, along with a cup full of pushpins. When a student leaves the classroom, she places a pushpin in the appropriate column, letting me know her destination. The kids are great about remembering to use the chart, and I always know where everyone is!

Gina Morrison—Gr. 5, Bowie Elementary, Grand Prairie, TX

For The Record

Anecdotal records are a valuable resource for teachers during conferences and around report-card time. Make keeping these records a simpler task with the help of adhesive file-folder labels. Keep a sheet of labels on your clipboard and carry it with you at all times. When you feel the need to document a student's behavior, write the child's name, the date, and a brief summary on one of the labels. Later, adhere the label inside the student's folder. Individualized record keeping was never easier!

Stephany R. Ezekiel—Gr. 4, Scotland Elementary
Scotland, AK

Emergency Packs

An emergency pack is just the thing for those students who run out of paper, pencils, or pens during a school day. Have each student bring in a Ziploc® bag, five folded sheets of ruled paper, two sharpened new pencils, and a black pen. Place all of the items inside the bag. Affix a name label to the front of each student's bag. Add a note to the bag like the one shown. Keep the packs at your desk until a student needs an item. Then send the note inside the bag home as a reminder that the item needs to be replaced.

Michael Williquette—Grs. 5–6, Faith Baptist School, Beecher, WI

The "Hole" Game

This management technique is sure to be a winner in any classroom! First divide your students into small groups; then list the names of each group's members on a small index card. Punch a hole in each card, thread string through the holes, and tie the string around your neck. Throughout the week, punch a hole in a group's card whenever you observe its members paying attention, following directions, volunteering, helping each other, or talking softly. At the end of the week, allow the group with the most holes in its card to choose prizes from a grab bag of treats. I keep the cards with me wherever we go. Students know that when my hole puncher is in my "holster" and the cards are around my neck, I mean business!

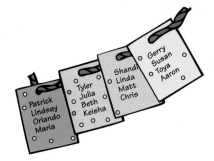

Deena Block—Gr. 4, G. B. Fine Elementary, Pennsauken, NJ

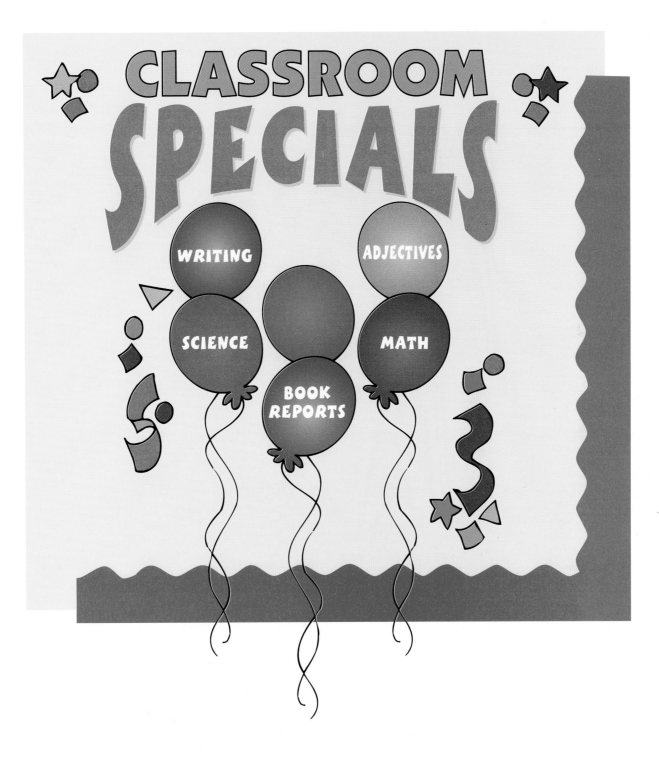

Miss Nelson's Writing Review

An Eight-Day Plan Aimed At Improving Writing Skills

Turn a beginning-of-the-year writing review into fun practice that targets five major forms of writing. Just use the familiar and well-loved picture book, *Miss Nelson Is Missing* by Harry Allard (Houghton Mifflin Company, 1985), as a springboard for improving descriptive, classificatory, persuasive, expository, and narrative writing.

by Kathy Sue Sanford—Gr. 6, Stephen F. Austin Elementary, Lake Jackson, TX

DAY ONE: Make Lists Of Character Traits And Descriptions

Dedicate this day to having students list character traits. Read the first half of *Miss Nelson Is Missing* aloud to the class, being sure to share the pictures. Ask students to listen specifically for words that describe Miss Nelson and Miss Viola Swamp. Have students also note the way the art describes each character. After reading and showing the pictures, give each student three to five minutes to produce a list of words that describe Miss Nelson. Have volunteers share their lists. Give students a few minutes to add any new words they heard to their lists. Then repeat the entire procedure for the character of Miss Swamp.

DAY TWO: Write A Description

Use this day to have students write a description of a character. Display a simple drawing of a clown to model for students how this is done. Describe the clown's physical traits—going from the head down to the feet—and his character traits to students. Have students note that you fully describe one of the clown's features before moving to another. Stress to students the importance of elaborating on each detail. Then have each student refer to her list from Day One and write a short description of either Miss Nelson or Miss Swamp. Challenge the student to word this description so vividly that her character's image could easily be reproduced by any reader.

DAY THREE: Make A Venn Diagram

On this day, review Venn diagrams with students. First model for students a Venn diagram that compares and contrasts the familiar characteristics of hamburgers and hot dogs. Then have students place their word lists from Day One in Venn diagrams that compare and contrast Miss Nelson and Miss Swamp.

DAY FOUR: Write A Classificatory Paper

Devote this day to having students write a classificatory paper. Use the hot dog/hamburger Venn diagram from Day Three to model this type of writing for students. As you write, show that all similarities of hot dogs and hamburgers should be detailed in one paragraph and their differences in another. Then have each student take out her Miss Nelson/Miss Swamp Venn diagram from Day Three. Ask her to consult it as she writes a paper that compares and contrasts the characteristics of Miss Nelson and Miss Swamp.

DAY FIVE: Write A Persuasive Letter

Set aside this day for having students write persuasively. Explain that students must first take a stand on a specific issue and then be willing to give reasons to support it. Give students an example about attending a traditional school versus a year-round school. Model how to write reasons for supporting one or the other in a logical way. Demonstrate the use of biased or slanted wording to show its effect. Then ask each student to pretend that she is tired of being a member of Miss Swamp's class. Have the student write a letter to Miss Nelson persuading her to return quickly and replace the awful substitute, Miss Swamp. Remind the student to support each of her reasons for asking Miss Nelson to return with an explanation or an example. Challenge the student to try using some biased wording.

DAY SIX: Write An Expository Paper

Devote this day to having students write a paper that explains a specific process. To model this type of writing, write the steps for making a banana split on the board or overhead. Point out to students that explaining how to make a banana split requires a list of ingredients. Show students how to position this near the paper's beginning. Explain that the steps needed to make the banana split must be given in a logical, sequential order. Stress, too, the importance of using specific words to convey exact meaning so that anyone following the written steps can be successful. Then hold a brief discussion about appropriate class behavior. Steer students toward discussing the actions of students who are thought to be well-behaved. Have students conclude that Miss Nelson's class was out of control before she left. Then ask each child to write a short paper explaining how to be a well-behaved student. Point out that the student is not to give classroom rules, but logical and sequential steps that any child could follow to become well-behaved.

DAY SEVEN: Write A Narrative Story

On this day have students write a real or fictitious story in which the main character overcomes a problem. Remind students that simple stories have three parts—a beginning where the problem is identified, a middle where the action builds, and an ending where the problem is resolved. Ask students to pretend that they are in either Miss Nelson's or Miss Swamp's classroom for one day. Have each student write a story about a problem she has in the class. Have her use specific details to describe the problem, develop two or three incidents related to the problem, and then resolve the problem.

DAY EIGHT: Culminate The Review

Use this day to have students complete any unfinished writings. Then read the rest of *Miss Nelson Is Missing* aloud to the class. Hold a session with students to find out how they felt about the writing assignments they'd been assigned. What was difficult about them? What was easy? If time permits, read another book by Harry Allard such as *Miss Nelson Is Back* (Houghton Mifflin Company, 1986) or *Miss Nelson Has A Field Day* (Houghton Mifflin Company, 1988).

The Themes Scheme

Fun With Thematic Book Reports

If you've experimented with integrated teaching, you probably agree that thematic units are a terrific way to get kids excited about learning. So why not apply this proven technique to your independent reading program? That's what Pat Garwich of Haverhill, Massachusetts, does. Every month, Pat presents her students with a list of books based on a simple theme, such as books with colors in their titles. Each student chooses a book to read independently; then the student completes a book report project to share with classmates. Use the following book lists to get started. Happy reading!

Mathematical Magic
(books with numbers or mathematical terms in their titles)

Be A Perfect Person In Just Three Days! by Stephen Manes
Nothing's Fair In Fifth Grade by Barthe DeClements
The Cricket In Times Square by George Selden
The Two-Thousand-Pound Goldfish by Betsy Byars
The Hundred Dresses by Eleanor Estes
The Twenty-One Balloons by William Pène du Bois
Absolute Zero by Helen Cresswell
Thirteen Ways To Sink A Sub by Jamie Gilson
The 18th Emergency by Betsy Byars
Eight Mules From Monterey by Patricia Beatty
The Book Of Three by Lloyd Alexander

Flavor Of The Month
(books with flavors in their titles)

Strawberry Girl by Lois Lenski
Chocolate Fever by Robert K. Smith
The Peppermint Pig by Nina Bawden
Superfudge by Judy Blume
Moonshadow Of Cherry Mountain by Doris B. Smith
Charlie And The Chocolate Factory by Roald Dahl
The Chocolate Touch by Patrick Skene Catling
The Pistachio Prescription by Paula Danziger
Do Bananas Chew Gum? by Jamie Gilson
James And The Giant Peach by Roald Dahl
Banana Twist by Florence Parry Heide
Banana Blitz by Florence Parry Heide
The View From The Cherry Tree by Willo Davis Roberts
Blackberries In The Dark by Mavis Jukes
A Taste Of Blackberries by Doris B. Smith

Animal Antics
(books with animals in their titles)

Owls In The Family by Farley Mowat
Tiger Eyes by Judy Blume
The Summer Of The Swans by Betsy Byars
The Wolves Of Willoughby Chase by Joan Aiken
Beat The Turtle Drum by Constance Greene
A Day No Pigs Would Die by Robert Newton Peck
The Midnight Fox by Betsy Byars
The Lemming Condition by Alan Arkin
The Elephant In The Dark by Carol Carrick
The Mouse Rap by Walter Dean Myers
The Valley Of Deer by Eileen Dunlop
A Dog Called Kitty by Bill Wallace
One-Eyed Cat by Paula Fox
The Dog Days Of Arthur Cane by T. Ernesto Bethancourt

M-m-m-m Good!
(books with foods in their titles)

Aldo Applesauce by Johanna Hurwitz
Hello, My Name Is Scrambled Eggs by Jamie Gilson
Jelly Belly by Robert K. Smith
Popcorn Days And Buttermilk Nights by Gary Paulsen
The Enormous Egg by Oliver Butterworth
Hurry Home, Candy by Meindert DeJong
Soup by Robert Newton Peck
Breadsticks And Blessing Places by Candy Dawson Boyd
The Celery Stalks At Midnight by James Howe
The Broccoli Tapes by Jan Slepian

Rainbow Reading
(books with colors in their titles)

Black Beauty by Anna Sewell
Island Of The Blue Dolphins by Scott O'Dell
Bingo Brown, Gypsy Lover by Betsy Byars
Where The Red Fern Grows by Wilson Rawls
Goodbye, Pink Pig by C. S. Adler
The Curse Of The Blue Figurine by John Bellairs
Shades of Gray by Carolyn Reeder
The Black Cauldron by Lloyd Alexander
The White Mountains by John Christopher
Delpha Green And Company by Vera and Bill Cleaver
A Blue-Eyed Daisy by Cynthia Rylant

Using Journals In Science

Leonardo da Vinci was one of the most gifted inventors and artists the world has ever known. Today we know about his ideas because he recorded much of what he saw and thought in his notebooks. His notebooks ranged from ones as large as wall posters to some that were small enough to carry on his belt. Some of Leonardo's notebooks have survived to this day. They're filled with lines and lines of neat print—written from right to left—along with numerous drawings and diagrams.

Journaling in science helps students reflect on skills they've learned, and creates orderly notes for later study. Use the suggestions below and the reproducible on page 60 to get your budding scientists into journaling.

by Irving P. Crump

Getting Started

Reproduce one copy of the journal cover (the top half of page 60) for each student. Have students color and decorate their covers; then have them cut lined paper the same size as the cover to make pages for their journals. Instruct each student to punch a hole in the top left corner of the cover and each journal page, then bind all of the pages behind the cover with a brad or ring. Make a journal for each major topic of study throughout the year.

Suggestions For Using Science Journals

Science Experiences:

Provide each student with a copy of the form on the bottom half of page 60 to complete after a science experiment or laboratory activity, a nature walk, or a field trip. Have the student follow the directions on the page, then add the completed page to his journal.

Free Writing:

Have students write about any aspect of a science or health topic of their choice. Let them express their opinions about a person, an event, or a thing. Anything goes!

Current Events:

Have students bring in magazine and newspaper articles dealing with science subjects. Share an article; then have students react to it in their journals.

Question Of The Day:

On the board write a question that relates to a topic you're studying, a news item, or a science-related subject. Examples: "Would you like to be a paleontologist? How would your family adjust if there were a gasoline shortage? What's the greatest environmental problem facing our community?" Have students respond to the question in their journals.

Vocabulary Words:

Have students write science words and their definitions in their journals.

Lists:

Have students list important facts, causes and effects of events, or statements comparing and contrasting the characteristics of objects or events. Examples: "List the characteristics of mammals. Compare and contrast tornadoes with hurricanes. List some of Leonardo da Vinci's ideas that have become realities in the past 300 years."

Observation Skills:

Have students observe an object or event over a period of time and record their observations. Examples: "Observe and record weather patterns for one month. Observe the growth of two plants: one that is fertilized and one that is not."

Writing From Another Perspective:

Have students write about an event from a different perspective. Examples: "Write about an oil spill from the perspective of a seal. How does a deer family feel about suburbs encroaching on its woodland home? How does a furniture manufacturer feel about a ban on the import of mahogany?"

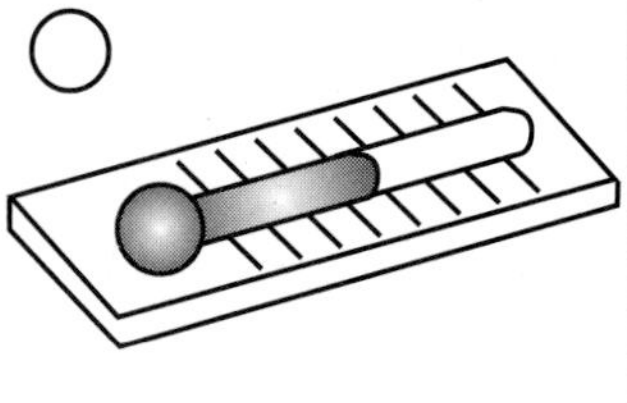

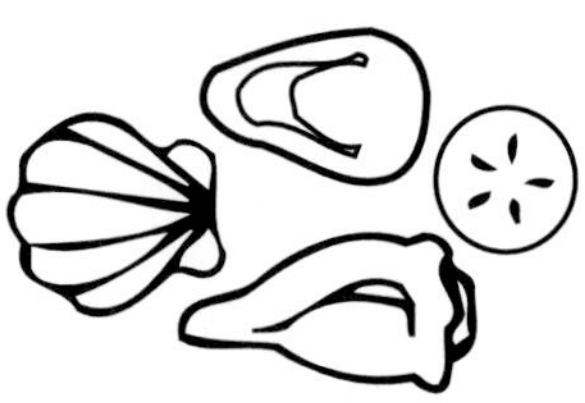

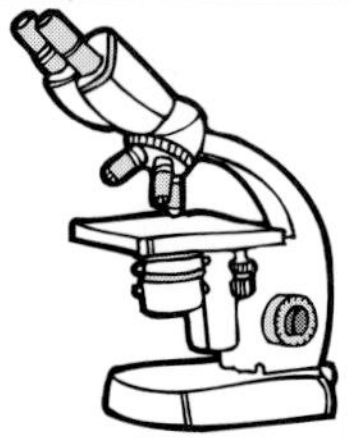

My Science Journal

_____
name

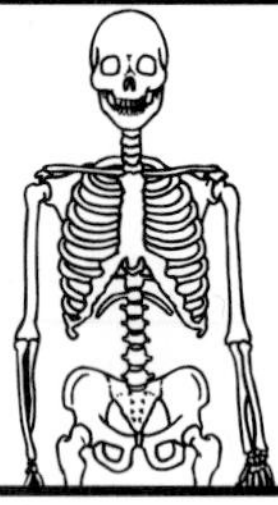

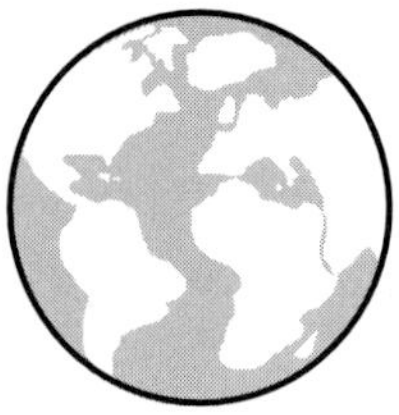

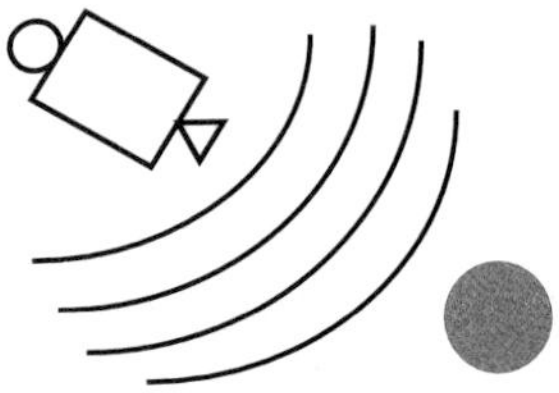

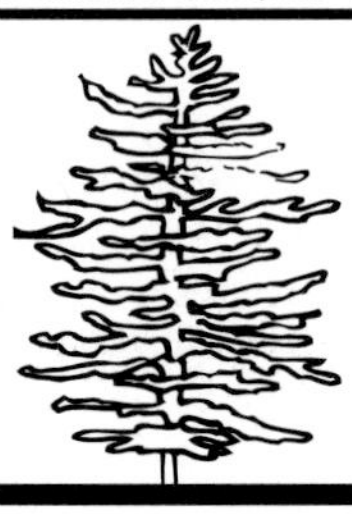

name _____ date _____

_____
science experience

1. Briefly describe the experience: _____
_____
_____

2. What special materials, if any, were used? _____
_____
_____

3. Write a sentence describing something new you learned. _____
_____

4. In the space below, draw a diagram or picture that would help you describe this science experience to a friend.

Mind-Bending Math

There's nothing like a little touch of mystery to capture students' interest. Challenge and delight them with the following baffling math tricks and puzzles.

by Irving P. Crump

Fast Figures

Amaze students with your fast figuring skills! Have a volunteer write two four-digit addends on the board. Then write a third addend, also having four digits, on the board. Challenge students to a race to see who can find the sum of the three numbers first. Follow the steps below and be the winner every time!

a. When you write your four-digit addend on the board, make sure each digit—when added to the digit directly above it—equals nine.

b. Write the five-digit sum: 1 followed by the first three digits in the top addend, followed by a digit that is one less than the digit in the top addend's ones place.

```
   7,362  } student's numbers
   3,918  }
 + 6,081  } your number: each
  ------     digit, when added to
  17,361     the one above it,
             equals nine.
```

one less than digit in top addend's ones place

1 — first three digits of top addend

Odd Versus Even

Have each student hold an even number of objects in one hand and an odd number of objects in the other hand. Or students may write numbers on slips of paper and hold the slips. Next have each student multiply the number in his left hand by three and the number in his right hand by two. Then instruct each student to add the resulting products. Ask a volunteer to share his sum. You can immediately determine which hand has the even number and which has the odd number!

If the student's sum is odd, then the left hand holds the odd number. If the sum is even, the left hand holds the even number.

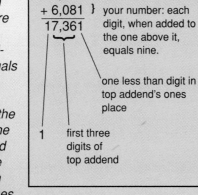

```
10    7
 L    R

10 x 3 = 30
 7 x 2 = 14
30 + 14 = 44
```
Sum is even. Left hand holds even number.

```
13    8
 L    R

13 x 3 = 39
 8 x 2 = 16
39 + 16 = 55
```
Sum is odd. Left hand holds odd number.

Clairvoyant Card Reading

Provide each student with five small index cards. Have each student number his cards from 1 to 10, writing 1 on a card, then 2 on the back; 3 on the next card, then 4 on the back; etc. Next have each student mix up his cards and lay them in any order on his desk. Without looking at his cards, ask a student to tell you how many odd numbers he has showing. You can then instantly determine the sum of his upturned cards!

The sum of 2, 4, 6, 8, and 10 is 30. Subtract the number of odd cards showing from 30.

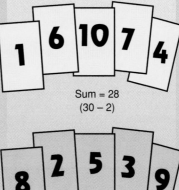

```
1  6  10  7  4
```
Sum = 28
(30 – 2)

```
8  2  5  3  9
```
Sum = 27
(30 – 3)

```
  632  } First number in
 -236  }   reverse order.
 -----
  396  } Difference (396)
 +693  }   in reverse order.
 -----
 1,089
```

```
  791
 -197
 -----
  594
 +495
 -----
 1,089
```

And The Number Is...

Have each student in your class write a three-digit number (consisting of three different digits) on a sheet of paper. Next instruct the student to reverse the digits in his number, write this new number below the original one, and subtract. (The sequence of the two numbers may be reversed if this step results in a larger number being subtracted from a smaller one. If the difference of the two numbers is 99, the student must choose a different number.)

Next tell each student to reverse the order of the digits in the difference, then add this new number to the difference. Then—drawing on your unbelievable psychic powers—inform students that they each have the same result (if everyone's computations are correct): 1,089!

Adventuring With Adjectives

Celebrate adjectives with a ferociously fun Adjective Adventure Day. The following magnificent modifier activities will lead your students down the trail to more descriptive writing!

ideas by Cheryl Schaeffer—Grs. 5–6, Lesterville, SD

Crazy Camouflage

To prepare for Adjective Adventure Day, instruct your students to dress up in outrageously colorful and contrasting outfits. Begin the day by having each student draw the name of a classmate out of a hat. Instruct each student to use adjectives to write a descriptive paragraph about the person whose name he drew, without revealing that person's identity. Exchange papers and have students take turns reading the descriptions. The class will enjoy trying to guess the identity of each person being described.

The Big Game

Your students will sink their teeth into this fun game, designed to broaden their adjective vocabulary. Have your class sit in a circle; then teach them the following clapping sequence:

slap, slap *(on knees)*
clap, clap
snap, snap *(with fingers)*
clap, clap

To begin the game, have the first student in the circle name a noun; then have the class start the clapping sequence. Starting with the person to the left of the first child, have each student add an adjective to the noun before the clapping sequence ends. For example, for the noun "cat," students could respond "fat cat," "clever cat," "furry cat," etc. If a player fails to come up with an adjective, then she is out. Play continues with the next student giving a new noun. Challenge students not to repeat any adjectives. When one player is left, start a new game.

It's A Jungle Out There!

Do your students get tangled up in homework and housework responsibilities? Help them cut through the workload and simplify their lives by inventing laborsaving devices for home and school. Instruct students to design inventions that will make their lives easier. After describing and illustrating their inventions, have students label them with descriptive names, such as Hassle-Free Homework Handler or Double-Duty Dishwasher and Dryer.

Armed With Adjectives

Shield students from dull writing with this descriptive coat-of-arms activity. Have each student draw a large coat of arms like the one shown. Instruct the student to draw a picture of the following in each of the four sections: a favorite pet or animal, a sport or hobby, a picture showing what the student wants to be when he grows up, and a favorite food. Instruct students to fill in the space around each picture with adjectives describing it. Have each student select his favorite section; then have him write a paragraph describing the picture in that section. Challenge the student to include as many of the section's adjectives in his paragraph as possible. Display the paragraphs and shields on a bulletin board entitled "Armed With Adjectives."

Me! King of the jungle!

Savagely Silly Stories

Students will roar with laughter while creating their own "Mad-Libs." Instruct each student to write a short adventure story using lots of adjectives. After editing the story, have each student erase her adjectives and replace them with numbered blanks. Working in pairs, have one student tell her partner the number of adjectives needed to complete her story. Have the partner make a list of adjectives—enough to fill the blanks in the story. The laughs begin when the first student reads her story aloud, filling in the blanks with adjectives from her partner's list.

Barry Slate

GAME PLANS

GAME PLANS

Sponge Board Baseball

Get ready to soak up information with Sponge Board Baseball. Divide your class into two teams. Draw a large square divided into nine equal parts on the blackboard. Label the squares as shown. After correctly answering a review question, a student throws a damp sponge at the board. His team earns whatever is in the square he hits. A scorekeeper keeps track of the bases reached as well as runs and outs earned. When a team has three outs, the next team takes a turn. The team with the most runs wins!

Deedra Bignar—Gr. 6, Nebo Elementary, Jena, LA

Out	Triple	Strike
Single	Home Run	Foul
Strike	Double	Out

Star Wars

The sky's the limit with a fun game of Star Wars! First program about 30 star cutouts with point values ranging from 5–25. Attach a small piece of magnetic tape to the back of each cutout so it will adhere to the blackboard. Place the stars in a basket so that students can't see the point values; then divide the class into four or five teams, writing each team's name at the top of the blackboard.

To play, have a member from each team go to the board. Call out a math problem to solve or a spelling word to write. Allow a reasonable amount of time for the players to complete the task. Let each student who arrives at the correct answer pick a star from the basket and attach it to the board below his team's name. At the end of the game, have each team total its points. The team with the highest total wins.

Jeffrey J. Kuntz—Gr. 6

5 20
10 25
15 5

Hop! Skip! Jump!

This challenging math game reinforces reasoning skills and pattern recognition. Divide students into four or five small groups. Draw a blank chart, like the one shown, on a chalkboard. Secretly select a three-digit number; then tell students that each group will work cooperatively to determine the number, but that only one group member will be allowed to announce his group's guess to the class. Next write the following code on the board:

- *Hop!* means none of the digits in a group's guess is correct.
- *Skip!* means that one digit in a guess is correct, but it's in the wrong place.
- *Jump!* means that a digit is correct, and it's in the correct place.

To play, have group 1 make a guess. Write the guess in the chart and code it according to the rules above. Let group 2 make a guess based on group 1's guess; then list the code word(s) in the chart. Continue play until a group identifies the secret number. As students get better and better at the game, try four- and five-digit numbers as well.

Coletta Preacely Ellis—Grs. 5–6
Wilson Elementary School
Lynwood, CA

Guess	Code
109	Hop!
823	Jump!
145	Skip!
265	Skip!
353	Hop!
426	Jump! Jump!
427	Jump! Jump! Jump!

Four-In-A-Row Spello

To play this spelling review game, divide students into pairs or small groups. (Pairing students promotes more individual practice.) Provide each group with a current spelling list and a game sheet consisting of an 8 x 8 grid. To play, students in each group take turns calling out words for each other to spell orally or write on paper. If correct, the speller writes his initials in any box on the game grid. If incorrect, play continues with the next player. The first student to claim four boxes in a vertical, horizontal, or diagonal row wins!

Jeffrey J. Kuntz—Gr. 6
West End School
Punxsutawney, PA

S	P	E	L	L	O
MC		SW		KJ		PB
MC			KJ			PB
MC					

Eraser Slide

To review any unit of study, my students play a game that's become one of their favorites. Students sit together in their cooperative groups. To play, I ask a question from the unit. Each group discusses the question and determines the answer. I then call on one student from a group. If that child gives the correct answer to the question, she gets a chance to slide the eraser down the chalk tray. Her team earns the number of points written on the chalkboard section where the eraser stops. If the answer is incorrect, I ask a student in the next group. This activity is a good team-spirit builder and a great review.

Susan Ely—Gr. 4, Churchville Elementary, Newtown, PA

Build-A-Word

Increase vocabulary and thinking skills with this fun word-building game. Give each student a grid of 36 squares. To begin play, ask a student to call out a letter. Have each child write that letter in a square on his grid. Continue having students call out letters and write them in their grids. Challenge students to form words of three or more letters horizontally, vertically, or diagonally. Explain that once a letter is written in a square, it cannot be erased, moved to another square, or changed. Have students circle their words as they build them. When all of the squares have been filled, declare the student with the most words the winner.

Joyceann Dreibelbis—Gr. 4
Kean Elementary
Wooster, OH

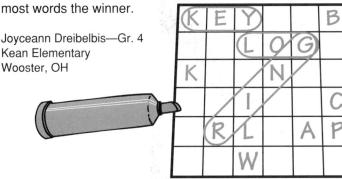

Fraction Dice Game

Wrap up a study of fractions with a roll of the die! Divide students into teams of three to five each and provide each team with a die. Instruct students on each team to take turns rolling the die two times: the first number rolled is the numerator for a fraction, while the second is the denominator. After everyone has rolled the die and recorded his fraction, students on each team compare their fractions with each other. The player with the greatest fraction—in its simplest terms—earns a point. Continue play until a student earns ten points. For a variation, provide each team with two dice or with 12-sided dice.

Sherri Kaiser—Gr. 4, Walnut Grove Elementary
Suwanee, GA

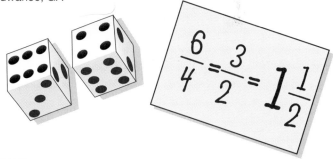

Table Race

For a fun math-practice game, I have students arrange their desks into groups of four or five each. I then provide each group with a sheet of bulletin-board paper large enough to cover its desks. I announce a page number that has math review problems corresponding to the skill we're studying. Students have a minute to open one math book in each group to that page; then they arrange themselves so that all group members can see the textbook and reach the paper. At my signal, groups work as many problems on the page as possible in a predetermined time. Students often divide the problems during their minute of planning time. I also encourage them to work others' problems too, since their teammates may make errors. When time is called, each correct answer earns a point for that team. What a fun way to review math!

Sherri L. McDonald—Gr. 4, Walnut Grove Elementary, Suwanee, GA

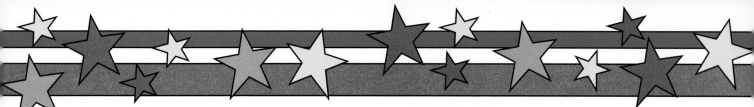

Pepping Up Parts Of Speech

Make reviewing parts of speech challenging for your class using the following game, which is similar to Scattergories®. Place a separate piece of paper labeled with each of the letters of the alphabet in a jar; then write the following categories on the chalkboard:

1. noun
2. verb
3. adverb
4. adjective
5. pronoun

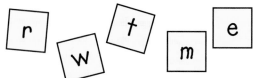

For each round of play, have the students number from one to five on their papers. Ask a student volunteer to select a letter from the jar and read it aloud. Instruct students to write a word that begins with the selected letter for each of the five parts of speech listed on the chalkboard. After students have recorded their responses, call on volunteers to share. A student earns a point only if the word she listed for a particular part of speech was not recorded by any other child in the class. This game is also fun when played in teams!

Tammy Johnson—Gr. 5, C. W. Harris Elementary, Washington, DC

Concentrate!

Build vocabulary and concentration skills with this blackboard review game. Write each vocabulary word for a current unit on a separate index card or cutout (one that matches the theme of the unit). Back each card with a piece of magnetic tape. Randomly arrange the cards on the blackboard. Allow students one minute to study the board. Then instruct them to close their eyes and put their heads down while you remove three to four cards. At your signal, have students look at the board, study it, and write the missing words and their definitions on their papers. Call on a student to correctly identify the missing words and their definitions. As an extra challenge, rearrange the position of the cards with each new turn.

Geri Laemers—Gr. 4
Durban Avenue School
Hopatcong, NJ

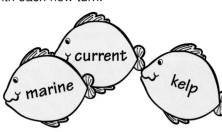

Ready To Review?

Throughout the year, write review questions and keep them in a jar. Use these questions to play the following exciting review game. First glue 20–40 die-cut shapes in rows on a piece of poster board. Write point values (50, 100, 200, 500) on the backs of small, self-sticking notes. Place each note on a shape so that the point value is hidden. Divide the class into cooperative teams; then ask the first team a review question. If the team correctly answers the question, have one of its members pull off

one of the self-sticking notes and reveal the points earned. If the first team does not correctly answer the question, then the next team gets a try. The team with the highest score wins the game.

Robin Halleran—Gr. 5
Livingston Elementary
Conyers, GA

26-Square Wipeout

My students love this game that provides plenty of basic math practice. I made a laminated gameboard with the numbers 1–26 on it (see the illustration). Students are divided into two teams. To begin play, I give Team 1 three numbers. That team then has one minute to come up with as many equations that will result in answers of 1–26 as possible. Students may multiply, divide, add, or subtract—or use any combinations of the operations. As players call out their equations and answers to me, I cross out each correct answer on the gameboard with a wipeoff marker. At the end of one minute, I count the numbers marked off. I then clean the gameboard and give the opposing team three numbers. After several rounds, the team that earns the most marked-off numbers gets to choose a math game to play on the following Friday.

Debbie Patrick—Gr. 5, Park Forest Elementary, State College, PA

+	1	2	3	4	−
5	6	7	8	9	10
11	12	13	14	15	16
17	18	19	20	21	22
×	23	24	25	26	÷

TEACHING *And* RESOURCE UNITS

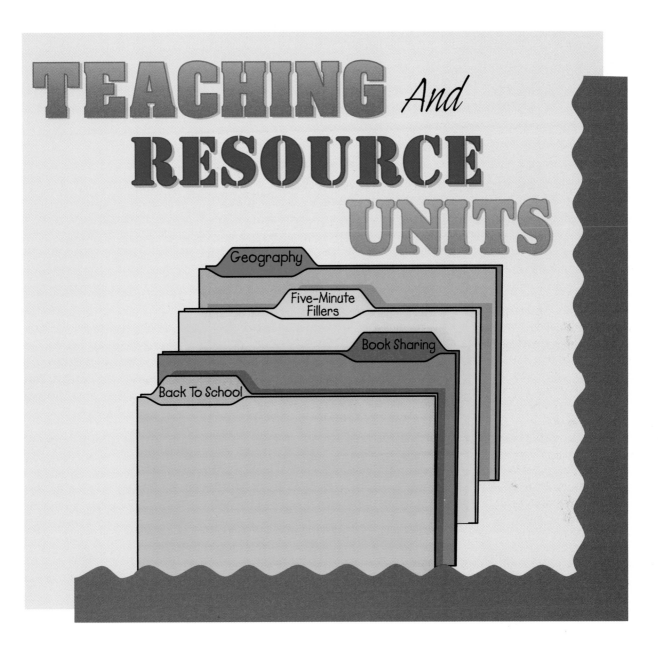

Geography

Five-Minute Fillers

Book Sharing

Back To School

Piecing Together A New Year

Back-To-School Ideas For Busy Teachers

Believe it or not, it's that time of year again. Time to dust off your favorite read-aloud, put up your "can't miss" bulletin board, and start fitting together the pieces of a new year. For a first week your students will love to pieces, try the following creative activities and practical reproducibles.

Picture Us, Piece By Piece!

On the first day of school, take two photographs of each student: one of a "normal" smiling face and one with a humorous, zany expression. Mount the smiling photos on a bulletin board, leaving space between the pictures. Cut each zany photo into four or five puzzle pieces; then mix all of the photos' pieces together. Distribute about ten pieces to each cooperative group. Tell students that during the next ten-minute period, only nonverbal communication—no talking—will be allowed. The class's goal is to reassemble all of the pictures, taping the pieces of each photo together on the back. Students are then to mount the pictures beside their matching photos on the bulletin board.

Once it's clear that everyone understands the directions, give the signal to start. Sit back and observe the interactions that take place as students first try to fit their pieces together and then realize that they will need to approach other groups for help. You'll notice which students are quick to seek help, which are so competitive they don't want to share their pieces, etc. The result is not just a fun bulletin board but also a unique opportunity to learn about your new students.

Stacy Kasse—Gr. 5, Taunton Forge School, Medford, NJ

We All Fit In!

Start the year off on the right foot with a team-building bulletin-board activity. To begin, draw a jigsaw puzzle design on a large piece of oaktag or bulletin-board paper, including a piece for each student in your class and for yourself. Cut out the pieces; then label the back of each piece with a number so that the puzzle can be reassembled easily later. Also indicate the top of each piece.

On the first day or during the first week of school, discuss with students the importance and contributions of each class member. Also talk about how, when someone is absent, the classroom environment just isn't complete—like a puzzle that is missing a piece. Give each student a piece of the paper puzzle. Have the student decorate his puzzle piece with his name and illustrations, colors, and symbols he thinks represent himself. After each child has decorated his puzzle piece, have the class reassemble the puzzle on a large bulletin board. Add the title "We All Fit In!" What a fitting way to start the year!

Gloria Munns—Gr. 6, Truman Elementary, Salt Lake City, UT

A Piece Of My Mind

Assessing students' writing skills is an important task during the first week of school. Let students give you a piece of their minds (as well as samples of their writing) by using the journal topics below.

Journal Topics:
- In some other countries, students stay longer at school each day than American kids do; plus, they attend for several hours on Saturday. What do you think would be the advantages of this type of schedule? The disadvantages?
- What makes a school a place that you look forward to going to each day?
- What is the best way for a teacher to deal with discipline problems?
- What is the best way for a teacher to help a student who is having difficulty understanding a new skill?
- What qualities does an excellent teacher have?
- What is the best way for two classmates who are arguing to solve their disagreement?
- What should a teacher do about a student who regularly fails to turn in his or her homework?
- Should students be rewarded for doing required tasks like homework or book reports? Why or why not?

We all fit in!

I Fall To Pieces!

Introduce the scientific method to students with an "eggs-ellent" science activity. Ask the class, "What will happen to an uncooked egg when it is dropped on the floor?" (The prospect of seeing an egg smash on the classroom floor will keep students' attention, while the obvious results will help you focus on teaching the scientific method.) After posing the question, explain to students that they will conduct an experiment in the manner that real scientists do. Label the top of a large piece of chart paper "The Scientific Method." Ask the class what they are going to find out about the egg. As they restate the question, explain that identifying the **question** or **problem** is the first step in the scientific method. List this on the chart as shown. Next ask students what they expect to happen when the egg is dropped. Explain that they have completed step two of the scientific method: stating their **hypothesis**. Discuss materials needed to conduct the experiment; then list them on the chart. Ask if students are ready to drop the egg; then have them explain the steps **(procedure)** to follow.

Before actually dropping the egg, discuss with students what they'll need to do as the egg falls and hits the ground. Point out the need to make a good **observation**; then add it to the chart. Once the egg has smashed on the floor, have students state the **conclusion** to add to the chart. This unforgettable experience will serve as a yearlong reminder of the scientific method.

Sarah Hilbert—Gr. 4, Mary B. Erskine Elementary, Seguin, TX

Bits And Pieces About Me

Help students get to know one another with a unique, high-flying display! If available, hang a few colorful kites in the upper corners of your classroom. Give each student a large kite pattern divided into 12 numbered segments as shown. Post the following directions on a large chart; then set students free to color their unique kites. Explain that if both colors in a direction apply to them, students should color that block with a design that uses both colors. Have students decorate the backs of their kites with stylized versions of their names or initials. Encourage students to add kite tails, including one paper or fabric bow for each family member (including pets). Suspend the kites from the classroom ceiling with fishing line. Students will soar into the new year while learning all about their classmates!

Directions:

1. Color section one red if you're a girl and blue if you're a boy.
2. Color section two yellow if you're an only child and green if you have brothers and/or sisters.
3. Color section three blue if you have a pet and green if you don't.
4. Color section four purple if this is your first year at this school and pink if you've been at this school for more than a year.
5. Color section five orange if you play on a sports team and red if you are involved in a non-sports, after-school activity.
6. Color section six green if you've always lived in this state and red if you've ever lived in another state.
7. Color section seven blue if you have your own bedroom and yellow if you share a bedroom with someone.
8. Color section eight green if you like math and orange if you like writing.
9. Color section nine purple if you prefer working with a group and red if you prefer working alone.
10. Color section ten blue if you like winter and yellow if you like summer.
11. Color section eleven green if you prefer being a listener and red if you prefer being a speaker.
12. Color section twelve orange if you like television and green if you like books.

Sara L. Ertl—Gr. 5, Lehigh Elementary, Palmerton, PA

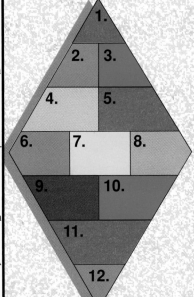

The Scientific Method

QUESTION: What will happen to an uncooked egg when it is dropped on the floor?

HYPOTHESIS: The egg will break when it is dropped on the floor.

MATERIALS: uncooked egg, paper towels

PROCEDURE:

1. Spread the paper towels on the floor.
2. Hold the egg high in the air above the paper towels.
3. Drop the egg.

OBSERVATION: The egg broke into pieces. The yolk—as well as the shell—broke. It made a real mess!

CONCLUSION: An uncooked egg will break when it is dropped on the floor.

Barry Slate

Piecing Together A Masterpiece

Emphasize the theme of cooperation early in the year with a fun cooperative art activity. Sketch a design—such as a simple picture of your school's mascot—on a large piece of paper. With a pencil, lightly divide the paper into squares (at least one per student). Using colored markers or crayons, indicate with a small dot the color of each section shown on the squares. Cut out the squares; then number the backs so that the picture can be reassembled later. Have students cut small squares of colored construction paper, storing them in plastic bowls at a center. During free time, each student glues appropriately colored paper squares into the labeled sections of his larger square. After each student has finished, reassemble your cooperative masterpiece by taping the sections together on the backs.

A Little Piece Of Advice

What student isn't at least a little apprehensive about his new teacher? On the first day of school, read aloud Mike Thaler's short book, *The Teacher From The Black Lagoon* (Scholastic Inc., 1989). After reading the book, have students discuss the qualities of a good teacher. Ask, "What little piece of advice would you give me about how to make this a positive year for everyone?" As a follow-up to the discussion, have each child write a letter to his favorite teacher, telling why he or she was so appreciated. Since the letters will likely contain mistakes, use this activity as an opportunity to reintroduce the writing process steps of editing, revising, etc. When the letters are complete, send them (use your school system's interoffice mail system if students have changed schools). How encouraging for any teacher to receive a letter of praise at the beginning of a new year!

Elaine Osteen—Gr. 6
Evers Park Elementary, Denton, TX

A Piece Of The Math Action

Inaugurate a new year of hands-on math explorations with a fun data analysis activity. Fill a bag with 500 Reese's Pieces® candies. Tell students that you want to know how many of the pieces are yellow, how many are orange, and how many are brown; but you don't want to take the time to count all 500 pieces. What would be the best way to solve this problem? Lead students to determine that the best method would be to take the pieces out in small groups, count the colors in each group, and make predictions based on that count. Divide the class into several cooperative teams. Have each team take a handful of candies and tally the number in its group. Let each group repeat this step 10–15 times, recording its tally each time on a chart (see the example); then have groups use their tallies to make a prediction about the number of each color inside the bag. Remind students that their predictions must total 500. List the predictions on the board. Discuss with students the difference between making a prediction based on information and making a "wild guess." Have volunteers count the actual candies inside the bag after school; then post the results. The next day, discuss with students real-life situations where it is impossible or impractical to count an entire group.

Small Group	1	2	3	4	5	6
yellow	10	6	6	8	10	9
orange	14	9	11	9	4	3
brown	4	12	12	7	9	7

70

We All Fit In!

If you're the least bit puzzled about the kids you'll be spending a year with, here's a chance to learn more about them! Find classmates who can sign their names in the puzzle pieces below. A student may sign no more than two pieces on the gameboard. Try to get five signatures in a row; then try to fill your entire gameboard.

GRADE-A READING MOTIVATION

Book-Sharing Activities From Our Subscribers

How do you motivate your students to read and even share about the books they're reading? When we asked you—our subscribers—to send in your ideas, we were overwhelmed with the grade-A ideas we received. When you want your students to crack open a book, look no further than these "eggs-ceptional" activities!

Reading "Hooks"

My students earn "Acerra Bucks"—our class incentive/reward—by "hooking" their classmates into books they have read. A student who wants to earn an Acerra Buck gives a brief introduction to his book; then he reads a portion he thinks will "hook" others into wanting to read his book. Since starting this program, my students' oral reading skills have improved. Their eyes have also been opened to a variety of authors and writing techniques.

Janet M. Acerra—Gr. 5
Forest Lakes Elementary
Oldsmar, FL

Sneak Peeks

To encourage my older intermediate students to read for pleasure—not just for a grade—I created "Sneak Peeks." Each Friday I preview an award-winning book selected from our media center. We note the title and author; then I read the first chapter aloud. I keep several copies of the book on hand for interested students to check out. My kids ask all week about the book that will be featured on "Sneak Peek," and this interest leads to avid readers.

Martha Ennis
Arnold Middle School
Columbus, GA

A Poppin' Good Idea!

Our class makes reading a feature presentation with this poppin' good idea. For each student, I mount a popcorn box on a bulletin board entitled "And Now For Our Feature Presentation: Reading!" Each time a student finishes a book, she writes a brief summary and evaluation on a popcorn-shaped cutout; then she places the cutout in her box. When each student has read four books, we have a popcorn party. While we enjoy the buttery treat, each pupil shares her book reports.

Neva J. Doerr—Gr. 4
Creighton Community Schools
Creighton, NE

Catherine,
Called Birdy
by Karen
Cushma[n]

Wal[k]

POPCORN

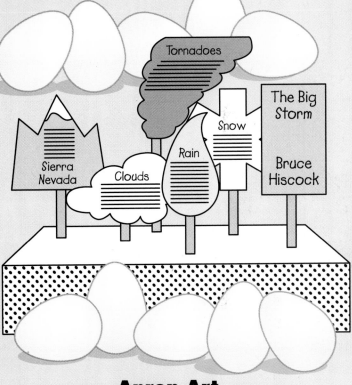

The Mark Of A Great Book

Capture the unique qualities of great books by creating these illustrative bookmarks. Provide each student with a bookmark pattern—either oversized to display on a wall or small enough to tuck into a favorite book. On the front of the bookmark, have the student draw an important scene from the book, and then add the book's title, its author, and her name. On the back, instruct the student to write a poem about a feeling the book evoked in her, including the event(s) in the story that produced this feeling. Laminate each bookmark; then punch a hole in the top for adding a yarn tassel.

Julia Alarie—Gr. 6
Essex Middle School
Essex, VT

Stabile Book Reports

Every teacher is familiar with the moving displays called mobiles. But have you heard of *stabiles*? Have students share their favorite books by creating these nonmoving displays. Each student needs a block of stiff Styrofoam® (the kind used in packages) and seven sticks (chopsticks, Popsicle® sticks, or wooden skewers). Have the student mount an illustrated portion of her book report onto the end of each stick; then have her insert each stick into the Styrofoam, securing it with a drop of glue. Instruct the student to include the following information on her stabile: the book's title and author, her name, the main characters, the setting, three main events in the plot, a rating for the book, and something she learned from reading the book. Display the finished stabiles on a table in your school's media center or foyer.

Julia Alarie—Gr. 6

Apron Art

To model the joy of reading for our students, each staff member at our school chose a favorite book to illustrate on the front of an apron. (As principal, I provided the pocketed aprons.) Using paint, markers, glitter, and even battery-operated lights, we brought the aprons to life. Props—such as finger puppets and items found in the story—were stored in the apron pockets to enhance the book sharing. We debuted the completed aprons at our school's "Reading Lock-In Party." Thereafter, the school celebrated "Apron Days" twice a month. On these special days, staff members visited classrooms to share their apron stories. Students were impressed by the talent, creativity, and dedication to reading exhibited by their school's staff.

Donna Neel—Principal
Lincoln Elementary
Norman, OK

Coupons For A Character

Which character in your book needed help during his/her adventures? Design some coupons for this character to use. Create a product that would have come in handy as the character dealt with his/her problem. Or design your coupons to provide opportunities or abilities that would have made a difference in the outcome of the adventure. Add colorful illustrations in the spaces provided.

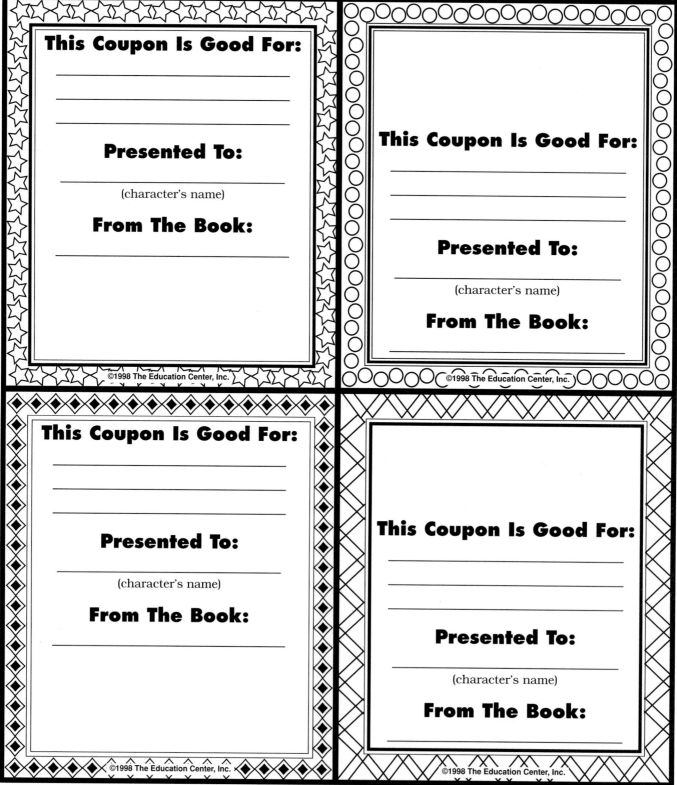

This Coupon Is Good For:

_____
_____
_____

Presented To:

_____

(character's name)

From The Book:

_____

©1998 The Education Center, Inc.

This Coupon Is Good For:

_____
_____
_____

Presented To:

_____

(character's name)

From The Book:

_____

©1998 The Education Center, Inc.

This Coupon Is Good For:

_____
_____
_____

Presented To:

_____

(character's name)

From The Book:

_____

©1998 The Education Center, Inc.

This Coupon Is Good For:

_____
_____
_____

Presented To:

_____

(character's name)

From The Book:

_____

©1998 The Education Center, Inc.

ARITHMETIC ARCADE

Creative Games To Reinforce Multiplication And Division Skills

Step right up, ladies and gentlemen, and get your tickets right here! Watch math skills *multiply* and groans *divide* and disappear with this collection of entertaining, challenging games.

by Irving P. Crump

Winning Facts

Skills: multiplication and division facts, calculator usage
Materials: pencils, paper, calculator for each player

To improve both speed and accuracy with basic facts, introduce this game as a whole-class activity. Once they catch on, students will want to play in pairs or small groups. Call out a basic fact for students to enter into their calculators—but instruct them *not* to press the equals key. Next have students record their responses on paper. When everyone has written his answer, students then press the equals key to check their work. Play rounds of 10 or 20 facts; then see who is most proficient. Or see who can correctly answer the most facts in succession without missing one.

Earning Dividends

Skill: division facts (or multiplication facts)
Materials: 35 small index cards for each group of 4–6 students

Have each group of students label four index cards with the word SKIP; then instruct the group to label the remainder of its cards 4, 6, 8, 9, 10, 12, 14, 15, 16, 18, 20, 21, 24, 25, 27, 28, 30, 32, 35, 36, 40, 42, 45, 48, 49, 54, 56, 63, 64, 72, and 81. These numbers represent the dividends of the basic division facts (or products of multiplication facts), omitting the factors zero and one. Ask students to underline each number so that it's easily identifiable. Then have each group double-check to make sure that its deck consists of the 35 cards programmed as described. Next ask one student in each group to shuffle the cards. Have each group sit on the floor or around a table so that each player can reach the cards, which are placed facedown in a stack in the middle of the group.

To begin play, a player in the group turns over the top card and lays it faceup. (If he draws a SKIP card, he loses his turn and play continues to the next person in the circle.) He then gives the division fact (9: 9 ÷ 3 = 3) or facts (16: 16 ÷ 2 = 8; 16 ÷ 8 = 2; 16 ÷ 4 = 4) that use(s) the dividend on the card. After naming all possible facts, the student keeps that card and says "pass." Play then proceeds to his right. If the second player agrees with the first player, he draws the next card and repeats the procedure. If the second player can name a fact that the first player forgot, then the second player wins the first player's card. Play continues around the circle until all of the cards have been used. The winner in each group is the student who holds the most number cards.

Race To $1,000

Skills: rounding, multiplying, calculator usage
Materials: product ads, calculators (optional), pencils, paper, die

On a bulletin board, post about 10–12 newspaper ads that feature items priced in the $10–$100 range (CDs, sports equipment, clothing, etc.). Or list items and their prices on a chalkboard. To play a whole-class game, roll a die and announce the number to the class. (If a one is rolled, announce *ten*.) Have each student select an item from the ads, round its price to the nearest dollar, then multiply that price by the number showing on the die. For example, if a four is rolled and a student chooses a CD priced at $14.95, he would estimate a total of $60 ($15 x 4). The student writes his estimate on his paper. Roll the die again and repeat the procedure, instructing each student to keep a running total of his purchases. (Students may buy more of the same items during subsequent rolls of the die.)

The object of the game is to have an estimated total that is closest to $1,000 without going over. Students may stop at any time they wish as long as they buy at least two items. For fun, have students use calculators to determine the actual cost of all the items they bought.

On Target!

Skills: multiplying two-, three-, and four-digit numbers by a one-digit number; calculator usage
Materials: pencils, paper, deck of cards with tens and face cards removed, a calculator for each pair of students

On his own paper, have each student make a diagram of three boxes (see the illustration) to represent a two-digit times a one-digit multiplication problem. Next draw a card from the deck and announce it to the class. (The value of an ace is one.) Instruct students to write that number in one of the boxes. After a number is written, it cannot be erased. Repeat this procedure with two more cards; then instruct students to solve the problem.

While students are working, write a digit from 0 to 9 on the chalkboard. Tell students that this digit is the "target." Have partners use calculators to check each other's products. If a product is incorrect, the student scores 0. If the product is correct, the student scores 10 points, plus bonus points for each target digit that his product contains: 5 points if the target digit is in the ones' place, 10 points if the target digit is in the tens' place, and 20 points if the target digit is in the hundreds' place.

Adapt this game for larger products by assigning points to additional place values.

Name Those Keys

Skills: multiplication, division, calculator usage, guess-and-check strategy
Materials: pencils, paper, calculator for each student or pair of students

Secretly write a multiplication problem on an index card. Draw boxes on the chalkboard to represent the problem, and write its answer. (See the samples shown.) Begin with basic facts; then progress to problems with two-digit numbers times one-digit numbers, then two-digit numbers times two-digit numbers. The object of the game is for students to use the guess-and-check strategy and their calculators to determine the missing factors. The order of the factors does not matter as long as the factors match the ones on your index card.

Adapt this game to reinforce division skills. Simply use division problems that do not have remainders.

Let's Play Pinball!

Complete this pinball game by filling in each bumper with < (less than) or > (greater than). Do <u>not</u> work the problems. Instead, round the numbers in each problem; then compute the product or quotient mentally.

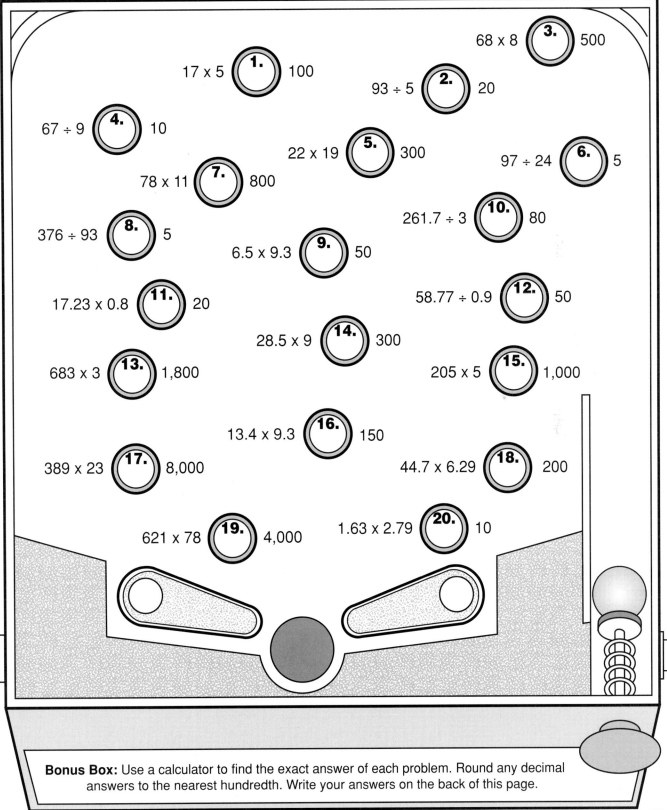

17 x 5 **1.** 100

68 x 8 **3.** 500

93 ÷ 5 **2.** 20

67 ÷ 9 **4.** 10

22 x 19 **5.** 300

97 ÷ 24 **6.** 5

78 x 11 **7.** 800

261.7 ÷ 3 **10.** 80

376 ÷ 93 **8.** 5

6.5 x 9.3 **9.** 50

17.23 x 0.8 **11.** 20

58.77 ÷ 0.9 **12.** 50

28.5 x 9 **14.** 300

683 x 3 **13.** 1,800

205 x 5 **15.** 1,000

13.4 x 9.3 **16.** 150

389 x 23 **17.** 8,000

44.7 x 6.29 **18.** 200

621 x 78 **19.** 4,000

1.63 x 2.79 **20.** 10

Bonus Box: Use a calculator to find the exact answer of each problem. Round any decimal answers to the nearest hundredth. Write your answers on the back of this page.

Test Your Strength!

A number is divisible by...

Step right up, and let's see how strong you are! First read the hints that help you know when a number is divisible by another number. Also study the examples.

Complete the chart below by making a check in each box that is true. The first row (16) has been completed for you.

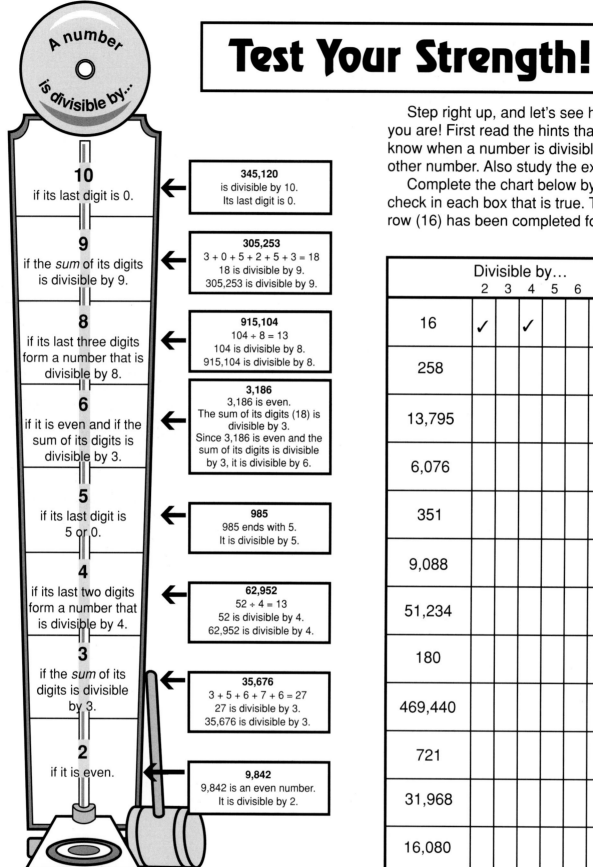

10
if its last digit is 0.

345,120
is divisible by 10.
Its last digit is 0.

9
if the *sum* of its digits is divisible by 9.

305,253
3 + 0 + 5 + 2 + 5 + 3 = 18
18 is divisible by 9.
305,253 is divisible by 9.

8
if its last three digits form a number that is divisible by 8.

915,104
104 ÷ 8 = 13
104 is divisible by 8.
915,104 is divisible by 8.

6
if it is even and if the sum of its digits is divisible by 3.

3,186
3,186 is even.
The sum of its digits (18) is divisible by 3.
Since 3,186 is even and the sum of its digits is divisible by 3, it is divisible by 6.

5
if its last digit is 5 or 0.

985
985 ends with 5.
It is divisible by 5.

4
if its last two digits form a number that is divisible by 4.

62,952
52 ÷ 4 = 13
52 is divisible by 4.
62,952 is divisible by 4.

3
if the *sum* of its digits is divisible by 3.

35,676
3 + 5 + 6 + 7 + 6 = 27
27 is divisible by 3.
35,676 is divisible by 3.

2
if it is even.

9,842
9,842 is an even number.
It is divisible by 2.

	Divisible by…								
	2	3	4	5	6	8	9	10	
16	✓		✓			✓			
258									
13,795									
6,076									
351									
9,088									
51,234									
180									
469,440									
721									
31,968									
16,080									

Bonus Box: Count the number of checks in your chart, including those for the completed sample, and write the total here: _____. Did you have a row with no checks?

Harvesting A Crop Of Responsible Students

By your example and the caring way you do your job every day, you're probably already teaching your students responsibility. But how can you make doubly sure that you're helping them learn how to cooperate with each other, show respect, be compassionate, and make wise decisions? Follow the advice of fellow subscribers by using the following teacher-tested ideas on encouraging students to be responsible.

Oh, Boy—It's T.G.I.F.!

To reward students for responsible behavior, the fifth-grade teachers at our school instituted T.G.I.F., or Time for Group Interaction on Friday. Students who turn in all assignments on time during the week and do not break any class rules are invited to a 30-minute get-together on Friday afternoon. The students—who are in five different self-contained homerooms—are thrilled with the chance to socialize with buddies from other classes. Students who don't earn the chance to participate in T.G.I.F. are grouped in several of the homerooms to work on missing/incomplete assignments or to read quietly. During this time, these children have a chance to catch up with their schoolwork so they can start fresh the next week. To help reinforce the concept of making responsible decisions, we stress to students that missing T.G.I.F. isn't a punishment, but a consequence of their choices. *Therese Durhman—Gr. 5, Mountain View School, Hickory, NC*

Grade Tracking

Intermediate students are very grade-conscious; yet most would say that it's the teacher's—not the student's—responsibility to keep track of grades. Not so in my classroom! To help my students learn how to keep track of their own grades, I give each child a blank grade sheet form. Each time I return a graded paper to students, I remind them to log it onto their grade sheets. If a student's grade sheet is correctly completed at the end of a six-week period, I reward the child with bonus points in the subject of his choice. Not only do students learn responsibility as they track their grades, but they also communicate their progress to their parents more frequently—an added bonus for me! *Betsy Fannin—Gr. 5, Bloom Middle School, South Webster, OH*

One Smart Cookie

Responsibility, good work habits, cooperation—all are ingredients in one smart cookie! To encourage my students to be responsible, I post a chef cutout on a small bulletin board entitled "What A Smart Cookie!" Also on the board, I place a student-generated list of "ingredients" for a smart cookie (see the example). At the end of the week, I name a student who exhibited these ingredients as the "Smart Cookie Of The Week." I write the student's name on a large cookie cutout and mount it on the board. In addition, I give the student a special certificate (see page 81) and a delicious cookie. *Lenore Kagan—Gr. 4, P.S. 150, Long Island City, NY*

What A Smart Cookie!

INGREDIENTS
- completes assignments
- is responsible
- is enthusiastic
- shares with others
- cooperates

SMART COOKIE OF THE WEEK

Tia

1st: H
2nd: HOM
3rd: HOME
5th: HO
6th: HOMEW
7th: HOMEWORK

Pam Crane

Handy Homework Tip

If you teach in a departmentalized setting, try this handy tip for helping students take responsibility for homework. Divide a large piece of poster board according to the number of periods you teach (see the illustration). Each time every student in a class turns in his homework, add a letter in HOMEWORK to the chart as shown. When a class finally spells HOMEWORK, treat it to a popcorn and video party. With this tip, students put the pressure to do homework on each other, so you don't have to! *Monica Moss—Special Education Grs. 5–8, Iuka, MS*

Recipe For Responsibility

Encourage responsibility at the beginning of the year with an eye-catching bulletin board. Have students brainstorm a list of "ingredients" for becoming a responsible student: be prepared for class, take responsibility for your actions, don't blame others for your mistakes, respect teachers and classmates, etc. Provide students with construction paper, scissors, and markers. Have each child draw and cut out a vegetable; then have him label it with one of the ingredients for responsibility. Post the cutouts on a bulletin board entitled "Our Recipe For Success? Be Responsible!" *Adapted from an idea by Kristen Murphy— Gr. 6, Laurel Elementary, New Castle, PA*

A Literature Helper

To help teach responsibility, track down a copy of Marilyn Burns's book *I Am Not A Short Adult: Getting Good At Being A Kid* (Little, Brown, and Company; 1977). This book offers kids insight about how to survive in an adult world. Its brief chapters make this book an excellent read-aloud choice. Share a chapter with students; then divide into cooperative groups to discuss it. The topics covered in the chapters also make terrific journal starters. *Susan Keller—Gr. 5 Reading and Language Arts, Plumb Elementary, Clearwater, FL*

Candy Contest

Use a favorite candy treat to encourage responsible behavior and better study habits. Divide your class into four groups. Have each group decide on a team name; then have the team label an empty baby food jar with its name. Label a small plastic bag for each team; then place 100 Skittles® candies into each bag. Explain to students that their teams can earn points (one candy per point) for the following behaviors:

- Everyone in a team is seated when class starts.
- All team members turn in a completed assignment on time.
- All team members return library books on time.
- Each team member is prepared for class.

Tell students that points will be lost for such behaviors as making excessive noise after class starts, not cooperating, turning in assignments late, etc. When a team earns a point, take a candy from its bag and place it in its jar. Remove candies when points are lost. Reward the first team to earn 100 candies with a special treat. *Adapted from an idea by Ellen Schoettle—Gr. 5, Tuttle Intermediate School, Tuttle, OK*

Student Self-Evaluations

When I talk to my class about responsibility, I suggest that success comes from six key elements: focus, participation, good work habits, a positive attitude, independent skills, and citizenship. To reinforce these elements every day, I give each student a copy of a weekly self-evaluation chart (see page 81). At the end of the day, students evaluate themselves by completing their charts. Each student who has a "yes" in each row receives a puzzle piece. When the student has earned 20 pieces, he assembles his puzzle, which is actually a free homework certificate that I've cut into 20 pieces. (You can also reward students with special coupons from area businesses such as a miniature golf park or pizzeria.) With this system of self-evaluation, students think about their behavior and take ownership of it. *N. Jane Bond—Gr. 5, St. Augustine Country Day School, St. Augustine, FL*

Was I On Target Today?

How responsible were you today? Think about the behaviors and attitudes you exhibited. Write YES or NO in each box.

	MON.	TUES.	WED.	THURS.	FRI.
FOCUS Did I concentrate and pay attention?					
PARTICIPATION Did I contribute in class and/or in my group?					
GOOD WORK HABITS Did I put forth my best effort?					
POSITIVE ATTITUDE Did I believe in myself?					
INDEPENDENT SKILLS When working alone, did I use my time wisely?					
CITIZENSHIP Did I treat others with respect?					

©1998 The Education Center, Inc. • *The Best Of* The Mailbox® *Intermediate* • *Book 3* • TEC835

You're One Smart Cookie!

Congratulations!

You've got all the right ingredients
to be named
"Smart Cookie Of The Week."
Keep up the good work!

Awarded to: _____

Signed: _____

Date: _____

INGREDIENTS

©1998 The Education Center, Inc. • *The Best Of* The Mailbox® *Intermediate* • *Book 3* • TEC835

Note To Teacher: Use the form with "Student Self-Evaluations" on page 80. Use the "Smart Cookie" award with "One Smart Cookie" on page 79. Before duplicating the award, write several of the ingredients your students chose on the recipe card.

Getting A JUMP On Geography!

A Collection Of Our Subscribers' Favorite Geography Activities

Making and reading maps, identifying landforms, using latitude and longitude—all these skills and many more go together to make geography-smart students. The next time you're jumping to give your students a fun geography lesson, try one of the following teacher-tested ideas from our subscribers.

Globe Mobiles

Ask your local pizza parlor to help your students review geography basics by donating a supply of the cardboard circles used to line take-out boxes (one per student). Instruct the student to draw the Eastern Hemisphere of the earth on one side of his circle and the Western Hemisphere on the other. After the student has painted each side and let it dry, direct him to use fine-tipped permanent markers to add details to the hemispheres: continent borders, the equator, the two tropics, the oceans, the prime meridian, the international date line, the highest point on each continent, other major bodies of water, etc. Attach a length of heavy yarn to each circle. Then hang all the mobiles from your classroom ceiling for a colorful vista that's a reminder of basic geography facts. *Gloria Jean Stevens—Gr. 5, Frank Jewett Elementary, West Buxton, ME*

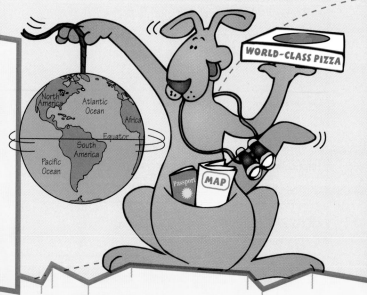

Take A Geography Cruise!

As part of our world geography study, I give each student a stamp from a foreign country and a copy of a cruise ship (see page 84). Each student adheres his stamp to the flag on his ship; then he researches his assigned country and fills out his ship pattern with the information. After cutting out his ship, the student mounts it around a world map posted on a large bulletin board. Then he uses a length of yarn to connect his ship to the country's location on the map. This is a great activity to do around National Stamp Collecting Day (November 2). *Kimberly Schwieren-VanHise—Grs. 4–6 Blended, Hines Elementary, Burns, OR*

Hometown Map

For a unique geography homework assignment, have each student choose one spot in your town. Direct the student to create a map that shows a visitor how to get from the student's house to that location. Inform students that the route must be the simplest and most direct way possible. Encourage students to add details that will help someone unfamiliar with your town to read their maps and find the special locations. Involve parents by asking them to help their child figure the mileage of his map's route. *Ruth Howell—Gr. 4, Carlisle Elementary, Spartanburg, SC*

Oui, Oui, mademoiselle! That is correct!

FRANCE by Simone Lepine

Country Wheels

Promote the sharing of newly learned information while your students travel the globe with this tactile research project. To begin, work together as a class to list ten questions that someone could research about a foreign country. Some suggestions include: "What type of government does this country have? In what continent is this country located? What are the major ethnic groups represented in this country? What is the size of the country in square miles?" List the questions on a piece of chart paper and display it in the classroom. Next have each student choose a country to research in order to answer the ten questions. Encourage students to write their answers as short, concise statements. After students have finished researching, give each a copy of page 85. Provide stencils of the cover (see the directions for making them, below).

After students have made their wheels, let them swap and share them. Or put all the wheels in a special box at a center so that students can read them during free time. *Simone Lepine—Gr. 5, Syracuse, NY*

Making cover stencils:
1. Trace the inside circle of the wheel (page 85) on tracing paper. Trace only one pie-shaped piece.
2. Draw a line across the tip of the "pie wedge" right before the number so that the number will still show (see the illustration).
3. Cut out the tracing. Use this outline to make several cardboard stencils of the cover.
4. Place the stencils, a supply of tagboard, scissors, and brads (one per child) at a table. Let students visit the table when they're ready to make their wheel covers.

Latitude And Longitude Cards

When it's time to introduce latitude and longitude to your students, provide them with this handy tool. Have each child copy the diagram as shown on a small index card. Tape each student's card to his desktop as a ready reference to use during lessons on latitude and longitude. *Karen Bryant, Rosa Taylor Elementary, Macon, GA*

Latitude/Longitude Rhyme

Trying to keep latitude and longitude straight can frustrate even the most able student. Before a recent map skills test, one of my social-studies classes wrote the poem on the right to help everyone remember the basic facts about latitude and longitude. *Gaylin Black—Gr. 4, Frontier Elementary, Angleton, TX*

latitude

longitude

Latitude lines run east and west,
But measure north and south.
If you learn these parallels,
You'll know what they're about!

Longitude lines run north and south,
But measure east and west.
Learn all about meridians
And you will pass the test!

Pattern

Use with "Take A Geography Cruise!" on page 82.

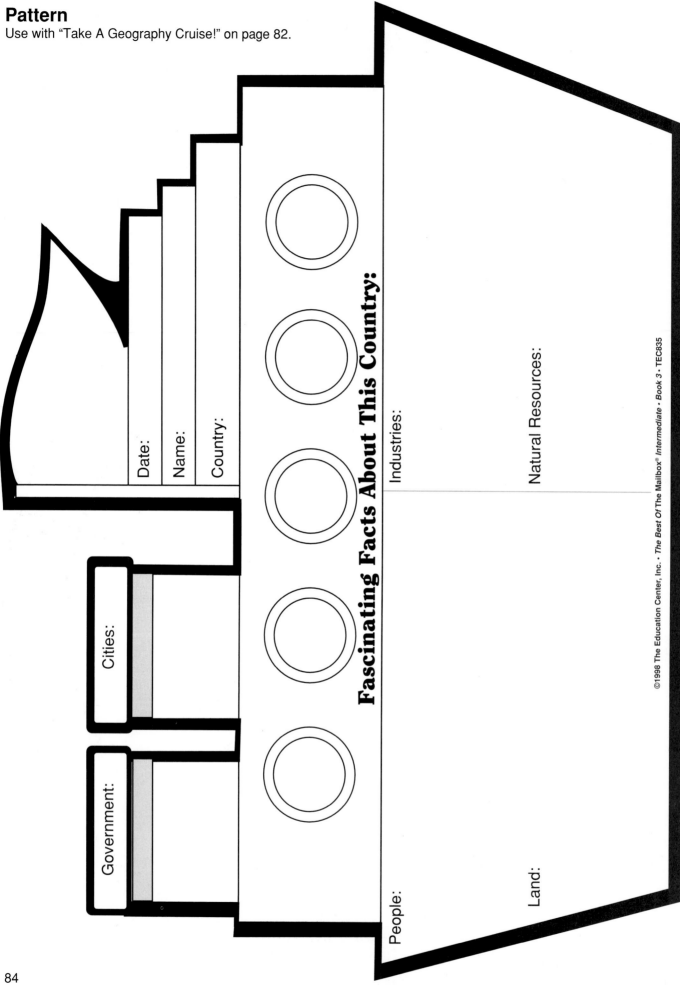

Date:

Name:

Country:

Cities:

Government:

Fascinating Facts About This Country:

Industries:

Natural Resources:

People:

Land:

A Country Wheel

Directions:

1. Cut out the wheel and glue it to a piece of tagboard; then cut out the wheel again.
2. In the outer, smaller section labeled 1, write research question number 1.
3. In the pie-shaped section that is numbered 1, write the answer to question 1.
4. Continue writing questions and answers in this manner until the entire wheel is complete.
5. Use a stencil provided by your teacher to make a cover for your wheel.
6. Decorate the cover with the name of your country, your name, and small illustrations.
7. Place the cover on top of your wheel so that the centers are aligned. Use a straight pin to poke a hole in the center of the cover and wheel.
8. Push a brad through the pinholes to attach the cover to the wheel.
9. Swap your wheel with a partner, and get ready to learn about another country!

©1998 The Education Center, Inc. • *The Best Of* The Mailbox® *Intermediate* • *Book 3* • TEC835

A Fractions Tune-Up

Hands-On Activities To Help Students Develop Fraction Concepts

BART'S PARTS
and
Service
*Taking Care Of Your
Whole Car For A
Fraction Of The Cost!*

Bart

All of a sudden, three plus four does not equal seven, and five can be less than four! What's an intermediate kid to do when the rules of math suddenly change? That's the challenge you may face when teaching fractions. Tune up your students' understanding of this complicated topic with the following number-sense activities and reproducibles.

by Irving P. Crump

A Half By Any Other Name...

A fraction can be represented in different forms and shapes. To help your class better understand this concept, provide each student with two sheets of 9" x 12" construction paper in two colors. Instruct each student to make squares with both sheets (see the illustration). Have the student fold one of the squares in half vertically and crease it; then have her reopen the square and cut along the crease. Finally have her fold the other square diagonally and cut along the crease.

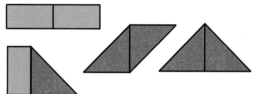

After each student has made these four pieces, guide the entire class through the following brief activities:

- Have each student make a rectangle with any two of his four pieces of paper. Then ask, "What part of this shape is each piece?" *(1/2)* Next instruct each student to use two pieces to make a parallelogram (other than a rectangle), a triangle, then a trapezoid. Repeat "What part of this shape is each piece?" after students make each shape. *(Each piece will be 1/2 of each new shape.)*

- Have each student make a rectangle with three of the four pieces. Ask, "What part of the shape is each piece?" *(1/3)* Instruct each student to use three pieces to make a parallelogram, then a trapezoid. Repeat the question after students make each shape. *(Each piece will be 1/3 of each new shape.)*

- Next have each student use all four pieces to make a rectangle. Ask, "What part of the shape is one of the pieces?" *(1/4)* Have each student use all four pieces to make a parallelogram and then a trapezoid. Repeat the question after students make each shape. *(Each piece will be 1/4 of each new shape.)*

- For fun, divide students into pairs and have each pair combine their pieces. Challenge each pair to use all eight pieces to make a large square. Ask, "What part of the square is one piece?" *(1/8)* "What part of the square is each student's pieces?" *(4/8 or 1/2)* "What part of the square is made up of the triangles?" *(4/8 or 1/2)* "What part of the square is made up of the rectangles?" *(4/8 or 1/2)* Challenge each pair of students to make other shapes with five, six, seven, and eight pieces. Have them write questions and answers based on the fractional relationships of the pieces to the shapes.

Barry Slate

"Tan-rrific" Fractions

Tangrams are unique, not only because of their geometric qualities, but also because of the fractional relationships between different pieces and between pieces and the whole. Duplicate page 89 for your students. Instruct them to answer all of the items on the page by first visually moving the pieces about and comparing them. Remind students that the tangram represents a unit (or whole) and that each individual piece is a fractional part of that unit. After students have completed the page, have them cut out the seven pieces, work with partners to check their responses, and then complete the activity at the bottom of the page.

Fraction Tool Kits

Divide students into groups of four to create fraction tool kits. Provide each group with scissors, rulers, and eight 12" x 18" sheets of construction paper: one each of red, light blue, dark blue, light green, dark green, yellow, pink, and white. Guide students through the following steps:

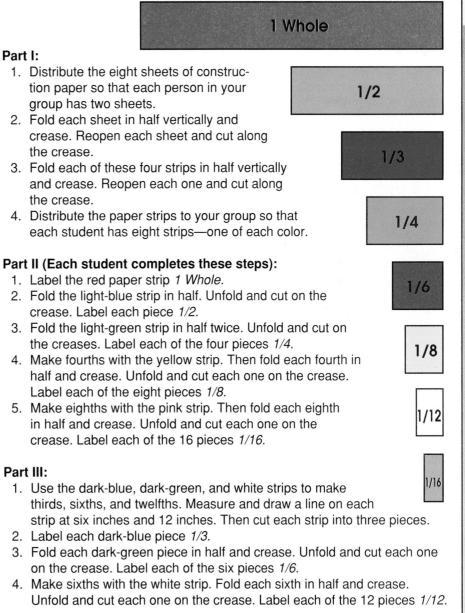

Part I:
1. Distribute the eight sheets of construction paper so that each person in your group has two sheets.
2. Fold each sheet in half vertically and crease. Reopen each sheet and cut along the crease.
3. Fold each of these four strips in half vertically and crease. Reopen each one and cut along the crease.
4. Distribute the paper strips to your group so that each student has eight strips—one of each color.

Part II (Each student completes these steps):
1. Label the red paper strip *1 Whole.*
2. Fold the light-blue strip in half. Unfold and cut on the crease. Label each piece *1/2.*
3. Fold the light-green strip in half twice. Unfold and cut on the creases. Label each of the four pieces *1/4.*
4. Make fourths with the yellow strip. Then fold each fourth in half and crease. Unfold and cut each one on the crease. Label each of the eight pieces *1/8.*
5. Make eighths with the pink strip. Then fold each eighth in half and crease. Unfold and cut each one on the crease. Label each of the 16 pieces *1/16.*

Part III:
1. Use the dark-blue, dark-green, and white strips to make thirds, sixths, and twelfths. Measure and draw a line on each strip at six inches and 12 inches. Then cut each strip into three pieces.
2. Label each dark-blue piece *1/3.*
3. Fold each dark-green piece in half and crease. Unfold and cut each one on the crease. Label each of the six pieces *1/6.*
4. Make sixths with the white strip. Fold each sixth in half and crease. Unfold and cut each one on the crease. Label each of the 12 pieces *1/12.*

Provide each student with a large Ziploc® bag in which to store all of the fraction kit pieces. (Fold the red strip so that it will fit inside the bag.) Duplicate the reproducible on page 90 to use with the fraction kits.

Pattern-Block Fractions

Besides being an obvious learning tool for geometry skills, pattern blocks also provide plenty of hands-on practice when exploring fractional relationships. Provide each pair or small group of students with a set of pattern blocks—about three or four blocks of each basic shape: hexagon, trapezoid, blue and white rhombuses, square, and equilateral triangle. Provide time for informal exploring as students note the relationships between the shapes. Use the questions below to lead a discussion as students manipulate the pattern blocks and place them on top of each other:

- What part of the hexagon is the trapezoid? *(1/2)*
- What part of the blue rhombus is the equilateral triangle? *(1/2)*
- What part of the hexagon is the equilateral triangle? *(1/6)*
- What part of the trapezoid is the blue rhombus? *(2/3)*
- What part of the hexagon is the blue rhombus? *(1/3)*

Have students use the pattern blocks to make various two-, three-, four-, five-, and six-piece designs. Then have them draw the designs on their papers and label the various fractional relationships depicted (see the examples). Ask students to verbally and manipulatively explain to their partners the fractions that they list.

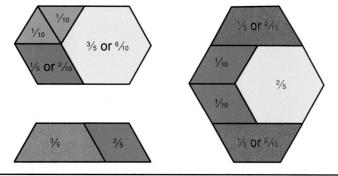

Fractions: An Owner's Manual

Experiencing real-life examples helps students better understand fraction concepts. Send your class on a fraction scavenger hunt. First have each student staple together seven sheets of notebook paper along the left margin. Then using old newspapers, magazines, catalogs, and photographs, have each student cut out graphics that illustrate these often-used fractions: 1/2, 1/3, 1/4, 1/6, 2/3, 3/4, and 5/6. Have the student cut out two illustrations for each fraction: one showing part of a whole and the other showing part of a set (see the illustration). After gluing the pictures on the seven pages, instruct each student to fold a 12" x 18" sheet of construction paper in half to make a cover for his manual.

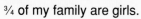

¾ of my family are girls.   ⅓ of the cans are green.

Additional Fraction Activities

- Bring in (or ask student volunteers to donate) a set of wrenches that are marked in various fractional increments. Tape over the fraction labels. Have students order the wrench openings from largest to smallest.

- Reading a ruler is a complicated chore for inter-mediate students. Draw a huge ruler on your chalk-board that models one inch. Make marks of various lengths to denote the 1/2 increment, the 1/4 increments, the 1/8 increments, and the 1/16 increments. Do not label the marks except 0 at the left end of the ruler and 1 at the right end (see the illustration above). Have two students stand facing away from the ruler; then draw an arrow to a particular mark. Next have the two students both turn around and identify the fractional name of the point you've marked in its lowest terms. The student who says the correct fraction name first wins a point for his side of the class. Erase the mark and continue with two more students.

- Play a fractions version of the game "Simon Says" using verbal clues about fractional parts of a whole or of a set. Direct the clues to either individuals, small groups, or the entire class. For example, Simon says:
  — Everyone: hold up 3/10 of your fingers.
  — Lance: open 1/2 of the file cabinet drawers.
  — Everyone: use textbooks to show 1/3.
  — Fran: become 1/5 of a team.

All Cracked Up!

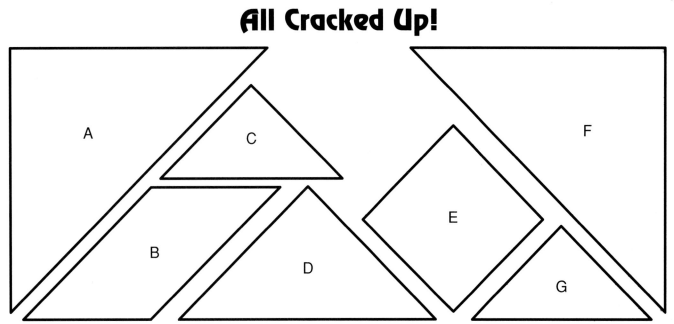

Bart and his assistant accidentally dropped a windshield. It broke into the seven pieces shown above, which Bart labeled A through G. The windshield's frame is shown at the bottom of this page.

The statements below describe how the seven pieces are related to each other. Fill in each blank with a fraction that makes the statement true. The first one is done for you.

1. G is __½__ of E.
2. G is _____ of D.
3. G is _____ of B.
4. D is _____ of A.
5. D is _____ of F.
6. E is _____ of F.
7. C is _____ of F.
8. B is _____ of A.
9. C is _____ of A.

10. A is _____ of the whole windshield.
11. F is _____ of the whole windshield.
12. A + F is _____ of the whole windshield.
13. D is _____ of the whole windshield.
14. B is _____ of the whole windshield.
15. E is _____ of the whole windshield.
16. C is _____ of the whole windshield.
17. C + G is _____ of F.
18. E + C is _____ of A.

Bonus: Cut out the seven pieces. Check your answers by moving the pieces around and placing them on top of each other. Work with a partner.

Now put the windshield back together in the frame.

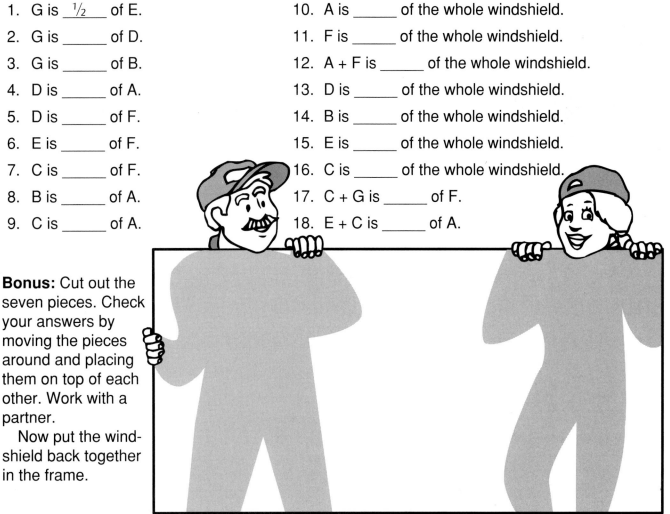

Using Your Fraction Tool Kit

Pair up with a partner to play each game below. You'll need two fractions kits and a die.

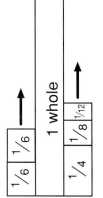

Game 1: Race To A Whole

1. Place 1 whole between players.
2. Each player rolls the die. The higher roll is Player 1.
3. Player 1 rolls the die and reads the matching fraction on the wrench.
4. Player 1 places that fraction piece beside the whole.
5. Player 2 rolls the die and reads the matching fraction.
6. Player 2 places that fraction piece on the other side of the whole.
7. Continue play by adding fraction pieces in a race to reach one whole.
8. When a player is near one whole, he can freeze.
9. The winner is the player who is closer to one whole, without going over.

$1=\frac{1}{6}$
$2=\frac{1}{12}$
$3=\frac{1}{16}$
$4=\frac{1}{16}$
$5=\frac{1}{8}$
$6=\frac{1}{4}$

Game 2: Race To 2 Wholes

1. Place the two wholes end to end and between players.
2. Each player rolls the die. The higher roll is Player 1.
3. Player 1 rolls the die and reads the matching fraction on the wrench.
4. Player 1 places that fraction beside the first whole.
5. Player 2 rolls the die and reads the matching fraction.
6. Player 2 places that fraction on the other side of the first whole.
7. Continue play by adding fraction pieces in a race to reach two wholes.
8. When a player is near two wholes, she can freeze.
9. The winner is the player who is closer to two wholes, without going over.

$1=\frac{1}{16}$
$2=\frac{1}{6}$
$3=\frac{1}{4}$
$4=\frac{1}{8}$
$5=\frac{1}{12}$
$6=\frac{1}{2}$

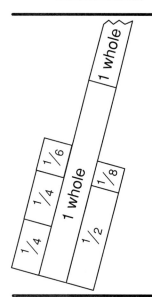

Game 3: Layer By Layer

The object of this game is to be the first player to stack all eight layers of the fraction pieces on top of the whole.
- For example, if 1/4 is placed on the whole first, then the entire first layer must be made up of fourths.
- A smaller fraction can be placed on a larger one. If 1/8 is rolled after 1/4, then it can be placed on top of 1/4 to begin a new layer.
- A large fraction can only be placed on top of an equal group of smaller fractions. For example, 1/6 can be placed on top of two 1/12 pieces.
- If a fraction cannot be placed, then that player loses his turn.

To play:
1. Place the two wholes between players.
2. Each player rolls the die. The higher roll is Player 1.
3. Player 1 rolls the die and reads the matching fractions on the screwdriver.
4. Player 1 chooses one of the two fractions.
5. Player 1 places that fraction piece on top of his whole strip, lined up at the end.
6. Player 2 repeats Steps 3, 4, and 5.
7. Play continues alternately until a player has made all eight layers.

$1 = \frac{1}{2}$ or $\frac{1}{12}$
$2 = \frac{1}{4}$ or $\frac{1}{16}$
$3 = \frac{1}{12}$ or $\frac{1}{6}$
$4 = \frac{1}{16}$ or $\frac{1}{8}$
$5 = \frac{1}{8}$ or $\frac{1}{6}$
$6 = \frac{1}{3}$ or $\frac{1}{16}$

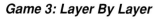

Note To Teacher: See page 87 for information on how to make fraction tool kits.

A Pinch Of Parts Of Speech

Mobile Words

Every good teacher knows that the best way to teach grammar is not with an isolated unit once a year but a review of important skills throughout the year. For a fun grammar review that's easy to add to any unit of study, challenge students to make parts-of-speech mobiles. Divide the class into several groups, one for each part of speech you wish to review; then provide each group with two or more wooden dowels and a variety of art materials such as construction paper, yarn, tape, and markers. Have each group use the materials to make a mobile based on its assigned part of speech and a current unit of study. For example, if the current unit of study is astronomy, the "pronouns" group might cut out paper stars and label each with a sentence (including underlined pronouns) such as "I told her that Orion is the constellation of the hunter." Challenge groups to be creative and design mobiles that review the parts of speech and show what they've learned about the topic of study. Hang the finished mobiles in your classroom—right above the heads of their proud designers!

Looking for just the right ingredients to spice up your grammar lessons? Season parts-of-speech practice with the following creative activities and reproducibles. But be prepared—students are sure to ask for second helpings!

by Beth Gress

Parts-Of-Speech Power Play

This fast-paced game can make parts-of-speech practice much easier to swallow! To prepare the game, write each letter of the alphabet on a small slip of paper; then place the slips in a bag. Duplicate the gameboard on page 94 for each student.

To begin play, draw a letter from the bag and announce it to the class. As soon as the letter is announced, each student tries to write a word beginning with that letter in each parts-of-speech column on his gameboard. The first student to fill in each category calls out, "Stop!" (Stop after three minutes if no student finishes by that time.) Quickly have each child call out the word he has recorded in the first column of his gameboard. If any students have duplicate answers, they must cross out those words on their gameboards; all incorrectly categorized words are also crossed out. Continue having students call out answers for the remaining categories. After all answers have been called out, have each student add his score for the round (one point for each word not crossed out) and record his score in the last column on the gameboard. Play several rounds; then have students total their scores to determine a class winner.

Pam Crane

Prepositional Poetry

You don't have to go *over* the river or *through* the woods to find a super activity for reviewing prepositions! Begin by having students brainstorm a list of prepositions. Next give each child a copy of the reproducible on page 93. Using the list of prepositions on the reproducible, have students give examples of prepositional phrases such as "over the river" and "under the table."

Now bring creative juices to a rapid boil by having students write a class poem using only prepositional phrases. Help students choose an activity to describe, such as washing the dishes, finding a treasure chest, going for an airplane ride, etc. Have students suggest about eight prepositional phrases to describe that activity from start to finish (see the example). Remind students not to repeat a preposition more than once and that the poem doesn't have to rhyme. After the poem is finished, add a title; then let students work individually or in pairs to write original prepositional poems on copies of the reproducible. Have students copy their finished poems on construction-paper cutouts that represent the activity (see the example in the illustration below). Post the cutouts on a "Prepositional Poetry" bulletin board.

On The Court

around the opponent,
down the court,
to the top of the key,
between the forwards,
toward the basket,
above my head,
near a victory,
in the hoop,
SWISH!

91

The Literature Link

Where else would you find the perfect parts-of-speech activity than between the pages of a quality children's book? The following books are wonderful tools for teaching or reviewing the parts of speech. After sharing a book with your class, have small groups create their own books on a part of speech, act out the book as a drama or puppet play, or add another chapter to the book.

Books to use:

A Cache Of Jewels And Other Collective Nouns by Ruth Heller

Merry-Go-Round: A Book About Nouns by Ruth Heller

Your Foot's On My Feet And Other Tricky Nouns by Marvin Terban

Kites Sail High: A Book About Verbs by Ruth Heller

I Think I Thought And Other Tricky Verbs by Marvin Terban

A Is For Angry: An Animal And Adjective Alphabet by Sandra Boynton

Many Luscious Lollipops: A Book About Adjectives by Ruth Heller

Up, Up And Away: A Book About Adverbs by Ruth Heller

Jabberwocky Wordplay

"Beware the Jabberwock!" warned Lewis Carroll, but this strange beast makes a great parts-of-speech tutor! Without realizing they're learning, students can apply their parts-of-speech prowess by analyzing the invented words of Carroll's famous poem "Jabberwocky." Check a local library for wonderful versions illustrated by Graeme Base, Kate Buckley, or Jane B. Zalben. After reading the poem with the class, discuss the possible meanings of such words as *slithy* and *vorpal*. Have students identify each nonsense word's part of speech, giving evidence from previous parts-of-speech lessons to support their answers. Follow the discussion by having each student label a large index card with his own invented word, plus its definition, dictionary pronunciation, part of speech, a sample sentence using the word, and an illustration.

Letter-Word Race

It may be a bit noisy, but the decibel level will be nothing compared to the parts-of-speech practice found in this fun class game! Write each letter (except *Q, X,* and *Z*) on an index card, making an additional card for each vowel. Distribute the cards to students (being sure to distribute all of the vowel cards first). At your signal, students group themselves to spell a word of at least four letters. Once a group of students has formed a word, they report to the teacher who writes the word on the back of each child's card. Each student, in turn, writes the correct part of speech beside the word; then he returns to the playing area and tries to regroup with other students to form another word. At the end of the playing time, have students total their scores, earning one point for each letter in a word on their cards. Have students check each other's cards and award two additional points for each correct part-of-speech label. Reward the highest-scoring student with a small treat or class privilege.

Bubbling Over With Prepositions

Bet you didn't know that you're just bubbling over with poetry-writing talent? Select an activity such as going to school, playing soccer, walking a dog, or painting a picture. On the lines, write eight prepositional phrases to describe the activity from start to finish. Use the prepositions in the bubbles to help you. Add a title for your poem on the top line.

by

behind

over   to

through

before

under

out   in

_____
title

up

on

after

below

inside

down

across

between

from

_____

_____

_____

_____

above

off

toward

along

_____

_____

beside

among

near   with

around

of

at

upon   into

©1998 The Education Center, Inc. • *The Best Of* The Mailbox® *Intermediate • Book 3* • TEC835

Name _____

Parts-Of-Speech

Power Play

Letter	Adjective	Noun	Adverb	Verb	Preposition	Interjection	Points
b	blue	~~basketball~~	brilliantly	~~bring~~	behind	Boy, oh boy!	4

Note To Teacher: Use with the "Parts-Of-Speech Power Play" activity on page 91.

ADJECTIVES AND ADVERBS FROM A TO Z

Adjectives and adverbs are all over the alphabet! To prove that fact, take this "A To Z" challenge. For each sentence, think of an adjective for the first blank and an adverb for the second blank. Both the adjective and the adverb must begin with the circled letter. Copy the entire sentence—with your new words—on your own paper.

EXAMPLE: (S) A _____ salmon swims _____.
A <u>slippery</u> salmon swims <u>silently</u>.

(A) An _____ armadillo ate _____.

(B) Both _____ badgers begged _____.

(C) The _____ coyote crawled _____.

(D) A _____ dog dug _____.

(E) Each _____ emu eats _____.

(F) Some _____ fleas flew _____.

(G) The _____ goose grabbed _____.

(H) Our _____ hen hopped _____.

(I) An _____ iguana implored _____.

(J) Some _____ jackals jumped _____.

(K) A _____ koala kissed _____.

(L) The _____llama leapt _____.

(M) Many _____ monkeys mumbled _____.

(N) Some _____ newts nibbled _____.

(O) Our _____ ostriches operated _____.

(P) Many _____ ponies pranced _____.

(Q) The _____quails quilted _____.

(R) A _____ raccoon rode _____.

(S) Some _____ skunks sank _____.

(T) The _____ tiger talked _____.

(U) An _____ unicorn unloaded _____.

(V) Some _____ vultures visited _____.

(W) A _____ walrus walked _____.

(X) You're excused from this one!

(Y) The _____ yak yawned _____.

(Z) A _____zebra zigzagged _____.

Bonus Box: Select your favorite sentence from the list above. On the back of this page, extend it to make a one- or two-paragraph story. Use as much alliteration with adjectives and adverbs as possible. (Hint: *Alliteration* is repeating the same beginning consonant in words. See the example sentence, which repeats the letter *s*.)

What Do You Do With A Minute Or Two?

Name That Category

For a quick mind-stretching game, think of a category such as things that melt, kinds of trees, or names of authors. Call out four or five words that fit the category; then have students try to guess the identity of the category. Make the game more challenging by using categories with two attributes, such as things that are soft and brightly colored, cities that are located east of the Mississippi River, or things that melt but can't be eaten. *Mary Ann Williams—Substitute Teacher, Franklin, PA*

A Musical Minute

When we have an extra minute between activities, I add a touch of music to our classroom. With record albums borrowed from our school's music teacher, we use those extra five minutes to learn a song related to an area of our curriculum. My students love learning American folk songs such as "Sweet Betsy From Pike" during our U.S. studies. For a multicultural tie-in, we also listen to music from other countries. Several of my students have even brought in classical recordings so that we can play a quick game of Guess The Composer. What a simple way to inject fine arts instruction into an already crowded day! *Susan Robinson, Lloyd Harbor Elementary, Huntington, NY*

Five-Minute Fillers From Our Subscribers

Making the most of every minute in the classroom—that's what exceptional teachers like you are famous for! When we asked our subscribers for five-minute fillers, we were swamped with terrific ways to extend learning into that extra minute or two between activities. We're quite certain that you'll use this collection of classroom-tested ideas time and time again!

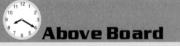

From "The Far Side"

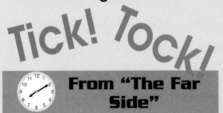

Provide students with a quick time-filling activity that will put smiles on their faces. Clip humorous cartoons, such as "The Far Side" or "Garfield," from the newspaper. Tape each cartoon to an index card; then file the cards in a file box on your desk. A student with an extra five minutes on his hands can take the cartoons back to his desk to read. You can bet that your students will enjoy this quiet, rib-tickling activity! *Dave York, Milliken Middle School, Milliken, CO*

Index Card Tip

I try to develop filler activities that review skills in need of a little extra practice. To make this task easier, I write each activity on a small index card and place it with my lesson plans for that day. Because of its small size, I can carry the card in my pocket to use at a moment's notice in the classroom or on our way to music, lunch, or recess. All cards are filed so that I have a handy supply of fillers to use year after year. *Mary L. Matthew—Gr. 5, Countryside Elementary, Olathe, KS*

Above Board

Fill an extra five minutes with this super review game. Divide the class into two teams. Choose a player from Team A to come to the front of the classroom and sit on a stool with his back to the chalkboard. On the chalkboard directly over the student's head, write a word that is related to a current unit of study, such as *Columbus* or *stalagmite*. Have the player's teammates give one-word clues to the word. Determine the score by the number of clues offered until a correct guess is given: the first clue is worth ten points, the second clue nine points, etc. After a correct answer is given and the score is recorded, choose a player from Team B to play. Your kids will beg for a chance to play this fun game! *Karen Lazarus—Gr. 5, James Monroe School, Madera, CA*

A Bad Case Of The Squiggles

When my class has a few extra minutes, I draw a simple series of lines or squiggles on the blackboard. Each student copies the drawing on his paper; then he uses those lines to create an interesting picture. If there's time, have students color the pictures or write paragraphs to accompany their creations. My sixth graders get a real kick out of this activity! *Xenia B. Young—Gr. 6, Stansbury Park Elementary, Stansbury Park, UT*

The Memory Game

A set of index cards is all you need for a "memorable" five-minute filler game. On each index card, I write a simple instruction, such as "Find something orange and bring it to your desk" or "Shake hands with the person sitting nearest the door." I store the cards in an index box. When we have an extra few minutes, I choose a student and ask how many cards he would like. I read each card to the student; then he tries to perform the tasks in order. If a child remembers all of the instructions, he takes another turn. If he forgets an instruction, classmates who have been good listeners supply the missing direction; then a new player is chosen. What an unforgettable way to hone listening skills! *Joan Koszalka—Special Education, Lindenhurst, NY*

Let's Link!

It takes only a few minutes to play a stimulating game of Links! Draw a series of "links" on the board to form a circle as shown above. Have a student start the game by writing a word in a link. The next player must write a related word in the next link. Continue calling on students to fill in the links until the circle is complete. Watch out for the last link—its word must relate to the links on both sides! *Susan S. Johnson, Long Valley, NJ*

Guess The Pattern

Five minutes is all you need for this fun activity. Begin by making a statement such as "I am going to the mall to buy a record and a doughnut." Challenge students to either identify the pattern you are using (the second item begins with the last letter in the first item) or respond with a similar statement such as "I'm going to the mall to buy candy and a yo-yo." Be prepared to continue giving examples until students guess the pattern. *Linda Silvidi—Gr. 6, Oakview Elementary, West Middlesex, PA*

Speak Out!

Set the stage for improved speaking skills with this terrific time-filler. Call out a thought-provoking question, such as "What would you do if you woke up one morning and discovered that you were invisible?" or "If you were selected to take a field trip to Mars, what would you expect to see?" Select a volunteer to stand up and "speak out" about the question for two minutes. (Use an egg or kitchen timer to keep time.) Give listeners a chance to ask the speaker pertinent questions about his response. Your students will love the chance to speak their minds! *Anita Swanik—Substitute Teacher, Ravenswood, WV*

Science For Kids By Kids

Science in your spare time? Why not? When one of my students sees a neat experiment (one that takes less than five minutes to complete) on television or in a book, he writes it on an index card; then he brings in the materials necessary to complete the experiment. I place the card and materials at a science center. When we have extra time during the day, my students and I go to the science center and try one of the experiments together. In less than ten minutes, we've completed and discussed an interesting science experiment. Now that's a good use of time! *Michele Smith, Hillcrest School, Logan, UT*

FROM HEAD TO TOE
Creative Activities For Studying The Human Body

It's the most marvelous machine ever created, composed of highly specialized parts doing their jobs with amazing efficiency. No, it's not a Ferrari—it's the human body, a walking wonder that fascinates everyone. Help students take a closer look at some of the human body's wonders with the following creative activities and reproducibles.

by Beth Gress and Becky Andrews

Paper Dolls And People Parts

"Hey, did you know your heart pumps about 100,000 times a day?" As students study the human body, they'll come across tons of fascinating facts they'll want to share with others. Give them the opportunity to do just that by providing several copies of the paper-doll pattern shown. Place the patterns at a center along with scissors, butcher paper, and reference books about the human body. Encourage students to use their free time to read through the books to find interesting information about the human body. When a student finds a fact he'd like to share, have him trace the pattern on butcher paper and cut out the tracing; then have him label the cutout with his fact. Tape the cutouts hand-to-hand on a wall to resemble a string of paper dolls. Challenge students to encircle your classroom with fact dolls. Or set an even bigger goal by challenging them to make a string of dolls that will stretch all the way from your classroom door to the principal's office!

Your skeleton has 206 bones.

Body Beautiful Flip Books

Review important vocabulary with a book-making activity that can double as an assessment tool. Write the letters of the alphabet vertically down a large sheet of chart paper. As you come across new vocabulary words during the course of the unit, list them beside the appropriate letter on the chart. At the end of the unit, have each student choose 25 words to include in a self-checking vocabulary flip book. Have students follow these steps to make their books:

Materials:

one 4" X 6" piece of cardboard	scissors	markers or crayons
twenty-five 4" X 6" index cards	hole punch	ruler
two metal rings	pencil	

Steps:

1. Punch two holes in the top of the cardboard piece as shown.
2. Use a ruler and a pencil to divide the index cards in half vertically.
3. Punch two holes at the top of each card half as shown, using the cardboard piece as a guide.
4. On the left side of each card, write a vocabulary word. On the right side, write the word's definition.
5. Cut the cards down the middle on the dividing lines.
6. Place the card halves containing the vocabulary words on top of the left side of the cardboard piece, aligning the holes; then insert a metal ring through the holes.
7. Place the card halves containing definitions on top of the right side of the cardboard piece, aligning the holes. BE SURE THAT THESE CARDS ARE IN A DIFFERENT ORDER FROM THE WORD CARDS. Insert a metal ring through the holes.
8. Flip the right side of your book to find the definition card for the first word on the left. On the back of both the word card and the definition card, write a 1.
9. Flip to the second word card on the left. Find the definition card for this word; then code the backs of both cards with a 2.
10. Continue labeling the backs of matching cards in this manner.
11. Swap books with a friend. Have your friend try to match each word card with its definition, looking on the backs of the cards to check his answers.

cerebrum — the largest part of the brain

capillaries — the smallest blood vessels

Barry Slate

98

The Match Game

Your students may already know that there are different blood types, but do they understand what those blood types may mean if they ever need a transfusion? Use the reproducible hands-on experiment on page 101 to help students understand transfusion reactions between different blood types. Divide the class into groups; then give each group the following materials:

clear plastic cup of water
clear plastic cup of water tinted with red food coloring
clear plastic cup of water tinted with blue food coloring
clear plastic cup of water tinted with red and blue food coloring (purple)
empty clear plastic cup (to use as a test cup)

eyedropper
copy of page 101
water for rinsing

Before beginning, explain to students that there are four main blood types, which are classified as A, B, AB, and O. In a blood transfusion, a person with one type of blood will become ill if he receives another type that doesn't match his. In this experiment, students will discover which blood types can be given in a blood transfusion to persons with any of the four blood types. They will also learn the type of blood that persons with any of the four blood types can receive. Be sure that students rinse the test cup and eyedropper thoroughly after each test. Also be sure students understand that clear water added to colored water doesn't represent a change; the color has only changed in shade, so the match is safe. But colored water added to clear does represent a change, indicating an unsafe match. See the answer key on page 190 to check students' results. After the experiment, have students identify the blood type that is a safe donor for any blood type (O, the *universal donor*); then have them identify the blood type that can safely accept blood from any donor (AB, the *universal recipient*). To check comprehension, ask questions such as "If you have B blood, to whom can you safely donate blood? (*people with B or AB blood*) If you have A blood and need a transfusion, from whom can you receive blood?" (*anyone with A or O blood*)

The "Blood Mobile"

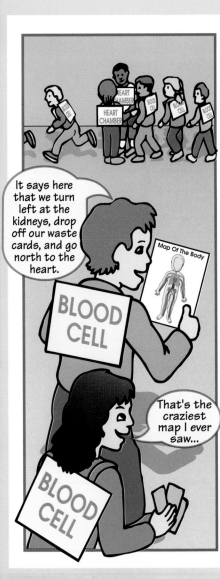

It says here that we turn left at the kidneys, drop off our waste cards, and go north to the heart.

Map Of The Body

BLOOD CELL

That's the craziest map I ever saw...

BLOOD CELL

Students often have a difficult time understanding that the same blood that goes out from the heart and lungs to different parts of the body also returns to the heart and lungs to begin the journey all over again. Give students an unforgettable lesson on this concept with a "mobile" circulatory system simulation. To prepare, have a parent volunteer label 80 index cards with the word food, 80 with oxygen, 80 with waste, and 80 with carbon dioxide. Assign the following roles to students:

chambers of the heart: four students
lungs: two students
kidneys: one student

small intestine: one student
body cells: four students
blood cells: remainder of class

Have each student make and wear a large nametag labeled with his role. Give the food cards to the small intestine students, the oxygen cards to the lungs, and the waste and carbon dioxide cards to the body cells; then head to the gym. Arrange students according to the diagram on page 100. (Duplicate the card on that page and carry it with you for easy reference.) Once students are arranged, direct them through the following steps:

1. The blood cells begin at the star and circulate by passing between two of the heart chambers.
2. The blood cells proceed to the lungs where they each pick up an oxygen card.
3. The blood cells move on through the other two heart chambers toward the small intestine where they each receive a food card. (*Explain that particles of food actually enter the bloodstream through the walls of the small intestine.*)
4. Each blood cell goes to a body cell to provide it with food and oxygen. To simulate this, the blood cell exchanges his food card for a waste card; then he exchanges his oxygen card for a carbon dioxide card.
5. Each blood cell goes to the kidneys where he deposits his waste card.
6. Each blood cell returns to the heart chambers and the lungs, where he exchanges his carbon dioxide card for an oxygen card. Then the cycle begins again.

Let students exchange roles and repeat the simulation until each student has had the chance to be a traveling blood cell. For fun, ask students how long they think it would take for a blood cell to complete a round-trip through the body and back. They may be surprised to learn that the trip takes less than a minute!

99

Fun puzzle

You're A Walking Wonder!

Did you know that you're a walking wonder? Well, you are! The human body is more amazing than any machine or computer. To prove that, look at the facts about your body below. Fill in each blank with a number from the box. Cross out each number as you use it. THIS ISN'T A TEST—it's just for fun!

60,000	40	100
9,000	106	22
4	100,000	600
90	300	20
206	13,000	100,000
500	85	32

1. You have _____ bones in your body.
2. _____ percent of your brain is water.
3. Your heart pumps _____ quarts of blood each day.
4. You have over _____ muscles in your body.
5. You use _____ muscles each time you take one step.
6. There are _____ miles of blood vessels in your body.
7. You have _____ bones in your feet and hands altogether.
8. Your heart beats over _____ times a day.
9. There are _____ miles of tiny tubes in each of your kidneys.
10. Your small intestine is _____ feet long.
11. You have _____ bones in your skull.
12. There are _____ million nerve endings in your skin that detect pain.
13. You have _____ taste buds in your mouth.
14. _____ percent of your blood is water.
15. Your mouth produces _____ milliliters of saliva every day.
16. You have about _____ trillion cells in your body.
17. You probably have about _____ hairs on your head.
18. You will have _____ teeth when you are fully grown.

The "Blood Mobile" Simulation

Reference Card

take a carbon dioxide card; give an oxygen card
give a food card
take a food card; give a waste card
take an oxygen card; give a carbon dioxide card
take a waste card

STUDENT ROLES:
Lungs:
Small Intestine:
Body Cells:

Kidneys:

CIRCULATION ROUTE

heart chamber → ☆ → heart chamber → kidneys → body cell → body cell → body cell → body cell → body cell → small intestine → heart chamber → heart chamber → lung → lung → heart chamber

Note To Teacher: Use with "The 'Blood Mobile'" on page 99.

Blood-Typing: The Match Game

How do doctors know what blood type to give someone who needs a transfusion? Follow your teacher's instructions and these steps to find out which blood matches are safe and unsafe.

1. Put a few dropperfuls of receiver A's "blood" in a clear cup.

2. Add one dropperful of donor A's blood to the cup; then circle YES or NO/SAFE or UNSAFE on the chart. Use these guidelines:
   - If the color of the receiver's blood stays the same (a darker or lighter shade is considered the same), then the match is SAFE.
   - If the color of the receiver's blood changes, then the match is UNSAFE.
   - Clear water donated to colored water is **not** a color change. But colored water donated to clear water does indicate a color change.

3. Rinse out the eyedropper and cup; then repeat the test for donor B.

4. Continue until you have completed all 16 tests (each patient's blood is tested four times).

	A donor (red water)		B donor (blue water)		AB donor (purple water)		O donor (clear water)	
A receiver (red water)	color change? YES NO	SAFE or UNSAFE?	color change? YES NO	SAFE or UNSAFE?	color change? YES NO	SAFE or UNSAFE?	color change? YES NO	SAFE or UNSAFE?
B receiver (blue water)	color change? YES NO	SAFE or UNSAFE?	color change? YES NO	SAFE or UNSAFE?	color change? YES NO	SAFE or UNSAFE?	color change? YES NO	SAFE or UNSAFE?
AB receiver (purple water)	color change? YES NO	SAFE or UNSAFE?	color change? YES NO	SAFE or UNSAFE?	color change? YES NO	SAFE or UNSAFE?	color change? YES NO	SAFE or UNSAFE?
O receiver (clear water)	color change? YES NO	SAFE or UNSAFE?	color change? YES NO	SAFE or UNSAFE?	color change? YES NO	SAFE or UNSAFE?	color change? YES NO	SAFE or UNSAFE?

Note To Teacher: See "The Match Game" on page 99 for a list of materials and steps for completing this project. See page 190 for an answer key.

Positively "PLANT-astic"!

Activities To Firmly Plant Your Students In Botany

Where would we be without plants? Don't even ask! Plants provide the food and oxygen that all creatures need for survival. Lead students on an exploration through the fascinating world of plants with the following hands-on activities, experiments, and reproducibles.

by Dean and Kelly Medley

Something New Under The Sun!

Scientists have recently discovered several new plant species in the remote jungles of Asia. Ask your students, "How do you think scientists recognize new plants?" Then have each student create a new plant species that he has just "discovered"! Follow these steps:

1. Gather a supply of craft materials such as colored paper, fabrics, pipe cleaners, straws, buttons, scissors, glue, and other scrap materials.
2. Instruct each student to draw a large diagram of his newly discovered plant on a 12" x 18" sheet of white construction paper. Remind students to include all important parts of the plant.
3. Have students select craft supplies and construct their plants, gluing the pieces on top of their diagrams.
4. Afterwards, have each student write a short article describing the environment in which his plant lives as well as any special adaptations or conditions necessary for its survival. Have each student present his plant and article to the class. Post these botanical discoveries around the room during your study of plants.

Examine students' projects to determine their knowledge of plant characteristics. Did your young botanists create *embryophytes*—plants with roots, stems, and leaves? Or did they portray *thallophytes*—plants that lack these structures (such as algae and fungi)? Use your kids' creations as a springboard for discussing the different classifications of plants.

Sticky Situation

Why be concerned about plant and animal extinction? The following game demonstrates the sticky situation that's created when even one element is removed from a delicately balanced food web.

Materials (per small group): 9" x 12" sheet of white construction paper, scissors, pencils, crayons, markers, 1 clean potato chip canister, 6 or more pipe cleaners, masking tape, six or more 1-inch squares of tagboard, paper cup

Directions:

1. Wrap the paper around the canister. Trim off any excess paper; then flatten the paper.
2. Research a food web that contains at least six components. Draw a diagram of the web on the paper. Label and number each component on the web. Wrap and tape the diagram around the outside of the canister.
3. Cut a 1/2-inch strip of masking tape for each food-web component. Label and number each tape strip with one component. Wrap each label around the end of a different pipe cleaner. Place the labeled pipe cleaners inside the canister.
4. Count out as many 1-inch squares of tagboard as you have components. Write a different number on each square. Place all the squares in the paper cup.

To Play The Game: Sit in a circle on the floor. Shake the canister and dump the pipe cleaners into a pile in the center of your circle. In turn, select a number from the cup. Then pick that pipe cleaner from the pile without moving or disturbing any of the other pipe cleaners. The student who successfully removes the most pipe cleaners before the teacher calls time wins.

After each student has had several tries, call time-out. Discuss any difficulties students had during the game. Lead students to realize that just as the pipe cleaners are difficult to separate, so are the relationships between animals and plants in a food web. When a species is removed through extinction, other members of the web are affected. Follow up by having students research specific endangered plant species and how their extinction will affect others.

Survival Of The Fittest

Plants grow almost everywhere. But what happens if the place in which they're growing doesn't receive enough sunlight, minerals, water, or clean air? Conduct the following simulation to predict the growth of four "plants" under different conditions:

Materials (per group of four students): 1 empty cereal box; scissors, 1 copy each of pages 104 and 105; 4 yellow, 4 purple, 4 green, and 4 orange Skittles® candies; glue stick; plastic cup

Directions:

1. Cut the front panel from the empty cereal box.
2. Glue the top flaps back together so that the box has four sides.
3. Glue page 104 faceup on the inside "bottom" panel of the box. Each circle represents the area in which a plant's roots have spread.
4. Cut apart the four graph pieces on page 105 and distribute one to each group member. Have each group member note the plant number indicated on his graph.
5. Place the candy pieces in the cup.
6. With the box sitting still on a desk, have one group member hold the cup three inches above the X and dump the candy pieces into the box.
7. Have each group member find column 1 on her graph and record the number of each colored piece that fell within her plant's circle.
8. Pick up all the candy pieces and repeat the process of dumping and recording nine more times.
9. Complete the group questions at the bottom of page 105. *(Rooted plants cannot move and are subject to the conditions of their locations. Many plants die for want of water, minerals, sunlight, or clean air. However, plants grow even where conditions are not always favorable. Plants adapt to survive in diverse environments.)*

Where Is The Water?

Students may already be aware that plants expel oxygen during *photosynthesis*. However, do they know that plants also release water through a process called *transpiration?* Most water is released through small openings in the leaves called *stomates.* Scientists use an instrument called a *potometer* to measure the amount of water expelled by a plant during transpiration. Challenge your students to prove the process of transpiration by using a student-made potometer and a *control.*

Materials (per small group): 2 identical 16-oz. foam cups with plastic lids, water, 1 small seedling, fine-point permanent marker, modeling clay

Directions:

1. Peel back the plastic from the straw hole in the lid; then carefully thread the seedling through the hole. Seal any openings around the hole with clay. Be careful not to injure the seedling.
2. Lay the lid on the cup to determine the location of the roots in the cup. Remove the lid and fill the cup with enough water to cover the roots.
3. Place the lid securely on the cup.
4. Mark the waterline on the outside of the cup with a marker. Write the date next to the line.
5. Create a control by filling the other cup to the same level with water.
6. Seal the straw hole with clay and place the lid on the control cup.
7. Expose both cups to light for two weeks.
8. Observe both cups each day. Record any changes in the water level by drawing a new line on each cup to mark the new level. Write the date next to the line.
9. Compare all data recorded on both cups. *(The students should note the decreased water level in the plant cup. This phenomenon occurs because the plant has released water during transpiration.)*

A Bibliography For Budding Botanists

Eyewitness Books: Tree
Written by David Burnie; Published by Alfred A. Knopf

Growing With Gardening: A Twelve-Month Guide For Therapy, Recreation, And Education
Written by Bibby Moore; Published by The University Of North Carolina Press, Chapel Hill

Grow Lab: A Complete Guide To Gardening In The Classroom and *GrowLab™: Activities For Growing Minds*
Both titles written and published by the National Gardening Association, 180 Flynn Avenue, Burlington, VT 05401

Let's Grow!: 72 Gardening Adventures With Children
Written by Linda Tilgner; Published by Storey Communications, Inc.

Plants And Flowers
Written by Brian Holley; Published by Hayes Publishing Ltd.

The Clover & The Bee: A Book Of Pollination
Written by Anne Ophelia Dowden; Published by HarperCollins

Flowers For You: Blooms For Every Month
Written by Anita Holmes; Published by Bradbury

"Survival Of The Fittest" Activity Board

Use with the "Survival Of The Fittest" activity on page 103.

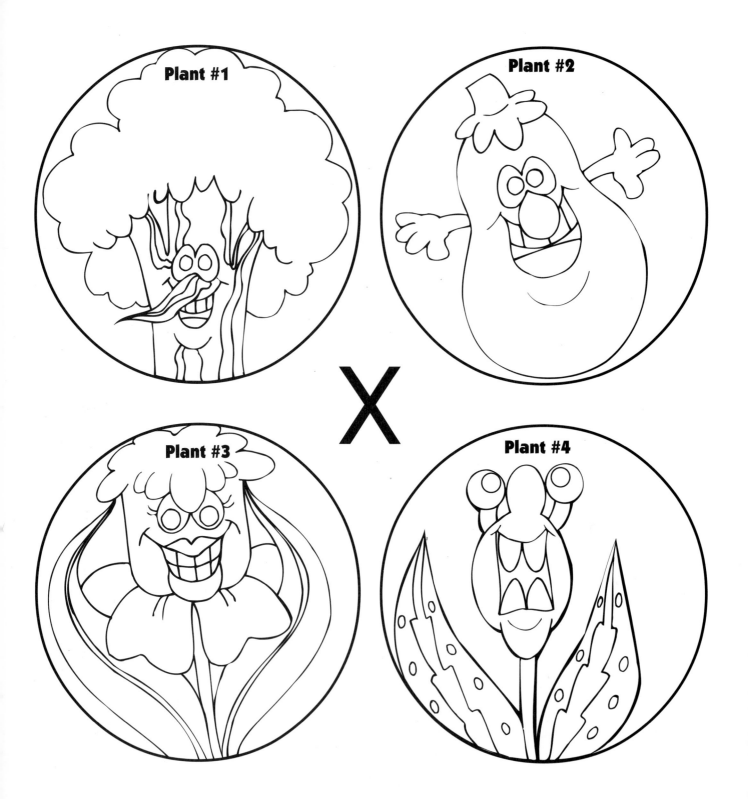

Plant #1	1	2	3	4	5	6	7	8	9	10	Plant #2	1	2	3	4	5	6	7	8	9	10
sunlight (yellow)											sunlight (yellow)										
minerals (purple)											minerals (purple)										
water (green)											water (green)										
clean air (orange)											clean air (orange)										

Plant #3	1	2	3	4	5	6	7	8	9	10	Plant #4	1	2	3	4	5	6	7	8	9	10
sunlight (yellow)											sunlight (yellow)										
minerals (purple)											minerals (purple)										
water (green)											water (green)										
clean air (orange)											clean air (orange)										

Names of group members: _____

Answer the following questions using the information on your graphs:

1. Which plant received the largest amounts of sunlight, minerals, water, and clean air combined?_____

2. How do you think this plant would have survived compared to the other three plants?_____
_____

3. Which of the plants received the least amount of water? _____

4. Could a plant survive if it did not receive much water? Explain your answer. _____
_____
_____

5. Could a plant receive too much water? Explain your answer. _____
_____

6. Could a plant survive if it did not receive sunshine or minerals? Explain your answer. _____
_____

7. How would a lack of clean air affect a plant? _____
_____

8. Have each group member research a different plant that manages to survive in adverse conditions (conditions in which the plant would not receive large amounts of sunlight, minerals, water, or clean air). On a separate paper, write your findings on how each plant has adapted to survive in these conditions.

Note To Teacher: Use this page with the "Survival Of The Fittest" activity on page 103 and the reproducible activity board on page 104. Examples of plants students can research in Step 8 include plants of the tropical rain forest or the high mountains, desert vegetation, or aquatic plants.

There's No Place Like Home!

Star-Spangled Ideas For Studying Your State

When we asked our subscribers to send us their favorite ideas on "studying your state," responses poured in from sea to shining sea! Add these star-spangled suggestions—all from creative teachers just like you—to your lesson plans.

(Many of the ideas that follow can also be used by students who are learning about United States regions, or studying states or countries other than their own. Adapt them to fit your teaching needs.)

Places To See

Here's a bright idea that sets its sights on your state's historical past! Duplicate the sunglasses pattern (page 108) on white construction paper for each student. In the left lens, have each child write two or three sentences describing one of your state's historical sites, making sure to explain its significance to your state's history. In the right lens, have the student illustrate the site. Instruct students to use colorful markers to decorate the frames of their sunglasses; then have them cut out the patterns and staple them to a bulletin board entitled "Places To See In _____ (name of your state)."

Pam Doerr—Substitute K–6
Lancaster County Schools
Mount Joy, PA

Digging Up Some Dirt

For an activity your students are sure to dig, try this! Before a student leaves on a trip that will take him to another state, give him a small baby-food jar (with a lid). Ask the student to fill the jar with a sample of soil from the state he visits; then have him bring the jar to school when he returns from his trip. Keep the labeled soil samples from year to year so that you can build a good collection. Have students compare soil samples from your state with those from the others in your collection. When you begin your U.S. regions unit, pull out the soil collection and have students look at samples from the particular states you're studying.

Jeri-Lyn Flowers
Cartersville Elementary
Cartersville, GA

Operation Alliteration

Help students remember important facts about your state with an exercise in alliteration. Begin by having each student list interesting facts about your state. Next have the student use a dictionary to list words that begin with the same letter as your state. As the final step, have the student use both lists—the state facts and the word list—to write an alliterative paragraph about your state. For a fun display idea, have students cut out samples of the letter they used from old magazines. Then have each child glue some of the letters around the edges of a sheet of construction paper. Finally have the student copy or paste her paragraph inside the frame of letters.

Kevin S. Spencer—Gr. 5
Raleigh Court Elementary
Roanoke, VA

Magnificent, Marvelous Minnesota

Fort Niagara

Happy Birthday To Our State!

Prior to our state's birthday, my students research to locate fascinating facts about Indiana. After the research has been discussed, we send teams of students to other classes in our school. The teams teach the students all about our state, from its symbols to important historical events and distinguishing physical features. At the end of the teaching sessions, all of the classes meet together in the gym where my students host a birthday party for our state. Set up around the gym are displays highlighting the projects we completed during our state study. After my students perform a skit about our state, everyone sings "Happy Birthday" and digs into a yummy birthday cake.

Julie Kaiser
Morgan Elementary
Palmyra, IN

Riddle Me This!

Whether your class is studying your state or researching other states, you'll love this fun bookmaking activity. After a student has researched his state, let him compose several riddles about it. Then have him type the riddles (one per page) on a classroom computer, using the fonts, styles, and sizes of his choice. Be sure the student types an answer key on a separate page. After printing the riddles and answer page, have the student staple them between two large paper covers cut in the shape of his state (with the answer key as the last page). Place the riddle books at a reading center for lots of free-time reading—and learning!

Marilyn Van De Venne—Gr. 5
Westwood Elementary
Portland, MI

Barry Slate

Souvenir Shop

Students will shop 'til they drop with this fun culminating activity. At the conclusion of your state unit, distribute large pieces of art paper. Challenge each student to draw the inside of a souvenir shop that might be found in your state's capital city. Every aspect of the shop—from the signs to the items featured in the display cases and on the racks and shelves—should help visitors remember their trip to your state. Provide time for each shopkeeper to explain the items and tell why she chooses to stock her shop with them.

Jean Frigm—Gr. 4
Stewartstown Elementary
Stewartstown, PA

State-In-A-Box

With this idea, a meaningful and fun assessment tool is in the bag—or, rather, the box! Ask each student to bring a large, unlidded box to school. After each child has a box, give him a copy of the "State-In-A-Box" project outline on page 109. Students follow the directions on the outline to transform their boxes into three-dimensional reports on your state. If desired, divide students into groups; then have each team create a boxed report on one aspect of your state, such as its geography, manufacturing, or history.

Maxine Pincott—Gr. 4
Oliver Ellsworth School
Windsor, CT

Pattern
Use with "Places To See" on page 106.

State-In-A-Box

Show everyone that you've got the facts on your state in the bag—or the box—by completing this unique project.

Materials you'll need: a large, unlidded box; glue or a stapler; paper to cover the box; art paper; scissors; crayons, markers, paints, or other art materials

Steps:
1. Read over this project outline; then jot down any questions you have in the box below. Be sure to ask your teacher these questions before you begin.
2. Fill in the due date that your teacher gives you.
   DUE DATE:_____
3. Cover the four sides and the inside of a large box with paper.
4. Store this sheet and any other papers in a folder for safe-keeping while you work.
5. Prepare the items in the "Must include..." list. Glue some of them on the outer sides of your box. Place other items inside your box. Put a check beside each item as you complete it.
6. If you want to earn extra points, include some or all of the items in the "Can include..." list.

Questions I Have About This Project

Must include on/in your box:
____ Illustration of your state's flag, including an explanation of the symbols on it
____ Map showing your state's natural resources (including a map key)
____ Illustration of the state bird, state tree, or state flower
____ Map showing some of your state's main tourist attractions (including a map key)
____ One-page report telling about two famous people who were born in your state
____ Three artifacts that represent your state

Can include on/in your box to earn extra points:
____ Written or tape-recorded interview with a famous contemporary state resident or a senior citizen who has lived in your state most of his/her life
____ Tape recording of your state's song
____ One-page report about a famous Native American from your state
____ Timeline showing at least five major historical events in your state's past
____ Additional illustrations and/or artifacts that give information about your state's geography, people, government, education, and industries
____ Anything else you think gives interesting information about your state

Note To The Teacher: Use this project outline with "State-In-A-Box" on page 107. Have each student bring in a large cardboard box (no lids needed). Provide each child with a file folder in which to store his work. If desired, fill in the due date (#2 in "Steps") before duplicating.

HOT ON THE TRAIL

Of Problem-Solving Skills

Ideas To Help Students Become Successful Problem Solvers

Whether it's drawing, estimating, measuring, listing, counting, asking questions, or listening to others, we all engage in problem solving every day of our lives. Turn your students into problem-solving super sleuths with the following creative teaching suggestions and reproducible. *by Irving P. Crump*

Tools Of The Trade

Problem-solving *strategies* are "tools" that students can use to approach and solve problems. Students should feel free to use any one or a combination of these strategies. Although they may be stated somewhat differently in various resources, the strategies in the list below can be very helpful to intermediate learners. Copy the list onto a chart to post in your classroom.

- **Make a table, chart, or graph.**
- **Make an organized list.**
- **Guess and check.**
- **Find a pattern.**
- **Draw a picture or diagram.**
- **Act out a problem.**
- **Make a model.**
- **Write a number sentence.**
- **Work backward.**
- **Work a simpler problem.**
- **Use logical reasoning; deduction.**
- **Brainstorm ideas.**

The following collection of teacher-directed activities are designed to be used at any time of the year. Adapt them to fit your needs: use them for "problem of the day" activities, copy them on transparencies for whole-class discussions, use them as homework assignments, or assign them to cooperative groups.

Make A Table, Chart, Or Graph

When generating data for a problem, it's helpful to organize it so that information is not repeated. A table, chart, or graph is the perfect organizer. Post the following problems for your students to try. After students have attempted different approaches to each problem, share and discuss each graphic shown. Then have students continue the patterns to arrive at a solution.

- Twenty bicycles and tricycles are entered in a neighborhood parade. There are 46 wheels in all. How many of the entrants are bicycles and how many are tricycles?
- Martha is ten years older than her brother. How old will Martha be when she is twice as old as her brother?

Martha	11	12	13	··········	20	
Brother	1	2	3	··········	10	

tricycles	wheels	bicycles	wheels	total wheels
19	57	1	2	59
18	54	2	4	58
17	51	3	6	57
↓	↓	↓	↓	↓
6	18	14	28	46

Organized Lists

Another way to organize data for problem solving is by listing. Guide students to make lists to solve the following problems:

- Draw a simple target like the one shown. Post a daily question to accompany the drawing. Examples: If two darts are thrown and they both hit the target, what are the possible scores? If three darts are thrown and they all hit the target, what are the possible scores? As an extension, draw a target of four concentric circles and ask the same types of questions. Or give students the total score; then ask them to determine where the darts landed.

- Draw the sign shown, or list the information on a chalkboard or transparency. Ask students: If you have $1 to spend, what combinations of supplies can you buy? Extend this activity by changing the prices of the items, adding another item and its price, or changing the amount that the student can spend.

Supplies	
Pencils	10¢
Pens	15¢
Paper	50¢

- Ask students to write down the last four digits in their telephone numbers. Instruct them to list all of the different four-digit numbers they can using those four digits.

Guess And Check

One way to solve certain problems is to make a guess and then check it. Sometimes the first guess is correct. At other times, several guesses must be tried before finding the correct solution. Instruct students to try this strategy with the following problems:

- On a chalkboard, draw the triangular arrangement of circles shown. Instruct students to arrange the numbers 1–6 in the circles so that the sum of numbers along each side of the triangle is nine. For extensions, have students arrange the numbers in the circles so that the sum along each side is 10; then 11; then 12.

- Show the L-shaped figure. Instruct students to divide the figure into four congruent pieces.

Draw A Picture Or Diagram

Not only is a picture (or diagram) worth a thousand words, but it also helps students see conditions that might not be so obvious when reading a problem. Share these problems with your students and direct them to solve the problems by drawing pictures or diagrams.

- Mark rides his bike to the library, which is ten blocks from his home. After riding seven blocks, Mark realized he had dropped a book. He rode back and found the book, then rode six blocks to the library. At which block did Mark find the book? (fourth) How many blocks did Mark ride back toward his home? (three) How many blocks did Mark ride in all to reach the library? (16)

- Suppose you have three measuring sticks of 8, 12, and 15 units. Show how you can use these three sticks to measure a length of five units. Have students use the line spaces on a sheet of notebook paper to help them reach a solution.

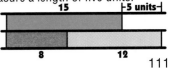

Act Out A Problem

Sometimes it's difficult to visualize the solution to a problem. Physically acting out the problem can be helpful. Have students "act out" these problems:

- Suppose you buy an antique for $100, sell it for $125, buy it back for $135, and then sell it for $150. How much money would you make (or lose) in buying and selling the antique? (You would make a profit of $40.) Have students use play money to solve this problem.
- Jenny is standing in the middle of a line of moviegoers. Five people are lined up behind Jenny. What's the total number of people in line? (11)
- A parking lot had a row of 24 numbered spaces filled with cars. All of the cars in the even-numbered spaces left. Then, of the remaining cars, every third one left. How many cars now remain in the parking lot? (8) Let students represent the cars.

Work Backward

Some problems involve a sequence of actions. The final result is known, but the beginning conditions must be determined. These types of problems can be solved by working in reverse.

- Draw the following flowchart on a chalkboard:

$$\boxed{} + 4 = \bigcirc \times 5 = \triangle - 4 = \bigcirc \div 2 = \boxed{18}$$

  Ask students to determine the numbers that belong in the shapes. (The first number, to be written in the square, is 4.) Review with students *inverse* (opposite) operations: add/subtract and multiply/divide.
- Challenge students to make up their own similar flowcharts to solve the following problem: Bob has saved $51 toward the purchase of a bike. He baby-sat each Saturday for four weeks, earned $12 for mowing the lawn, and received $15 for cleaning out the garage. What was his pay for one night of baby-sitting? ($6)

$$\left(\text{4 x babysitting}\right) + \boxed{\$12} + \left(\$15\right) = \left(\$51\right)$$

Work A Simpler Problem

When a problem seems difficult, it is sometimes helpful to break it down into one or more problems that have similar conditions. Then by solving these simpler problems, a pattern emerges that helps in solving the original problem.

- All the lockers in a hallway are numbered 1-150. How many locker numbers contain at least one digit 5? (25) Brainstorm with students ways to solve this problem without counting every number to 150.
- What is the sum of the following series of numbers: 1 + 2 + 3 + 4 + ...99? Hint: tell students to make pairs of 100: 1 + 99; 2 + 98; 3 + 97; etc. (The answer is 4,950, or 49 100s plus 50.)

Pam Crane

112

America's Most Wanted

Dastardly Dan has been on the lam for years, thanks to his clever disguises! Solve each problem below on another sheet of paper. After you solve the problem, add a bit of disguise to Dan's photo. When you're finished, not even Dan will recognize himself!

1.
List all the possible ways a football team could score 12 points. Remember: a touchdown is six points, a point-after touchdown is one point, a safety is two points, and a field goal is three points.

(Add a brown mustache.)

2.
A van holds a driver plus seven passengers. How many vans will be needed to take the sixth grade—Miss Reid's 26 students and Mrs. Wright's 28 students—on a field trip? If neither teacher drives, how many total people (drivers and passengers) will go on the trip?

(Color Dan's hair yellow.)

3.
I am a two-digit number greater than 40. If you divide me into groups of seven, four are left over. The sum of my digits is eight. Who am I?

(Add bushy, black sideburns.)

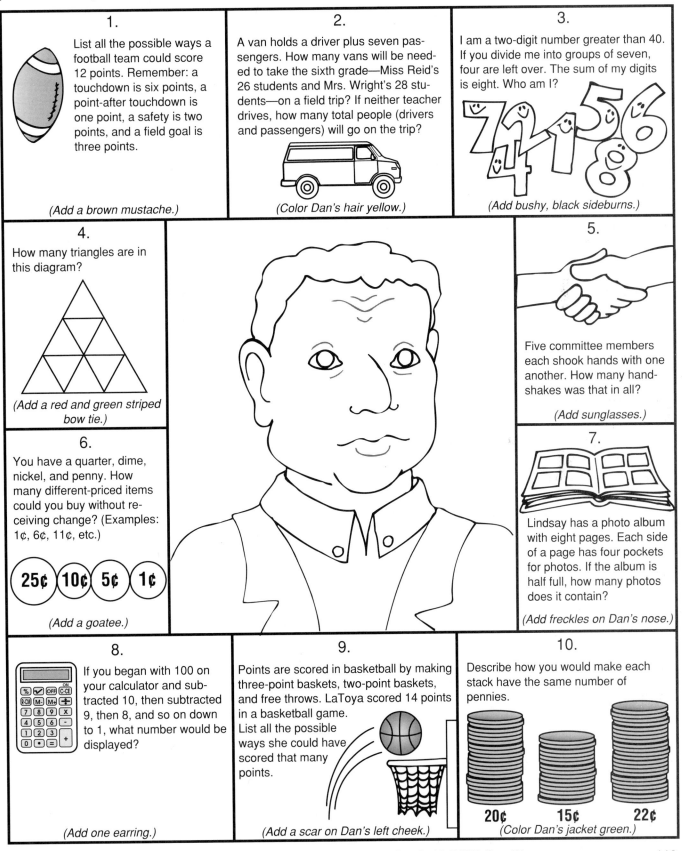

4.
How many triangles are in this diagram?

(Add a red and green striped bow tie.)

5.
Five committee members each shook hands with one another. How many handshakes was that in all?

(Add sunglasses.)

6.
You have a quarter, dime, nickel, and penny. How many different-priced items could you buy without receiving change? (Examples: 1¢, 6¢, 11¢, etc.)

25¢ 10¢ 5¢ 1¢

(Add a goatee.)

7.
Lindsay has a photo album with eight pages. Each side of a page has four pockets for photos. If the album is half full, how many photos does it contain?

(Add freckles on Dan's nose.)

8.
If you began with 100 on your calculator and subtracted 10, then subtracted 9, then 8, and so on down to 1, what number would be displayed?

(Add one earring.)

9.
Points are scored in basketball by making three-point baskets, two-point baskets, and free throws. LaToya scored 14 points in a basketball game. List all the possible ways she could have scored that many points.

(Add a scar on Dan's left cheek.)

10.
Describe how you would make each stack have the same number of pennies.

20¢   15¢   22¢

(Color Dan's jacket green.)

Make A Splash With Spelling!
Teacher-Tested Ideas From Our Subscribers

When we began searching for terrific spelling ideas, we sought help from the best source around—you! Dive into these teacher-tested games and activities from our subscribers for a spelling curriculum that's sure to make a splash with your students!

Barry Slate

Coordinating Words

Blend a little math into an entertaining spelling activity! Give each student a piece of graph paper. Have the student label a horizontal and vertical axis as shown; then have him write the letters A-Z on the graph, placing letters randomly at intersecting points (see the illustration). On the back of the graph paper, have the student write the coordinates of the letters needed to spell each of his spelling words. Have him staple an answer key to the back of his graph. The next day, let students swap papers and try to "decode" each other's coordinates. *Sherri L. McDonald—Gr. 4, Walnut Grove Elementary, Suwanee, GA*

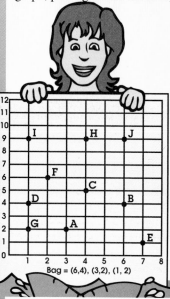

Bag = (6,4), (3,2), (1, 2)

Spelling Posters

Give each student a sheet of colorful construction paper. Have the student use a pencil to write his spelling words randomly on the paper, trying to cover as much area as possible. Have students swap papers to check spelling. After corrections are made, have students trace their words with brightly colored markers or crayons; then have them outline the words as shown. This activity allows students to "study" their words four times in a nonthreatening manner. Let students take home the weekly posters to decorate their rooms. *Melinda Prather, Forest North Elementary, Austin, TX*

flower

Spelling Beach Ball

Here's a great game to introduce or reinforce spelling or vocabulary words in any subject. Write each word on a small index card; then use clear packing tape to attach the cards to an inflated beach ball. Toss the ball to the students. The child who catches the ball looks at the word touched by his left thumb; then he completes one of these activities:

- says the word ten times as fast as he can
- spells the word for the class
- uses the word in a sentence
- gives a synonym or antonym for the word
- divides the word into syllables
- gives a brief definition of the word.

Let students continue passing the ball until each child has a turn. *Deena Block—Gr. 4, G. B. Fine Elementary, Pennsauken, NJ*

Spelling Auction

To motivate my students to study their spelling words, I hold a Spelling Auction at the end of each grading period. Each week I add several bonus words, gleaned from other units of study, to my students' spelling list. Each correctly spelled bonus word on a test is worth one point. Points for each student are recorded in my plan book. At the end of the six-week grading period, I give each student his point total to use during our auction. Students bid on such items as sugarless candy, extra bonus points, free computer time, and other special class privileges. My students work hard to earn bonus points. They even check their test papers more closely to make sure they receive credit where credit is due! *Betsy Fannin—Gr. 5, Bloom Middle School, South Webster, OH*

Find The Misspelled Word

Occasionally I grade and return a spelling test without marking it except for the grade and the number of words missed. My students then must use their word lists to check their tests and identify the words they missed. If a student correctly identifies all of the words he missed, I raise his grade by subtracting two, rather than five, points for each word. Not only does this method improve proofreading skills, it also helps my students master their words before moving on to the next list. *Kristen McDonald, Pamplin, VA*

Using Spelling Words In Journals

To learn spelling words you must use them. Try posting words students tend to misspell on a special bulletin board. Then have students use the words to write their own journal starters for the week. For example, if *friend* is frequently misspelled, a student might suggest a starter such as "A good friend is someone who...." Or have students use the posted words in their journal entries, underlining each word as it's used. *Susan Paprocki, Northbrook, IL*

Great Gumballs!

To motivate better spelling, I draw a large gumball machine on a piece of poster board. Inside the machine, I pin brightly colored paper gumballs. Each Friday I remove a gumball for every student who maintains or improves his grade from the previous week's spelling test. If more than half of the class meets this goal, I double the amount of gumballs removed. When the machine is emptied, we have a minicelebration in our classroom. *Kathleen Smith—Gr. 4, Calvary Baptist Academy, Muskegon, MI*

Taping And Typing

One spelling method I've discovered is an individualized "tape and type" program. I keep an individualized record of misspelled words for each child. I tape-record the list, pausing after each word to allow time for the student to write it on his paper or type it on a word processor. After the pause, I give the correct spelling of the word. This practice activity is very effective because each student has his own personalized tape to which words can be added. Plus, students can take home their tapes for further practice. *Susan Paprocki*

Edited By The Big Guys

Turn your students into spelling spies with this motivational idea. Display a gift certificate from a fast-food restaurant or ice cream shop. Announce that a student can win the certificate by finding a spelling mistake in any professional publication, such as a textbook, newspaper, or library book. Encourage your young proofreaders to write a letter to the publication notifying it of the error. What a super way to make students aware of the importance of good spelling! *Susan Paprocki*

Barney Blowfish A+

Word Maps

To individualize my spelling program, I have each student select four new words from any subject or library book to add to his weekly list. For each extra word, a student completes a word map. The map tells where the word was located and gives a synonym or antonym, a definition, and a sentence using the word. Students turn in their word maps on Friday to earn extra bonus points. *Betty L. Foti—Gr. 4, Truman Elementary, Lafayette, LA*

Word Map

pleasant expectation

I was full of anticipation about our trip to Disney World.

From *The Indian In The Cupboard*

anticipation

Synonym: expectation

Spelling Games

"Did You Write...?"

For this fun game, provide each student with a small slate and a piece of chalk. Write the spelling words on the chalkboard. Select one student to be the "leader"; then ask him to write one of the words secretly on his slate. One at a time, let the leader's classmates guess which word he wrote by asking, "Did you write _____ (spells the word)?" If the guess is incorrect, the student responds by saying, "No, I did not write _____ (spells the word)." Classmates write the incorrect guess on their slates; then the next person tries to guess the word. Play continues until the word is identified. The student who guesses the word becomes the next leader. *Ann Gerber—Academically Talented Grs. 3-6, North Central Local Schools, Creston, OH*

Spell And Roll

For a fast-paced review game, divide the class into two teams. Call out a spelling word; then have each student write the word on his paper. Next select a student from Team A to spell the word aloud. If correct, the student rolls a die and adds the number rolled to his team's score. If incorrect, the student subtracts the number rolled from his team's total, and the opposing team gets a chance to spell the word. My class asks to play this great game every week! *Geraldine Swartzbaugh—Gr. 5, Delahunty Middle School, Hermitage, PA*

Heart Attack!

My students named this rapid-fire game Heart Attack, and for good reason! Divide the class into four or five teams. Have each team arrange its desks in a straight line. Call out a spelling word; then say "Go!" At this signal, the first student on each team writes the word on his paper, then passes the paper behind him to the next player on his team. That student writes the word on the paper and passes it behind him, continuing in this manner until each student has written the word. Members of the team that finishes first raise their hands. Check that team's paper to make sure the word was spelled correctly by each team member. If all spellings are correct, the team earns a point. I give Hershey's® Kisses® to the winning team at the end of the game. *Melinda Gribben—Grs. 5-6, Indiana County Christian School, Avonmore, PA*

Spelling Kickball

When the weather is nice, my students head outdoors to play a special spelling version of kickball. Rules are similar to regular kickball. I take the role of pitcher for both teams. As I roll the ball towards a student, I call out a spelling word. The student kicks the ball and spells the word aloud as she runs to first base. The student is out if she is caught or tagged out (as in regular kickball), if she doesn't spell the word before reaching first base, or if she misspells the word. My students love this fast-paced game! *Teri Deaton Taylor, DeWitt Elementary, Cuyahoga Falls, OH*

Spelling Basketball

Divide the class into two teams; then place a wastebasket against a door or wall. Secure long strips of masking tape on the floor at three different distances from the wastebasket. The line closest to the wastebasket is the one-point line, followed by the two- and three-point lines. Wrap tape around a large wad of paper to make a ball. In turn, ask a team member to spell a word. If correct, the player earns a chance to score points for his team by shooting a basket from the line of his choice. *Candace Jackson—Gr. 5, Dry Ridge Elementary, Dry Ridge, KY*

LITERATURE

The Cay
A Powerful Novel Of Survival

Use the following activities and reproducibles to extend Theodore Taylor's story of two unlikely friends and their struggle for survival on a tiny Caribbean island.

with ideas by Lynn Greco

Book summary: Eleven-year-old Phillip Enright is in a struggle for survival. The freighter on which he and his mother are traveling from the Dutch island of Curacao to the United States is torpedoed by the Germans during World War II. Phillip awakens to find himself floating on a raft with an elderly West Indian named Timothy. After a crack on the head leaves Phillip blind, the castaways land on a tiny barren island, or cay. How these two mismatched companions build a friendship and challenge nature's elements makes for an unforgettable story.

Before reading: Place a class set of page 120 (duplicated on white construction paper) at a center. Before you begin reading, have each student select a chapter from the book (which has 19 chapters). After a chapter has been read, direct the student who selected that chapter to get a copy of page 120 and complete the mini-mural activity about his chapter. Display the completed mini-murals on a large table or windowsill. By the end of the book, you'll have a visual summary of the story.

After reading Chapter 3: All Phillip notices are the differences between himself and his raft mate. One of those differences is Timothy's calypso-like dialect. Discuss dialect with students; then have them find examples of Timothy's speech from Chapter 3. List these examples on the board for students or pairs of students to translate. Provide more examples of Caribbean dialect with *A Caribbean Dozen: Poems From Caribbean Poets* (Candlewick Press, 1994). Edited by John Agard and Grace Nichols, this rich volume recalls the childhood memories of 13 Caribbean poets, and includes many poems written in the distinctive dialect of the region.

After reading Chapter 5: After reading this chapter, give students two minutes to list things they would do with a good friend if they could spend three days with him or her. After students have shared their lists, review Phillip and Timothy's situation: adrift on the open sea, little to eat or drink, scorched by a blazing sun, surrounded by unfriendly waters. Set a timer for another two minutes; then have pairs of students list things they might do to pass the time while adrift. After this exercise, let students pretend to be Phillip or Timothy and write in their journals about the days in the raft.

After reading Chapter 7: The two castaways find themselves on a small Caribbean island in what Timothy calls the "Devil's Mouth"—a U-shaped group of islands with sharp coral banks on either side. After briefly reviewing map skills, give each student a sheet of art paper and challenge him to draw a bird's-eye view of the cay. Remind students to reread portions of the chapter to help them locate information about the island. Provide time for students to compare their finished maps. At the conclusion of the book, take a second look at the maps and discuss how the students' views changed as they read further.

After reading Chapter 10: Phillip began his adventure with racial prejudices inherited from his mother. When he asks Timothy why there are different colors of skin, Timothy replies that he thinks "...beneath d'skin is all d'same." Let students communicate their own ideas about this statement in original collages. Begin by brainstorming with students reasons why people have prejudices about others who are different from them. Then give each student a sheet of construction paper, scissors, and a glue stick. Have the student cut out pictures, words, and phrases from old magazines to illustrate "beneath d'skin is all d'same." After students have glued their cutouts collage-fashion to the paper, provide time for them to share their thought-provoking creations.

After reading Chapter 12: In this chapter, Timothy contracts malaria and is nursed back to health by Phillip. Write the last line of the chapter on the board: "He never really regained his strength." Without reading any further, have students or student groups list their predictions as to how this statement might be a foreshadow of upcoming events. Let students share their predictions as you list them on chart paper. Post the list so students can compare their ideas to actual events as the story continues to unfold.

After reading Chapter 15: A massive hurricane has just swept over the island with devastating results. Depending on where you live, it's likely that you and your students have never experienced a hurricane. Invite a meteorologist to speak to your class about hurricanes and their effects. Perhaps he/she can bring news videotapes taken before, during, or after a hurricane. Have students compare the information gathered from this talk with the author's description of Timothy and Phillip's ordeal.

After reading Chapter 16: It isn't until after Timothy dies that Phillip realizes the love behind the old man's stubbornness. Discuss the qualities Phillip found in Timothy that made the gentle sailor such a good friend. What qualities do your students look for in a friend? After this discussion, give each child a copy of page 121. Tell students that their mission is to find out what other people look for in a friend. Go over the directions on the reproducible so that each child understands how to complete the survey. After the surveys have been completed, let students compare them and graph the results, noting the most frequently mentioned qualities.

Culminating activity: Ask your librarian for a copy of *If Once You Have Slept On An Island* by Rachel Field (Boyds Mills Press, Inc.; 1993). In this enchanting picture book, a simple 14-line poem about life on an island is illustrated with descriptive watercolors. Share the book with students, and discuss how both the author and Phillip felt about their islands. Then challenge your class to write a version of the poem as it might have been written by Phillip a few months after his rescue. Copy the lines of the poem on chart paper to post in the classroom as a reference. Work with students to create a class-written poem that follows Field's pattern. After the poem is polished, assign two or more lines to each cooperative group. Instruct the groups to write each line at the top of a separate piece of art paper, and then illustrate it with scenes from the book. Bind the finished pages together into a class book that honors a memorable story.

Make A Mini-Mural

Before you begin reading the book: Select a chapter from *The Cay.*

After reading your chapter: Follow the directions in each panel. Then cut out the three panels along the heavy lines only. Write your name on the back of the panels. Then fold on the two dotted lines to make a standing mini-mural.

Fill in the blanks to write an "If... Then..." statement about the chapter.

If...

_____
_____
_____
_____
_____

Then...

_____
_____
_____
_____

Write some thoughts you had while reading the chapter.

Chapter _____

Draw a scene from the chapter.

Duplicate student copies on white construction paper. Use with the "Before reading" activity.

Note To The Teacher: Before you begin the book, have each student select a chapter on which to complete this activity. activity on page 118.

Finding A Friend

Timothy and Phillip—at first sight, they seemed unlikely to ever become friends! Phillip didn't understand Timothy's stubborn insistence that he learn to take care of himself despite being blind. It wasn't until after Timothy's death that Phillip realized his friend had been so strict because he wanted young Phillip to learn how to survive on his own. Timothy proved to be the best friend Phillip had ever had.

What qualities do people look for in a friend? Interview ten people to find the answer to that question. Write the name of each person and his/her relationship to you (relative, friend, teacher, neighbor, etc.) in the chart below. Then check off the qualities that person looks for in a friend. If necessary, add qualities to the chart by writing them in the starred blank boxes.

Information About Interviewees			Friendship Qualities									
Name of interviewee	Relationship to interviewer	M = Male F = Female	Fun to be with	Something in common with me	Easy to talk to; listens	Caring	Clever/smart	Sense of humor	Helpful	★	★	★
1.												
2.												
3.												
4.												
5.												
6.												
7.												
8.												
9.												
10.												

Note To The Teacher: Use after reading Chapter 16 of *The Cay*. See the activity on page 119.

Not Just For

Using Picture Books With Intermediate Students

Ever catch one of your students lingering over a picture book in the library? Intermediate students aren't immune to the allure of an intriguing picture book. So why not use picture books to liven up your curriculum? Get started with these creative teacher-tested suggestions from our network of subscribers.

Friendship Books

One of the most important topics I discuss with my students during the year is friendship. To help with the discussions, I use three favorite picture books: *We Are Best Friends* by Aliki, *Best Friends* by Steven Kellogg, and *Silly Fred* by Karen Wagner. After discussing these books and the characteristics of a good friend, each of my students writes a poem about friendship. We bind the finished poems, with illustrations, into a class book entitled *A Friend Is....* The simple truths in these picture books really challenge my students to think about friendship. *Brenda Myers—Gr. 6, Greenlawn Elementary, Bainbridge, NY*

Primary Reading Buddies

Pair up with a primary class for a picture book experience that pays back big dividends. Begin by modeling the reading of picture books to your students. Show them how to hold a book so the entire audience can see it, how to read with expression, and how to select a good picture book. Finally, let students choose their own books and practice reading them aloud to each other.

The next step is to divide the class into five groups (one for each day of the week). On Monday, have the members of group 1 visit the primary classroom and read their books to small groups of younger students. On Tuesday, send group 2 to the primary class to read, and so on. Your students will increase their reading fluency, become more responsible, and grow more comfortable being in front of a group. *Leslie Ann Rake—Gr. 5, Kimball Elementary, Seattle, WA*

Wordless Books

For a wonderful writing activity, ask your librarian for a stack of wordless picture books. Give a book to each of several cooperative groups. Challenge each group to write a sentence for each illustration in the book. After the writing is completed, give groups time to share their stories. You can bet your students will have a much better idea of the hard work involved in being an author with this stimulating activity! *Cathy Woodward, McKinley Elementary, Newton, KS*

Bear Festival

You're never too old to love teddy bears or a good bear story! My fourth graders gathered a collection of books on a bear theme (see the suggested list that follows). After reading and studying the books, I divided the class into groups of four students each. Each group wrote and illustrated an original bear picture book. To celebrate our success as authors, we invited a primary class of students to bring their stuffed bears to a "bear festival." At the festival, my students shared their original books and then presented them to our guests for their class library. I read *Corduroy* by Don Freeman to both classes; then I paired each of my students with a younger child to complete a related art activity. Before sending our guests back to their classroom, we treated them to a snack of Teddy Grahams® and juice. What a "beary" special way to celebrate books! *Kathleen MacLeod— Gr. 4, Sound Beach School, Miller Place, NY*

Bear Books
Jamberry by Bruce Degen
The Bear's Toothache by David McPhail
We're Going On A Bear Hunt by Michael Rosen
Old Bear by Jane Hissey
Blackboard Bear by Martha Alexander
Little Bear by Else H. Minarik

Little Readers

Picture Books In The Content Areas

Add a picture book or two to your science or social studies units. For example, after completing a science unit on light, share a simple picture book on the topic. Have students discuss how they would amplify the simplistic text based on their newly acquired knowledge of the topic. It's a great way to review a just-finished unit! *Bette Baldwin—Gr. 4, Westwood School, Stillwater, OK*

Picture Book Contest

Instead of completing a regular book report, my students focus on picture books one month of the year. I begin by selecting 30–40 picture books, choosing a variety of types such as wordless, alphabet, Caldecott winners, fairy tales, and those using different art styles. We spend quite a bit of time discussing the books and their illustrations. Next I divide the class into four groups: A, B, C, and D. Groups A and B are given half of the books to read; groups C and D receive the other half. Students are encouraged to make notes as they read each book. After groups have spent a couple of weeks reading and studying the books, we hold a contest. I prepare a set of question cards, with five to seven questions on each book. Groups A and C are combined to make one team, while groups B and D comprise the other team. The team that correctly answers the most questions is the winner. My students love the change of pace and even learn to appreciate "baby" books! *Sharon Mander—Gr. 4, Wayne School, Elgin, IL*

Recognizing Story Elements

During the first month of school, review the various elements of a fiction story: setting, characters, plot, problem, solution, etc. To aid in this review, have students identify these elements in several picture books. Take the opportunity to discuss how the illustrations support the various elements in the text. Even your slower readers will experience success with this activity. *Ben Boerkoel—Gr. 4, Oakdale Christian School, Grand Rapids, MI and Sheryl Block, Simpsonville Elementary, Simpsonville, KY*

Comparing And Contrasting Fairy Tales

Even intermediate students are drawn to fairy tales, and today there are hundreds of versions from which to choose. Have students compare and contrast different versions of the same fairy tale (see the list of titles below). After comparing the books, let students write their own modernized versions of favorite fairy tales. Is that a Nintendo® in Baby Bear's room? *Bonita Tomcheck—Gr. 4, Howard Chapman Elementary, Strongsville, OH and Lydia Piper—Media Specialist, Wilkinson Gardens Elementary, Augusta, GA*

Titles To Compare/Contrast

Red Riding Hood by James Marshall—*Lon Po Po: A Red Riding Hood Story From China* translated by Ed Young

The Three Little Pigs by Paul Galdone—*The True Story Of The Three Little Pigs* by Jon Scieszka

Deep In The Forest by Brinton Turkle—*The Three Bears* by Paul Galdone

Hansel And Gretel retold by Rika Lesser—*Nibble Nibble Mousekin: A Tale Of Hansel And Gretel* by Joan W. Anglund

Stone Soup by Marcia Brown—*Stone Soup* by Ann McGovern

Cinderella retold by Amy Ehrlich—*Princess Furball* by Charlotte Huck

Jack And The Beanstalk retold by Susan Pearson—*The Giant's Toe* by Brock Cole

I'll Always Love You

Written & Illustrated by Hans Wilhelm
Published by Crown Publishers, Inc.

In Hans Wilhelm's endearing picture book, a boy grows up with his beloved dog, Elfie. When Elfie dies, the boy is comforted knowing that every night he told Elfie he would love her forever. After sharing the book, discuss the love and caring illustrated in the story. What did the boy get from the dog? What did he give back? Why was it important that the boy tell Elfie he loved her? Why is it important to tell people that we care about them? After the discussion, have each child write a letter or make a card for a parent, grandparent, or other significant person to share his feelings of love. *Betty Adams—Gr. 5, Staunton Elementary, Staunton, IN*

Animals Should Definitely Not Act Like People

Written by Judi Barrett & Illustrated by Ron Barrett
Published by Atheneum

In this humorous picture book, the author uses alliteration to depict animals in ludicrous human situations (for example, "...it would be outrageous for an octopus to play outfield."). After reading the book aloud and discussing it, have students brainstorm a list of animal names; then have them pair each animal with a human activity that uses alliteration and has possibilities for a humorous illustration. Have each student choose one animal/activity to illustrate, using the format in *Animals Should Definitely Not Act Like People*. Bind the finished pages into a class book. *Susan M. Copher—Grs. 3–5, Red Oak School, Highland Park, IL*

Oral Reading Practice

Picture books are the perfect tools for practicing oral reading. I have each of my students choose a favorite picture book and practice reading it fluently with expression. After the practice sessions, I let each child tape-record himself reading his book. With the tapes, I can evaluate each child's oral reading at my convenience; plus, my more timid students can practice reading without the fear of facing a live audience. After listening to a tape, I record my feedback right onto the tape. Students can take their tapes to the listening center during free time to hear my feedback. By using the same tapes throughout the year, students are able to hear and evaluate their progress. Tapes can also be played for parents during conferences. *Ben Boerkoel—Gr. 4, Oakdale Christian School, Grand Rapids, MI*

I'm In Charge Of Celebrations

Written by Byrd Baylor & Illustrated by Peter Parnall
Published by Charles Scribner's Sons

The joy of celebrating the glorious, yet often unnoticed, wonders of each day is beautifully detailed in this unusual picture book. After reading the book aloud to my class, we make a list of traditional celebrations such as Christmas, Labor Day, and birthdays; then we list the celebrations described in Byrd Baylor's book. After comparing the two lists, we discuss personal celebrations for each of us such as being invited to a sleepover, enjoying the first day of summer camp, or sitting in front of a roaring fire on a chilly day. I have each student write a paragraph about his own personal celebration and illustrate it. Then we make a lasting memory by binding the pages together in a class book entitled *Our Celebrations*. *Patricia Shulman— Gr. 5, Hillside Elementary, Needham, MA*

The Pain And The Great One

Written by Judy Blume & Illustrated by Irene Trivas
Published by Bradbury Press

This inventive book by popular author Judy Blume is a great springboard for a lesson on comparisons. Half of the book presents a sister's commentary on her younger brother, "The Pain." The other half is the brother's equally heated opinions about his older sister, "The Great One." After reading the book, discuss how two different people can have totally different perceptions of the same event. Have each student write a journal entry in which he describes an event from his perspective; then have him describe the same event from a sibling's, parent's, or friend's perspective. *Adapted from an idea by Anne Runyon, Littleton, CO*

Q Is For Duck: An Alphabet Guessing Game

Written by Mary Elting and Michael Folsom
Illustrated by Jack Kent
Published by Houghton Mifflin/Clarion Books

"Q is for duck." Why? Because a duck quacks! In this creative alphabet book, readers are challenged to make the connection between a letter and the word paired with it. After sharing the book and its pattern with students, assign a letter of the alphabet to each child. Have the student write and illustrate two pages for his letter, using the pattern in the book. Bind the finished pages into your own version of this guessing book. *Holly Ford—Gr. 4, East Elementary, Baraboo, WI*

Swimmy

Written & Illustrated by Leo Lionni
Published by Knopf

In this popular tale of teamwork, Swimmy joins another school of fish after his family is eaten by a bigger fish. When the bigger fish threatens his new school, Swimmy creates a solution that proves cooperation is the key to success. To emphasize the teamwork theme, I share this book with my intermediate students. Then we join together (like the fish in the story) to create a huge mural of Swimmy and his friends. We draw a large fish shape on butcher paper; then we place the paper on a table. Small groups of students use fish-shaped, Styrofoam cutouts and red paint to fill in the fish shape with prints of smaller fish. One black fish print is used for Swimmy (who, in the story, pretends to be the eye of a huge imaginary fish). As one group is filling in the fish with prints, the other students illustrate the sea around the huge fish or paint various cutouts to add to the mural. When everything has dried, we have a beautiful display—the result of outstanding teamwork! *Deborah A. Roettgers—Gr. 4, St. James of the Valley School, Cincinnati, OH*

People

Written & Illustrated by Peter Spier
Published by Doubleday

If you're eager to make students more aware of multiculturalism, this is the book for you. Peter Spier's story celebrates the differences in people around the world, from their hairstyles to their clothing to their homes. After sharing the book with students, have each child respond to the following question in his journal: Are differences good or bad? Have students support their opinions with examples from the book. *Susan Myers—Gr. 4, Lockport Catholic Intermediate, Lockport, NY*

The Hating Book

Written by Charlotte Zolotow & Illustrated by Ben Shecter
Published by Harper & Row

A misunderstanding between friends is resolved by a simple conversation in Charlotte Zolotow's classic little picture book. Use the story as a model to create *The Loving Book*, a class book in which students give reasons why they love their friends. Or have each student write about a time when she had a misunderstanding with a friend and resolved the conflict. For a role-playing activity, have students act out effective and non-effective communication skills to use with family members and friends. *Georganne Leopard—Resource Grs. 4–6, Crestview Elementary, San Antonio, TX*

The Trumpet Of The Swan
A Children's Classic By E. B. White

This classic tale of a mute trumpeter swan named Louis speaks directly and delightfully to every child who's realized with horror that he's somehow different. Cheer as Louis triumphs over his handicap to win fame, fortune, and the love of the beautiful Serena; then soar to new learning heights with these creative activities that extend E. B. White's masterpiece.

with contributions by Mary Anne Haffner

Setting The Stage

Louis starts his rather unusual life on a pond deep in the Canadian forest. Use this marvelous fantasy to introduce a lesson on pond/wetland habitats. Provide students with books and other resource information about forest wetlands. Cut through one corner of a large appliance box to make a large, folded mural panel. Have one group of students research, sketch, and paint a forest wetland scene on the panel. Next have each student or pair of students research a wetland animal (see the list below); then have the students draw and cut out pictures of their animals to mount on the mural. Provide time for students to share their research on the wetlands animals. Stand the completed mural in a corner of the room; then add a few soft pillows to make a cozy corner for silent or shared reading of *The Trumpet Of The Swan*.

muskrat	moose
beaver	otter
red-winged blackbird	woodpecker
mosquito	Canada goose
chipmunk	sparrow
bullfrog	mallard duck
chickadee	striped skunk
marsh wren	raccoon
red fox	snowshoe hare

Separating Fact From Fiction

In his fantasy about Louis, author E. B. White includes factual information about trumpeter swans. But how accurate is White's information? Ask your media specialist to provide information on swans duplicated from encyclopedias, bird field guides, and other resource books. After reading each of the first four chapters of *The Trumpet Of The Swan*, list as a class any facts about trumpeter swans on a large piece of chart paper; then ask students if they think White's information is accurate. How can they be sure? Divide students into groups; then give each group copies of the resource information about swans. Assign each group the task of using the information to verify the accuracy of several facts on the class list. Have groups share their findings with the rest of the class.

After this exercise, discuss how E. B. White's research on trumpeter swans added appeal to his book. How might the book have been different without the factual information on swans? To extend this activity, have each student choose a particular animal to research for several days. After keeping a log of facts about his animal, have each student write a short fictional story about his animal, weaving some of his factual information into the tale just as E. B. White did.

Buddy Up!

Louis's human buddy, Sam Beaver, writes nightly in a journal, concluding each entry with a question so that he will have something to think about while falling asleep. Often he includes an illustration with his text. Stimulate student writing with this "buddy up" journal activity. Duplicate two copies of the swan booklet cover on page 128 on white construction paper for each student. After cutting out the covers, have each student trace one copy of the cover onto several sheets of lined notebook paper and cut out the tracings. Have students decorate their front and back covers, then staple these lined pages between them. Provide class time for students to write responses to each day's reading of *The Trumpet Of The Swan*. Challenge students to end each day's entry with a question, similar to Sam's. During the next day's writing period, have each student switch journals with a buddy. Have the buddy write a response to his partner's question; then have partners share their responses with each other.

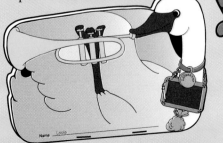

Overcomers, Inc.

"Remember that the world is full of youngsters who have some sort of handicap that they must overcome. I am sure you will overcome it, in time." So speaks Louis's father as he confronts his young son with the disturbing news that he can't speak. It will be a rare student who doesn't identify in some way with Louis's uneasiness at discovering he's "different." Discuss with students how Louis must have felt at not being able to speak and the positive attitude he developed about his handicap. What are some obstacles that your students have overcome with hard work and a positive attitude? Challenge students to begin searching in newspapers and magazines for examples of inspiring overcomers. Set aside a small bulletin board entitled "Overcomers, Inc." on which students can post articles about people who have surmounted challenging handicaps. In addition, encourage students to add to the display brief notes of praise recognizing friends or relatives who they think should be honored as overcomers.

Let Me Toot My Horn About...

For an easy student-made display, draw a simple horn pattern (see the example on page 128); then duplicate copies of it on yellow construction paper. Have student volunteers cut out the horns and store them in a shoebox. On a bulletin board, mount the title "Toot Your Horn About…." Every few days post a large index card labeled with one of the sentence endings listed below. During free time, let each student label a horn with his opinion about the statement posted on the bulletin board. Set aside time to review and discuss the opinions expressed on the display. After the discussion, take down the horns and post a new ending.

Let me toot my horn about...

- what Sam might be when he grows up.
- Sam's practice of writing in a journal every night.
- the way that Louis's father told Louis about his "defect."
- whether Louis's father was right in saying that "the world is full of talkers, but it is rare to find anyone who listens."
- Mr. Brickle's statement that "everyone is entitled to his likes and dislikes and to his prejudices."
- the fact that Sam never told his father about Louis and the trumpeter swans.
- whether Louis's father did the right thing in stealing the trumpet.
- whether it is frightening to be different from everyone else.

National Geographic Presents...

If the adventures of Louis had actually happened, you can bet that *National Geographic* would have been right on top of the story! For a fun culminating activity, divide your class into several "investigative teams." Tell students to pretend that they work for the National Geographic Society. Each group has been asked to create a brief television program about Louis. Before setting groups free to begin planning their presentations, discuss features that might be included in a program about Louis. How about interviews with Sam Beaver, Mrs. Hammerbotham, Mr. Brickle of Camp Kookooskoos, and the manager of the Ritz Hotel? Or an "on-location" visit to the pond where Louis was born or the music store that Louis's father robbed? After groups have practiced their programs, videotape each team's presentation. Then pop some popcorn and invite a neighboring class to join yours for an afternoon of viewing enjoyment.

127

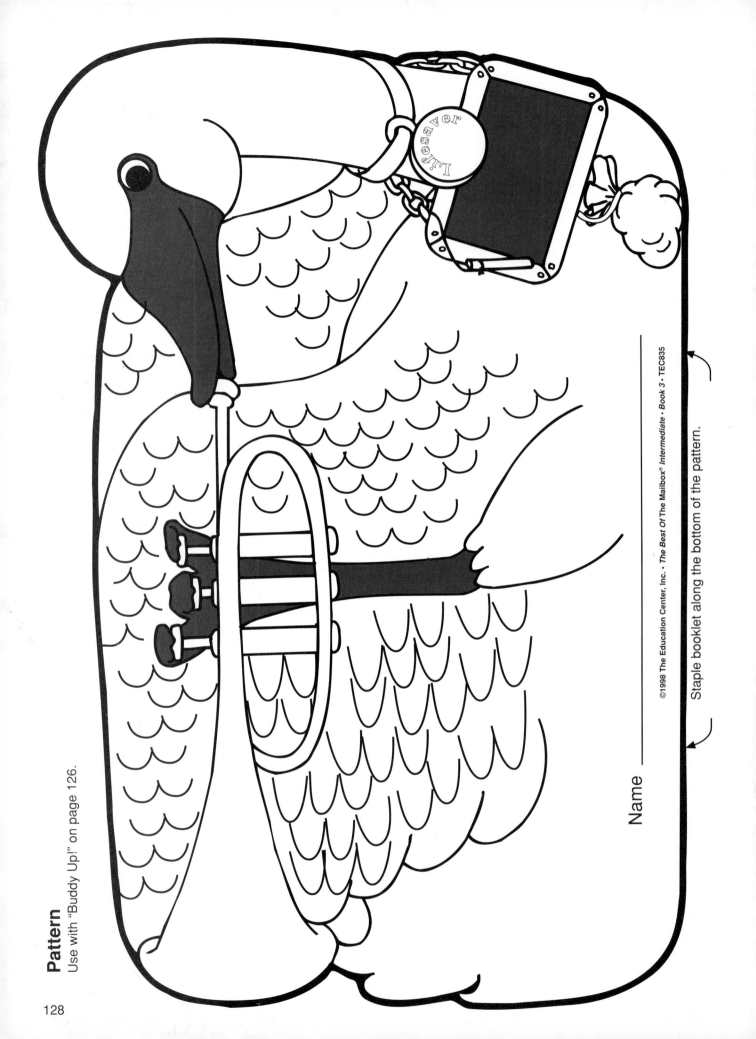

Pattern
Use with "Buddy Up!" on page 126.

Name _____

Staple booklet along the bottom of the pattern.

©1998 The Education Center, Inc. • *The Best Of The Mailbox® Intermediate • Book 3 • TEC835*

128

An Occasional Cow

A Humorous Novel By Polly Horvath

Imogene Spark is more than a little relieved to hear that the summer camp she was supposed to attend has burned down. Imagine—getting to spend an adventure-filled, glamorous summer at home in New York City! But Imogene's dreams are shattered when she learns she'll be spending the summer in Iowa with her cousins. A pig talent show, the snoopy Anderheimerhooper kids, and cousins as adventuresome as Imogene make for a sidesplitting story your kids will relish. Add some "spark" to your reading program with this hilarious novel and the following chapter-by-chapter activities and reproducibles.

by Beth Gress and Becky Andrews

Chapter 1: Summer camp means one thing to Imogene and her best friend Edie: making wallets. Have each student make his own wallet to hold a character-development project. Have each student fold one 9" x 6" piece of construction paper in half lengthwise; then have him punch holes at 3/4-inch intervals along the two ends and the folded edge. Using a 3'–4' length of yarn, show students how to sew an overcast stitch around the edge of the wallet on three sides, tying a knot at each end as shown. Have students decorate the outsides of the wallets with their names.

Next duplicate the character bills on page 132 on green paper. Give each student approximately 15 bills to place in his wallet. As a character is introduced in the story (or later, as students learn more about the character), have each child draw a picture of the character in the center of a bill; then have him write descriptive words or phrases around the picture. Finally have the student draw symbols representing that character in the four corner circles of the bill. Have students keep the bills in their wallets; then use them to complete the character-development activities on page 132.

Chapter 2: In this chapter, Imogene commiserates with her best friend Edie about the dismal prospects of spending the summer in Iowa. After reading this chapter, ask students, "On what is Imogene basing her negative opinions about Iowa? Are her opinions valid? What do you think she'll find in Iowa?" Have each student write a conversation that Imogene's cousin Josephine might be having with her best friend about Imogene's impending visit.

Chapter 3: As Imogene gets off the plane, she easily spots her cousins—they're the ones standing on their hands in the terminal. Ending the chapter with that mental picture may give your class some ideas about what the Reinstein clan will be like. Have students brainstorm a list of predictions about Imogene's cousins, Aunt Bobo, and Uncle Bud. List their predictions on a chart. As students continue reading, check the chart periodically to see if any of the predictions were accurate.

Chapter 4: At the end of this chapter, students—as well as Imogene—will have a better picture of life in Iowa and the Reinsteins. Have student groups meet to make lists comparing Imogene's life in New York City with her life in Iowa.

Chapter 5: After reading this chapter, post the following tasks on a small bulletin board under the title: "I challenge you to…"
- find out what an *agate* is.
- survey ten people to find out if they've ever belonged to a secret club.
- research to find out the name of a famous spy.
- find out what *sotto voce* means.
- find out how intelligent pigs are compared to other common animals.

Let students who accept a challenge share their information with the class.

Chapter 6: Before video games, lots of kids amused themselves by making gum-wrapper chains like Imogene's or creating games such as the Reinstein kids' "bathtub walking." For a creative-thinking activity, have small groups design rainy-day games using only equipment found inside the average house. Remind students that the games must be safe enough to play without adult supervision. Have groups share their games; then vote on the one most likely to be a favorite of the Reinstein kids.

Chapter 7: In this chapter, Imogene and her cousins try to utilize special techniques to induce sleepiness (so they can take a nap during the day and then spy on Mr. Ferguson all night long). With students, brainstorm a list of methods students have heard of for inducing sleepiness. For homework, have each student survey ten people to find out what they do when they have problems falling asleep. The next day in math class, have students graph the combined results of their surveys.

Chapter 8: In this chapter, Josephine gives Imogene a taste of what it means to be a member of the LCCS—the Laundry Chute Climbing Society. The Reinstein kids formed two other "secret societies" also known by their abbreviated names: the AGAC (the Association Of Great Agate Collectors) and the BTWS (the Bathtub Walking Society). List the following abbreviated names; then have students guess what they stand for:

IBM—International Business Machines
NABISCO—National Biscuit Company
NASA—National Aeronautics and Space Administration
GASP—Group Against Smoking In Public
ABC—American Broadcasting Company
ACTION—American Council To Improve Our Neighborhoods

Chapter 9: Aunt Emma has only two words for her niece and nephew when they come asking for money: "Think ahead." After reading this chapter, have students list evidence proving that the Reinstein kids didn't think ahead in devising a plan to spy on Mrs. Ferguson.

Chapter 10: Edie Finkelstein, Imogene's best friend, is missing! Wanting to prove that she can be just as adventurous as anyone, Edie skips out of summer camp and heads to Iowa to join Imogene. Feeling caught between new friend Josephine and old friend Edie, Imogene is relieved to learn that Edie will be heading back to camp in a week. In their journals, have students write about times when they have felt caught between two friends. Have them answer questions like "What did you do about the situation? Can someone have two best friends? Why or why not?" Let volunteers share their entries.

Chapter 11: Fights with friends are inevitable and always painful. Use this chapter to discuss fighting and friends. Write the following sentence starters on the board:

Friends usually fight when...
When you're angry with a friend, you should...
When I have a fight with a friend, I...
When I know that a friend is angry with me, I feel...

Have volunteers finish the sentences. At the end of the discussion, staple white background paper on a small bulletin board. At the top of the board, write "Friendship is…." During free time, let students use colorful markers to write endings to the sentence, graffiti-style, on the board.

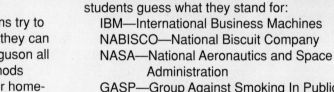

Chapter 12: Aunt Emma stirs up a lot of suspense with her story of how she discovered her "inheritance." Reread that section to students, pointing out the times when Aunt Emma almost tells the climax, then leaves the kids hanging to build suspense. Challenge each student to write a short fantasy entitled "How I Found My Fortune," adding elements of suspense just as Aunt Emma did.

Chapter 13: Imogene's gum chain gets its just reward at the fair when it wins first prize for best oddity. Have students create oddities of their own using the reproducible entry form on page 133. Display the entry forms on a bulletin board; then have the class vote on the best oddity.

Chapter 14: If Imogene and the Reinstein children had exchanged parting gifts, what would they have given each other? Have each student make a list suggesting the gift each Reinstein child would have given Imogene and the present Imogene might have given each of her cousins.

Culminating Activities

- April is National Humor Month, the perfect time to read *An Occasional Cow.* After finishing the book, let students nominate their favorite parts for the "First-Place Funny Bone Award." Have students describe their favorite parts on large cut-out bones. Post the cutouts on a bulletin board.

- With its descriptions of life at the Reinsteins' home, *An Occasional Cow* is a terrific novel to read while studying the midwestern states. Use this book as an introduction to individual projects on other states or regions. Have each student choose a state and research its climate, physical geography, agriculture, major cities, etc. After all notes have been taken, have students pretend that they have been asked to make suggestions for a sequel to *An Occasional Cow.* The sequel will have Imogene spending another summer in a state she's never visited. Have each student use her notes to write a letter to Polly Horvath, suggesting a sequel set in the state she studied. Instruct students to include at least three possible adventures that Imogene could experience in their states. For example, since pigs are a major farm industry in Iowa, Imogene encountered a pig talent contest on her visit. After sharing their letters, have students staple them inside originally designed book jackets for their sequels.

- Imogene felt that anyone who chose to live in Iowa couldn't be trusted; but her attitude about Iowa changed over the summer. Duplicate the "Iowa: Before And After" reproducible on page 133 for each student to complete. Then dare students to take the "Big Ten Challenge." Encourage each child to use his free time to research Iowa and develop a list of ten "favorable facts" about the midwestern state. Let students trace the reproducible's Iowa outline onto construction paper; then have them cut out their tracings and label them with their ten facts. Post the cutouts on a bulletin board entitled "Iowa, You're 'I-o-WOW'!"

131

Patterns

Use with the Chapter 1 activity on page 129.

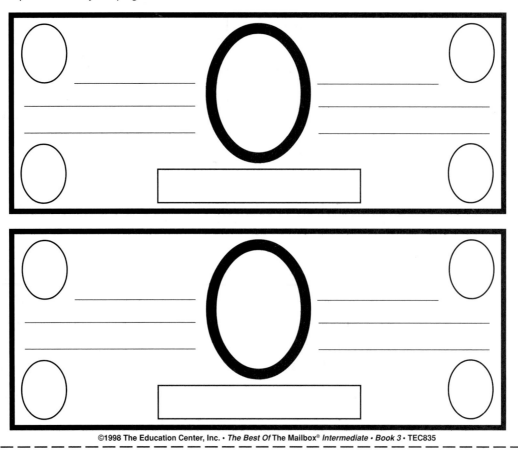

Name_____

Holy Cow, What A Character!

Characters:

Imogene Spark	Mrs. Spark	Mr. Spark
Edie Finkelstein	Josephine Reinstein	March Reinstein
Annie Mae Reinstein	Nathan Reinstein	Bobo Reinstein
Bud Reinstein	Loulou Ferguson	Sara Anderheimerhooper
Aunt Emma	Myrtle Hassenfeffer	Betula Beefay

Make a character bill for each of the characters listed at the left. Then choose ___ activities to complete using the bills.

Activities:

• Stack the bills in order from your favorite to your least favorite character. On the back of your favorite character's bill, write at least two reasons why he/she is your favorite.

• Use the following code to figure the "cash value" of the bills in your wallet. Write the value of each character on the back of the bill; then write the total value of the bills on the outside of your wallet.

very important to the story:	$100
important to the story:	$ 75
somewhat important to the story:	$ 25
unimportant to the story:	$ 5

• Choose one character. Use the words and phrases you listed on the bill to write a description of that character that uses exactly 40 words.

• Choose one character. List ten items that the character might place in a box to be opened on his/her birthday 200 years from now. The items should help people of the future learn about that character's personality.

• Pretend that you've just discovered a formula guaranteed to make you invisible—but only for 24 hours. Now you can observe your favorite character all day long. Make a log listing your observations. Base your observations on the character's personality and interests as described in the book.

Note To Teacher: Use with the Chapter 1 activity on page 129 and the character bill patterns above. Before duplicating, fill in the blank in the speech bubble with the number of activities you want students to complete.

Iowa: Before And After

Imogene was suspicious of anyone who chose to live in Iowa—but her opinions about this midwestern state changed after spending a summer with the Reinsteins. In the state outline below, list Imogene's opinions before and after her experiences in Iowa.

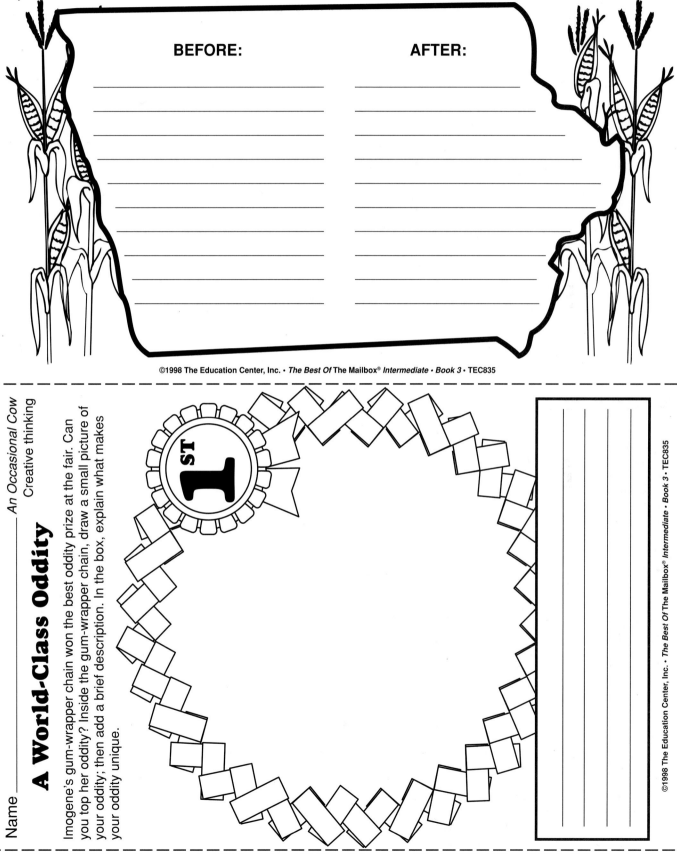

BEFORE:

_____
_____
_____
_____
_____
_____
_____
_____

AFTER:

_____
_____
_____
_____
_____
_____
_____

©1998 The Education Center, Inc. • *The Best Of* The Mailbox® *Intermediate • Book 3 •* TEC835

Name_____

An Occasional Cow
Creative thinking

A World-Class Oddity

Imogene's gum-wrapper chain won the best oddity prize at the fair. Can you top her oddity? Inside the gum-wrapper chain, draw a small picture of your oddity; then add a brief description. In the box, explain what makes your oddity unique.

©1998 The Education Center, Inc. • *The Best Of* The Mailbox® *Intermediate • Book 3 •* TEC835

Note To Teacher: Use "Iowa: Before And After" with the culminating activity on page 131. Use "A World-Class Oddity" with the Chapter 13 activity on page 131.

133

The House Of Dies Drear

A Spellbinding Mystery by Virginia Hamilton

The huge, isolated mansion of white abolitionist Dies Drear was a former Underground Railroad station. Now it's home to 13-year-old Thomas Small and his family. Is it really haunted by slaves who were once housed there? And why are all these frightening things happening only hours after the Smalls arrive? Use the following literature activities and reproducibles to extend the reading of this edge-of-your-seat mystery about a black family caught in a web of suspense and danger.

by Loraine Moore

For Rent: A Most Unusual House

For the past 100 years, the house of Dies Drear hasn't been lived in for more than three months at a time—a challenge even the best real-estate agent might run from! For a fun creative-writing activity, collect a variety of real-estate ads from newspapers and local real-estate agencies. Have small groups of students study the ads. Discuss the characteristics of the house of Dies Drear (huge size, hidden passages and tunnels, steeped in history, etc.) and how those qualities could be seen as positives by the right customer. Then have each group design a flyer to convince prospective renters to give the house of Dies Drear a try! Post the flyers on a bulletin board entitled "For Rent: The House Of Dies Drear."

Student Detectives

As students read this suspenseful novel, they'll encounter more questions than answers. Well, that's the lot of a good detective! Let your students become regular gumshoes while they practice their critical-thinking skills. Cut a supply of duplicating paper in half so that each student has about ten pages. Have each student staple his pages inside a folded sheet of construction paper to make a clue book. After your students read a chapter (or you read a chapter aloud), write the critical-thinking question listed below on the board. Have students copy the question at the top of a page, then answer it either individually or after discussing it with a partner or small group. As students progress through the book, let them go back and revise their answers using clues from the book.

Critical-Thinking Questions To Answer After Chapter…

1 — Why do you think there aren't any complete plans for the house?
2 — Why do you think Mr. Small insisted that Thomas talk to no one about the foundation's report on the house or the legend of the three slaves?
3 — Why do you think the Smalls' furniture had already been arranged for them?
4 — What do you think Mac Darrow meant when he told Thomas, "But I suspect you'll be needing me later"?
5 — What, if anything, do you think Mr. Small is keeping from Thomas?
6 — What do you think Mr. Pluto meant when he shouted, "I have found it before you, and you ought to see it!"
7 — Why do you think Mr. Small was looking so strangely at Mr. Pluto?
8 — What do you think is haunting Mr. Pluto?
9 — What or who left the triangles in the Smalls' house and Mr. Small's office?
10 — Why do you think Mr. Darrow and his sons came to church that Sunday?
11 — Why do you think the Darrows have something in for Pluto, like Carr said?
12 — Who do you think vandalized the Smalls' kitchen?
13 — What do you think Thomas and his dad saw when the wall slid open?
14 — Who do you think is the "other" Mr. Pluto?
15 — What do you think might be Mayhew's plan for the Darrows?
16 — What secret about Mr. Pluto, Mayhew, and the Darrows do you think Mr. Small knows about?
17 — How do you think Mayhew plans to scare the Darrows?

There's History In This Mystery!

In her novel, Hamilton weaves information about the Underground Railroad, the hardships of the slaves who "traveled" on it, and the work of abolitionists who staffed it. The theme of the importance of history is even personified in old Mr. Pluto, who passionately tries to preserve the history of Dies Drear and the slaves he helped escape to freedom.

Use this fascinating novel as a springboard to a study of the Underground Railroad and the time period in which it flourished. Have students study the lives of actual abolitionists and "conductors" on the Underground Railroad (see the list that follows). Read aloud excerpts from the following books to give students additional background information about slavery, the abolitionist movement, and the Underground Railroad:

Books:
- *Now Is Your Time! The African-American Struggle For Freedom* by Walter Dean Myers (HarperCollins): gives historical accounts taken from actual documents written by and about slaves.
- *Many Thousand Gone: African Americans From Slavery To Freedom* by Virginia Hamilton (Alfred A. Knopf, Inc.): draws on actual slave narratives.
- *Sojourner Truth: Ain't I A Woman?* by Patricia McKissack and Fredrick McKissack (Scholastic Inc.): a highly acclaimed biography about one of the most famous black abolitionists.
- *Underground Man* by Milton Meltzer (Harcourt Brace Javanovich): tells the story of a white abolitionist who risks his life to rescue slaves from Kentucky.

Abolitionists:

James G. Birney	John Brown	Sojourner Truth
Frederick Douglass	William Lloyd Garrison	Elijah Parish Lovejoy
James Russell Lowell	Lucretia Mott	Alexander M. Ross
Elizabeth Cady Stanton	Harriet Beecher Stowe	Levi Coffin
Harriet Tubman		John Greenleaf Whittier

Live From The House Of Dies Drear

A lot of creepy things have been going on at the house of Dies Drear—just what a hungry news reporter likes to hear! Culminate the reading of this mystery classic by having students write and produce their own television news program. To prepare students for this activity, videotape suitable television interviews for the class to view and discuss. Next divide the class into pairs. Assign a character from the book to each pair: Thomas, Mr. Small, Mrs. Small, Mr. Pluto, Pesty, Mayhew, Mac Darrow, or one of the three Darrow brothers who were tricked. Have each pair write a five- to ten-question interview between a reporter and its character. Remind students of the following pointers about interviewing:
- Questions should be written to match the sequence of events in the book.
- Questions should be short and general so that the person being interviewed does most of the talking.
- Include questions that ask for the character's feelings and opinions.

Once students have written their interview questions and the character's answers, have each pair decide which partner will take the role of the reporter and which will be the character. Provide class time for students to practice their interviews. On the performance day, encourage students to come dressed in suitable costumes. Videotape the interviews; then watch the tape with students over a snack of hot popcorn.

The Black Trunk

At the end of the book, Thomas notices a black trunk hanging from the ceiling in the cavern. He decides to let the trunk remain a mystery—at least for now. Tickle your students' imaginations by asking them to think about what might be in the trunk. What would happen if the trunk fell? Tell students you want each of them to write a new mystery for Thomas and Pesty that starts when the trunk falls. Since mystery can be a difficult genre for young writers, help them get started by having each child divide a large piece of paper into thirds. Have the student label the tops of the three sections "Characters," "Setting," and "Plot"; then have her fill in the sections with information for her story. In the Plot section, encourage students to develop a problem the characters face and a solution to the problem. Once students have developed these plans, have each child write a short sequel to *The House Of Dies Drear.*

For students eager for a real sequel, never fear! Introduce them to *The Mystery Of Drear House* by Virginia Hamilton, which continues the story of the Small family and their life in Drear House.

Chapter 1	Chapter 2	Chapter 3	Chapter 4	Chapter 5
dismal	relic	eaves	serene	varicolored
calamity	eccentric	quatrefoil	slimy	miniature
veranda	plunder	fertile	forlorn	crestfallen
sinister	caretaker	limestone	paralyze	tamper
desolation	agile	opaque	frantically	meander

Chapter 6
ancient
eerie
jowls
emerald
massive

Chapter 8
superstitious
cubicle
stealthily
ornate
doorjamb

Chapter 10
segregated
refuge
congregation
pulpit
hostility

Chapter 13
ambush
sconce
falcon
recoil
forge

Name _____ *The House Of Dies Drear*
Spelling contract

Spelling At The House Of Dies Drear

Choose ___ words from *The House Of Dies Drear* for this week's spelling list. Circle the words you've chosen; then list them on the back of this page. Complete ____ of the activities listed below for homework this week.

Activities:

- Type your spelling words using our class computer.
- Write your words in *reverse* alphabetical order. Example: zebra, yellow, xylophone,…
- Make a set of flash cards for studying your words.
- Write newspaper headlines using your words.
- Estimate how much time it would take for you to copy your spelling list; then have a friend time you while you write each word one time. How close was your estimate to the actual time?
- Use the following code, a red marker, and a blue marker to write your spelling words.
  Code: *red* = vowels; *blue* = consonants.
- Draw or trace a simple shape, like a heart. Fill it in with your spelling words. Use colorful markers if you'd like.

★ ★ ★ ★ ★ ★ ★ ★ ★ ★ ★ ★ ★ ★ ★ ★ ★

Note To The Teacher: Have each student create his own personalized spelling list by choosing words from this page. Before duplicating the page, fill in the number of words and activities you want students to complete for homework during the week. If desired, pair students at the end of the week and have them test each other on the meanings and/or spellings of their words.

Chapter 7
threshold
cordial
spasm
specter
agitated

Chapter 9
hypotenuse
intruder
confide
misshapen
bellows

Chapter 11
aloofness
garret
musty
vicious
vandalism

Chapter 12
expanse
sprawling
comical
dread
delicately

Chapter 14
sentinel
cavern
tapestry
ledger
legacy

Chapter 15	Chapter 16	Chapter 17	Chapter 18	Chapter 19
grimly	anguish	elaborate	phosphorous	independent
obsessed	reprimand	shroud	gossamer	vaulted
fanatical	corridor	premonition	flimsy	intricate
heritage	hasty	squatter	alibi	inventory
mortal	lever	ancestor	malice	bulged

A Chain Of Events

Events in a story are often related in a chain of causes and effects. An event that leads to other events is a *cause*. What happens as a result of the cause is its *effect*. The following questions can help you to identify whether a statement is a cause or an effect:

To find a cause, ask: "Why did it happen?"
To find an effect, ask: "What happened as a result?"

A single event can lead to many different effects. Fill in the blanks in the chart with what you think are the most important causes or effects.

Cause	Effect
1.	The house of Dies Drear has basically been empty for the past 100 years.
Someone sets up all the furniture in the house before the Small family arrives.	2.
3.	Thomas is trapped inside the kitchen wall.
4.	Thomas thinks Mr. Pluto is a devil.
Someone sneaks into the house through a secret passage while the Smalls sleep.	5.
6.	Thomas and his father find the hidden cavern of treasures.
7.	Mr. Pluto becomes terrified of the Darrows.
8.	Mayhew dresses up like his father.
Thomas, Mayhew, Mr. Pluto, and Mr. Small dress up like ghosts.	9.
Mr. Small decides to inventory the treasures in the cavern before telling anyone about it.	10.

Bonus: If Thomas and Mr. Small had never discovered the cavern, the mystery of Dies Drear's treasures would have remained a mystery. Pretend that Mr. Small has finished cataloging the treasures in the cavern. The foundation has asked him to hold a press conference to inform the public about the mystery of Dies Drear's treasures. On the back of this page, write the announcement that Mr. Small will make.

A Chain Of Events

Focusing On
Famous Folks

Using Biographies And Autobiographies With Intermediate Students

Next time you're surprised to see one of your students select a biography to read (instead of a joke book), don't be! Today's nonfiction shelves are bulging with compelling biographies and autobiographies written especially for intermediate students. Get your kids focused on books about famous folks with the following creative activities.

To Begin

Ask your media specialist to help you track down excellent biographies and autobiographies for intermediate children. Send home a note with students asking parents to donate used biographies suitable for intermediate students. Try to collect books about people from a wide variety of backgrounds, nationalities, time periods, and professional fields.

Famous Folks On Film

Have each student read a biography or autobiography; then divide your class into pairs. Announce that students will be making a "Famous Folks" television documentary to inform other classes about the people they read about. Begin by having each pair meet to tell each other about their famous person; then have the pair work together to write live interviews with their famous folks. Explain that each student will have two roles: the person he read about AND a reporter interviewing his partner's famous person. For example, if Frank read *On Top Of The World: The Conquest Of Mount Everest* by Mary Ann Fraser (published by Henry Holt), he'll pretend to be Edmund Hilary. His partner, Missy, will take the role of Hilary's interviewer. If Missy read *Ruth Law Thrills A Nation* by Don Brown (published by Ticknor & Fields), she'll pretend to be daring pilot Ruth Law, while Frank pretends to interview her.

On the day of filming, have each student dress as his/her famous person. Encourage students to make or bring any props which their famous people might use during the interviews to explain their answers. Let interviewers sit off-camera to ask their questions. After viewing and discussing the film in class, make it available to other classes for checkout.

Make biographies and autobiographies a part of your classroom all year long with these easy ideas:

- Each week read an interesting passage from a different biography or autobiography. Share a few interesting facts about the person featured in the book (check inside the book jacket). Include a bonus question about the person on your weekly spelling test.

- Start a Famous Folks Book Club. Each month have club members eat their lunches in your classroom. During the lunch, have each student discuss the biography or autobiography he is currently reading. For an extraspecial touch, provide a dessert based on the biography you're reading. For example, if you've just read *George Washington: Leader Of A New Nation* by Mary Pope Osborne, bring cherry tarts or cherry-decorated cupcakes.

- Each time you're getting ready to start a new science or social studies unit, ask your media specialist to help you collect several related biographies to incorporate into your unit. For example, if you're studying aviation, look for biographies about the Wright brothers, Sally Ride, or Charles Lindbergh.

- Once or twice a week, stop class activities by announcing, "Let's take a bio break!" Any student who can share a fact about a famous person he's reading about earns a point. Award prizes for the highest-scoring students at the end of the grading period.

OUR READERS WRITE

Our Readers Write

Manners Banner

To foster good behavior and a sense of class pride, my class creates a "Manners Banner" at the beginning of the new school year. Using student ideas, we make the banner out of felt, fringe, yarn, buttons—you name it! I attach the banner to a dowel and hang it outside our classroom. When students exhibit good behavior in the cafeteria or in special classes (such as music, art, etc.), the banner remains where it is. If the behavior has not been as good as it should be, the banner comes down. I'm always amazed when students take the responsibility to suggest that the banner remain or come down.

Susan Jennifer Trice—Gr. 4
Grand Avenue Elementary
Orlando, FL

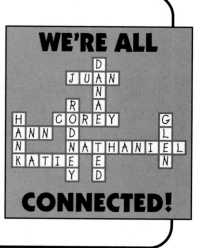

Boxed In

For a fun, back-to-school art project, ask each student to bring an empty, cardboard food box to class. Have students cover their boxes with colorful construction paper. On each of the four sides of the box, a student writes and illustrates a positive statement about himself. The student then attaches a current snapshot of himself to the top of the box. These completed boxes make a great display for Open House!

Nancy Thorrington—Grs. 5–6, Burt Township School, Grand Marais, MI

Designer Stationery

During the first week of school, I give my fifth-grade class the unusual assignment of designing stationery for me to use throughout the year. After each student has completed an original design, the class votes on the one it likes best. That design becomes the one that I photocopy for notes to parents, students, and administrators.

Mary Koeck—Gr. 5
Winneconne School
Winneconne, WI

Folder Labels

Want your students organized from day one? On the first day of school, give each student a strip of address labels that have been programmed with his name and the headings for all his folders and notebooks. (If your school has a computer with a label maker, it will make production of the labels very easy.) All the students have to do is peel and stick, and they're better organized!

Eleanor Maxwell—Gr. 4, Thornton Elementary, San Antonio, TX

All About You

Ask each child to select a number between 1 and 15 and write it inside a circle at the top of his paper. Then have the student write facts—equal to the number written at the top of his paper—he'd like to share about himself. Since some students would be more comfortable communicating via a written format than they would be if speaking before a group, you're sure to gain valuable information about your less-outgoing kids. And you'll also reap insights into students' writing and vocabulary skills!

Jo Farrimond, Foster Middle School, Tulsa, OK

We're All Connected!

Use this creative bulletin-board idea to post your students' names at the beginning of the year. Write each student's name in large print on an enlarged piece of grid paper; then cut out the name. Arrange the names to look like a crossword puzzle on a bulletin board titled "We're All Connected!"

Randee Bonagura
Fairfield Elementary
Massapequa, NY

Scientists At Work!

Encourage enthusiasm for science with an easy-to-make display. Take photos of students as they work on classroom science activities and experiments. Post the photos on a bulletin board along with samples of student-made charts, graphs, lab reports, etc. Add the title "Scientists At Work!" Your students will love being the stars of this motivating display.

Julie Johnson—Grs. 3-4
Colonial Hills Elementary
Houston, TX

Holiday Recordings

Right before the Christmas season begins, I ask each student to choose a favorite traditional or modern-day Christmas story or poem. After each student has made his selection, he tape-records it. I encourage students to enlist family members and friends to help with their recordings. Background music and original sound effects help liven up the readings. As the holidays approach, we take time to listen to the tapes in class. Our holiday recordings provide practice with oral reading and help put everyone in the holiday spirit!

Sr. Bernadette Mary Hiester—Gr. 4
Holy Family Elementary
Philadelphia, PA

Food Boxes For The Needy

Instead of a class gift exchange at Christmastime, our students create food boxes for needy families. Groups of three to five students each are formed. Each group is responsible for decorating a box, filling it with nonperishable food items, and writing a poem that is placed on the box. The boxes are presented to a representative from our local community care center on the day before Christmas vacation. Each group reads its poem aloud and then loads its box in the truck. The box will be given to a needy family that day. This is a fun and productive way to teach our youth that giving is better than receiving.

Claudia Cerasani, Barbara Schwab, and Laurie Tracey—Gr. 6
Pioneer Middle School
Yorkshire, NY

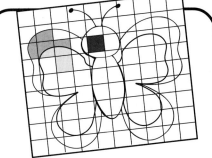

Positive Behavior Grids

Interested in a monthly or thematic method for reinforcing positive behavior? Duplicate for each team a simple, seasonal picture on which you've drawn a grid. Display the grids on a bulletin board in the classroom. Whenever a group is observed following directions, working cooperatively, or staying on task, allow one square on the group's shape to be colored. When all of the shape's squares are colored, award a homework pass or other reward to each member of the group. When every group successfully colors in all squares, hold a class popcorn party to celebrate.

Julie Bliss—Grs. 4–5
Holy Family School
Des Moines, IA

Celebrity Stockings

Here's a holiday activity that's stuffed with creative- and critical-thinking practice! With students, brainstorm a list of famous people—both living and deceased—from all walks of life: sports, politics, television, science, etc. Have each group of three students select one celebrity and design items that would go in that person's stocking. Instruct each group to mount its items on the outside of a stocking (an inexpensive fabric stocking or a large paper one), being careful not to identify the celebrity anywhere on the stocking. Display the stockings on a wall in the hallway; then invite other classes to guess the identity of each stocking's celebrity.

Susan Robinson—Gr. 5
Kings Park, NY

Heart Of Cards Collage

I have been teaching for 13 years and have received many Valentine's Day cards from my students. Each year I display all of the cards from students past and present in a special way. I draw and cut out a large heart from poster board. As a card is received, I write the name of the student who gave it to me at the top. All of the cards are mounted, collage fashion, on the front and back of the heart (be sure not to cover student names). The year is written at the top, and the heart is displayed along with those of past years. This creates a display of delightful Valentine memories.

Bev Huffman—Gr. 4, Riverdale-Forest Elementary, Forest, OH

Lucky To Be Me!

Aren't we lucky that everyone in the world is unique? Send that message to your class this St. Patrick's Day with a student-made bulletin board. Provide students with plenty of old magazines; then instruct each child to cut out words or pictures that describe and illustrate his uniqueness. Have the student glue the cutouts, collage-fashion, on a large shamrock pattern that's been cut from green construction paper. Post the one-of-a-kind shamrocks on a bulletin board entitled "Lucky To Be Me!" or "Lucky Me! I'm Special!"

Theresa Hickey—Gr. 4, St. Ignatius School, Mobile, AL

"OARP"

To add a twist to my students' literature circles, they now "OARP." When a group is given a reading assignment, each student writes an OARP response in his journal. OARP stands for the following:

Opinion: how the student felt about the selection
Action: what happened in the selection
Reaction: how the characters react to the action
Prediction: what the students think will happen next

My students love to OARP, and I love listening to their discussions!

Ellen Mucha—Grs. 5–8 Language Arts
Immaculate Heart of Mary–St. Luke's
Minneapolis, MN

Weekly Journalist

Building a class scrapbook of a different sort is a snap with my simple idea! Each Monday I select one student to be the journalist of the week. This student uses a disposable camera to take a picture of anything he chooses. Once the film is developed, the student writes a description to go along with the picture that he took. I put all the pictures and descriptions into a scrapbook for free-time viewing.

Melanie Bruse—Gr. 5, Jordan Ridge Elementary
South Jordan, UT

Fact/Opinion Book

Incorporate the language arts skill of recognizing facts and opinions into other curriculum areas. After studying Asia, my students created a class fact/opinion book. Each student wrote and illustrated two pages: one page with a fact and one page with an opinion. We combined all of the pages into a class book. Adapt this idea to any science or social studies topic. The completed book is a great tool to use when reviewing a topic.

Marion Young—Gr. 4
Weigelstown School
Dover, PA

```
      5
   5x1=5
   5x2=10
   5x3=15
   5x4=20
   5x5=25
   5x6=30
   5x7=35
   5x8=40
   5x9=45
```

```
      3
   3x1=3
   3x2=6
   3x3=9
   3x4=12
   3x5=15
   3x6=18
   3x7=21
   3x8=24
   3x9=27
```

Multiplying Like Rabbits

Use this idea to help "everybunny" in your class learn his multiplication facts. Write each set of multiplication facts on a piece of chart paper. Design and cut out rabbit ears to place above each set of facts. Display all facts on a bulletin board titled "We're Multiplying Like Rabbits."

Brandi Lampl—Gr. 4, W. A. Fountain Elementary
Forest Park, GA

"Geo" Questions

Start your students' day with an activity that will make them world-geography experts in no time! First thing in the morning, I give each team a geography question from my Trivial Pursuit For Juniors® game. Teams have one minute to discuss their answers. If a team answers its question correctly, it earns a point. The team with the most geography points at the end of the week is allowed to choose our recess activity for Friday.

Debbie Patrick—Gr. 5, Park Forest Elementary, State College, PA

Ordering Time-Saver

To simplify ordering new materials in the spring, I attach a Post-it® Brand note to the inside front cover of each catalog that I receive. On the note, I list items that I may want to order later. When ordering time rolls around, I don't have to go through each catalog again, page by page.

Linda Nelson—Grs. 1–8 Chapter I, Piscataway Township Schools, Piscataway, NJ

Time To Read And Write

Develop fluent readers and writers with the help of your class calendar. Use the day's date to determine the amount of time students spend on sustained reading and writing. For example, on March 28 have students write for 28 minutes and then read silently for 28 minutes. Students will look forward to the time to read and write without interruptions.

Wendy Rodda—Grs. 5/6
Middleton, Nova Scotia, Canada

Photo Posters

Students love to have their pictures taken and then displayed. But they really get excited when prints are enlarged into posters! I try to choose one print from each roll of film I shoot and have it enlarged to poster size. This is accomplished inexpensively with a color copier. There's no better way to brighten up a classroom than with posters of your kids' favorite subjects—themselves!

Julia Alarie—Gr. 6, Essex Middle School, Essex, VT

Zany Zoo

Practice parts of speech with some absurd animal antics. After thinking of an animal, have each student write a sentence to describe his animal using this pattern: article + adjective + noun + verb + adverb. For example, "The furry kitten purred loudly." Next have each student print his sentence on a sentence strip and cut it in half to separate the subject from the predicate. Gather the subjects and predicates into two separate piles; then shuffle the piles. In turn, have each student select a subject and a predicate to tape together. The resulting silly sentences will leave your students hooting like hyenas and cackling like cockatoos! For extra fun, have students illustrate their zany creatures.

> The huge elephant
> slithered slowly.

Sherri Kaiser—Gr. 4, Walnut Grove Elementary, Suwanee, GA

Drop Me A Line!

Practice letter-writing skills all year long with this simple idea. At the beginning of the year, have each student bring stationery, a few stamps, and the addresses of several friends or family members to school. Store each child's supplies in a special folder. Each grading period, pull out the supplies and have each student write a letter to one of his chosen recipients. A great activity for Friday afternoon!

Candy Whelan, Garlough Elementary, West St. Paul, MN

Made In The Shade!

Here's a bright idea for this year's hall passes. Take advantage of summer sales by purchasing two pairs of inexpensive sunglasses. Write "Pass" and your name on the earpieces of each pair. Students will enjoy wearing these cool shades as they perform duties that require traveling from the classroom and back.

Stella Bizzio—Gr. 5
LeRosen Elementary
Lafayette, LA

Yellow-Page Recycling

When new phone books arrive, don't throw the old ones out! Have students bring their old phone books to class; then divide students into teams. Have each group design a Yellow-Pages scavenger hunt with which to challenge another team. What a great way to familiarize students with the wealth of information found in today's phone books!

Christine A. Baughman—Gr. 5, St. James The Less School, Columbus, OH

Daily Survey

Looking for a new way to motivate your students as soon as they walk through your door in the morning? Place a chart labeled "Daily Survey" on an easel at the entrance to your room. Include a different question on the survey each day, such as, "What time period would you most like to live in?" or, "If you could travel to any one of the seven continents, which would it be?" Students enjoy not only answering the questions, but also coming up with questions of their own. You'll have students from other classes coming to your room as well to check out the daily survey!

Debbie Patrick—Gr. 5, Park Forest Elementary, State College, PA

Wanted: Class Helpers

Make a job chart that's both striking and easy to maintain. Enlarge and laminate the classifieds section of your local newspaper. Mount the resulting poster on a wall, door, or small bulletin board. On Monday, write each job and the name of a student volunteer on a self-sticking note; then stick all of the notes on the poster. Change the notes weekly.

Debbie Tucker—Grs. 4–6
Ojibway Heritage School
Shoal Lake, Ontario, Canada

Fraction Garden

Here's a creative way to teach fractional parts of a whole! Divide your math class into groups. Give each group a total number of flowers and a fraction to represent each flower's color. For example, tell students they have 30 flowers, and that three-fifths are yellow, one-third are red, and one-fifteenth are purple. Have each student group determine how many flowers there are of each color. Then challenge the group to design a flower garden that shows the correct number of flowers by color on a piece of art paper. The completed flower gardens make a terrific math bulletin board!

Mary Spina—Gr. 4, Bee Meadow School
Whippany, NJ

Just One Look

Here's an easy way to help a student catch up on a literature-based book after being absent. Assist your class in completing sentence strips that document and illustrate each important event in the book as it is read. Display the completed sentence strips in order on a wall of the classroom. When the absent student returns, he finds that catching up isn't so difficult after all.

Andrea McMahan, Munford Middle School, Munford, TN

Find A Pencil? Leave A Pencil!

It seems students are always finding pencils and turning them in, or losing pencils and trying to find them. To avoid such interruptions, I borrowed an idea that convenience stores often use with pennies. Simply label a cup with "Find a pencil? Leave a pencil. Need a pencil? Take a pencil." Begin by putting a dozen pencils in the cup. Then students know where to put pencils that they find, or where to borrow pencils if they lose theirs.

Jonathan S. Cohen—Gr. 4 Student Teacher
Maple Shade, NJ

Review Sheet Signatures

My students take home a unit review sheet two days before a unit test. At the bottom of the sheet are two lines for a parent's signature. If the student studies with a parent two nights in a row and gets the parent's signature for each night, I add bonus points to that child's test grade.

Eleanor Maxwell—Gr. 4
Thornton Elementary
San Antonio, TX

Good News Calendar

Display a large calendar within easy access of all of your students. Each morning, allow the children to write good news about themselves in the block for that day. At the end of the month, review all of the accomplishments students have shared on the calendar. What a self-esteem builder!

Cathy Ogg—Gr. 4
Happy Valley Elementary, Johnson City, TN

"Pop" Quiz

Before reviewing for an upcoming test, I bring an inexpensive, two-liter bottle of pop and small paper cups to class. I distribute the cups to students before I begin quizzing them. If a student correctly answers a question, she gets a cupful of pop. What a fun and tasty way to review!

Julie Leingang—Gr. 6, Grimsrud Elementary
Bismarck, ND

Homework Stars

To motivate my students to complete homework assignments, I give each child a construction-paper star labeled with 16 dots. Each child's star is stored in a labeled paper pocket stapled onto a "Homework Stars" bulletin board. Students turn in their stars with their homework assignments. If a student's work is neat and complete, I punch out one dot on her star. When all 16 holes are punched, the star becomes a homework pass. The student receives a new star so she can tackle the homework challenge again.

Anne H. Warnke—Grs. 4–5 Emotionally Handicapped
Sandston Elementary
Sandston, VA

Writers' Blocks

Whenever my students are writing in Writing Workshop, they have an easy way of letting me know when conferences are needed. Instead of raising his hand and sitting idly, a student picks a toy alphabet block from the writing center and places it on his desk. This allows the child to continue working until I see the conference-needed signal. "Downtime" for student writers is virtually eliminated!

Robin Kennedy—Gr. 5
Ashley River Creative Arts
Elementary School
Charleston, SC

"Things I Know About..."

I've found the following technique to be a quick way to review my students' knowledge of any subject matter. Each student is asked to write four statements about an assigned topic, with each statement beginning "I know that...." Students also add illustrations at the bottoms of their pages. At the end of the year, each student compiles her pages into a book that is placed in her yearlong portfolio. Students like this format because it allows them to decide what to write. This activity also leads into writing paragraphs, from which students can easily develop essays.

Tami Bird—Gr. 5, Liberty Elementary, Murray, UT

Place-Value Cards

To help my students learn place value, I give each child a wipe-off pen and a laminated index card labeled as shown. When it's time to practice, I call out a large number. Each student writes the number on his card; then he holds the card up for me to check. Having the spaces labeled so clearly on the card reminds my students that each spot needs a number.

Kate Luchtel—K–8 Tutor
Gardena Valley Christian School
Gardena, CA

The Smarties® Board

What to do with early finishers or students who need an extra challenge—that's a problem many teachers face. My solution is to set up a Smarties® Board. On a bulletin board I post a list of extra activities covering all areas of the curriculum. For each extra project completed, a student earns a roll of Smarties® candy and a "Smartie® star" to place beside his name on a class chart. When a student has earned five Smartie® stars, he is awarded a special certificate. How's that for a smart idea?

Nancy Galliher—Gr. 4, Tapteal Elementary, Richland, WA

Animal Quotations

I've found a really amusing and motivational way to teach my students how to write direct quotations. Using animal pictures from old calendars, I ask my students to write what they think that animal would say if it could talk. The results are often hilarious. The class votes to decide the funniest quote, but I only allow students to choose from quotations that are correctly written. It's amazing how interested my kids have become in punctuating their ideas correctly!

Vivian Kannon—Gr. 4, Lakeview Annex, Nashville, TN

"Look, it's Superman!" quipped Pierre the penguin.

Cellophane Tangrams

Tangrams are a very useful manipulative in my math class, but the cost of purchasing a transparent set for each student was prohibitive. We tried construction-paper sets, but they tore easily. My students and I preferred the commercially made tangrams because we wanted to use them on the overhead and see through them for pattern duplication. My solution was to laminate inexpensive colored cellophane. I cut the laminated cellophane into four-inch squares and then cut each square into the seven tangram pieces. Each student now has his own sturdy tangram set, for little or no cost.

Marie Blum—Gr. 5
Ellis B. Hyde Elementary
Dansville, NY

Cream-Filled Geology

Enjoy an edible science lesson! Teach students about the three layers of the earth with cream-filled cupcakes. Give each student an iced cupcake and a clear drinking straw. Instruct each student to push her straw into the cupcake to mimic drilling into the earth. Next have her carefully pull the straw from the cupcake to observe evidence of its three layers—the cream-filled center (core), the cake (mantle), and the icing (crust). Then direct the student to break the cupcake open to view a cross section of the "earth" before it's munched away!

Tammy Nelson—Gr. 5, St. Leo's School, Ridgway, PA

Staff Appreciation Day

At the end of the year, express appreciation to cafeteria staff and custodians by holding a "Thank-You Shower." Divide your class into groups. Instruct each group to compose a poem, rap, or song lauding the hard work of these employees. During the shower, have each group perform while others serve donated refreshments. Through this process, students will recognize the contributions of these vital but behind-the-scenes staff workers. Meanwhile the staff will know they're appreciated!

Cathy Ogg, Happy Valley Elementary, Johnson City, TN

Easy Birthday Display

Here's a simple birthday display that's a snap to make. List each month—along with students who have birthdays in that month—on a sticky label attached to the center of a paper birthday-party plate. Attach the plates to a bulletin board, door, or wall space. The result—a birthday display that's colorful and eye-catching, and that doesn't require tons of time to make!

Sharon Wilkens—Gr. 4
Imbler School District
Summerville, OR

Hard Work Pays Off

Reward your honor students with a display that also results in unique awards. Enlarge a ten-dollar bill; then duplicate a supply of these big bills. Photograph each honor-roll student. Trim each child's photo and glue it inside an enlarged bill as shown. Display the bills on a "Hard Work Pays Off!" bulletin board. After you take down the display, give each student his bill to take home.

Marilyn Davison—Grs. 4 & 5, River Oaks School, Monroe, LA

Reading Recommendations

Who better to recommend a good book to next year's class than your graduating students? At the end of the year, I have each of my students create a bookmark illustrated with the title and author of a book she'd recommend to a rising sixth grader. At the beginning of the next year, I randomly distribute the bookmarks to my new students. They love getting recommendations from the kids who have already been in my class.

Nancy Nixon—Gr. 6 Reading
Heritage Middle School
Middlebury, IN

WALK TWO MOONS
BY SHARON CREECH

Personal Spellers

Need a simple way to help children record their misspelled words correctly? Ask each student to bring a blank address book to school. When she misspells a word, have the student find the correct spelling and write it in her address book under the appropriate letter. This simple idea will build a personal speller that really works for each student!

Merrill Watrous
Eugene, OR

IT COMPUTES!

Make Mine E-Mail!

Hesitant about giving out your home phone number or address to students and parents? Give them your E-mail address instead! E-mail is a teacher's "e-friend." Why?

- It never interrupts you at dinner or takes up more time than you have available. You're in; you're out; it's over!
- You can use E-mail to keep in touch with students who are absent.
- You can write parents who have the same question one note as a group.
- You can use it to keep in touch with colleagues at other schools.

Start small and soon your "e-confidence" will grow!

Merrill Watrous, Eugene, OR

A Disk To Call My Own

Working between the computer lab and the classroom computer is a snap when each student has his own personal disk. Early in the year, have each student initialize and title a disk with his name. Whenever a student must stop midstream while working on a program in the computer lab, he has only to save his work to his disk. He can then take his disk back to the classroom and continue working on the classroom computer. This saves a lot of stress when computer lab time runs out before a student has completed a project.

Patricia Novak—Gr. 4, Meadowbrook School, Eatontown, NJ

Computer Owners

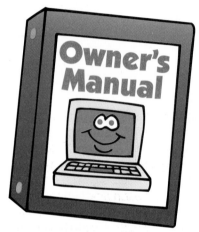

My students take turns using our two classroom computers by rotating "ownership" on a weekly basis. Each week two students in the room "own" the computers. Each owner may use his computer during recess and lunch, or he may lend it to someone else. If another student has free time during the day, she may borrow the computer from an owner. Computer owners must also keep the computer work stations organized and tidy. If desired, store an "Owner's Manual" containing the ownership rules at each computer station.

Shannon Renwick—Grs. 5–6 Peepeekisis Pesakastew School Balcarres, Saskatchewan Canada

Sticky Keys

Does your classroom computer have a case of sticky keys? Help your students keep the keyboard and mouse clean by providing a box of baby wipes nearby. Have each student use the wipes to clean her fingers before using the computer. This small task will keep your high-tech baby as clean as the day it arrived!

Julie Eick Granchelli—Gr. 4, Lockport, NY

Font IDs

Help students easily identify your computer's fonts with this tip. Make a list of all the fonts on your computer by typing the name of each font in its own style. Print a copy of the font list and attach it to the wall near your computer. Students can quickly scan the list to decide which fonts they want to use.

Jennifer Overend—Gr. 6, Aprende Middle School, Chandler, AZ

Hanging Shoe Bag

Simplify diskette storage by using a hanging shoe bag. Label each pocket with the name of one of your software programs. Or provide storage for personal disks by labeling each pocket with a student's name.

Julie Eick Granchelli—Gr. 4, Lockport, NY

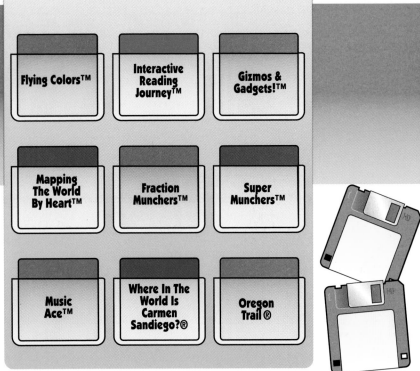

Computer Keyboard Covers

Looking for an inexpensive way to help your students practice memorizing the computer keyboard? Obtain the lid from a box of duplicating paper and cut away a flap from one of the long sides. Place the lid over the keyboard with the open side facing the student. Direct the student to place his hands inside the opening, under the box lid, and onto the keyboard. This allows the student to type without looking directly at the keyboard. Decorate the lid with Con-Tact® paper for a more attractive cover.

Kelly Howell—Gr. 6, Macedonia Elementary, Canton, GA

What's New?

Keep parents up-to-date with your own computerized classroom newsletter. Begin Monday by opening a new document. At the end of each day, have two to three students collaborate on a summary statement telling what happened in school that day. Have them sign the summary and save the document. Edit each day's summary. At the end of the week, print out and duplicate the resulting page to send home. Students practice real-life writing as they keep their parents informed.

Julie Eick Granchelli

Computer Station Organizer

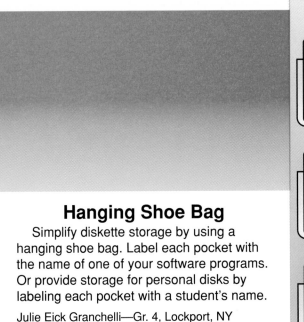

Want to eliminate the question, "Whose turn is it?" Organize your computer station with a three-ring binder filled with laminated construction paper cut to fit (one sheet per student). Open the binder so that it stands freely (similar to a chart stand). Use a wipe-off marker to write a student's name on each page. When a student is finished with the assigned computer task, he flips the page over to show the next person in turn. When all of the sheets have been used, simply flip the entire set back to the first sheet and repeat the process. Using wipe-off markers will enable you to reuse the notebook again and again.

Patti Derr—Gr. 5
Northwest Area Elementary
Reading, PA

Class History

Expand the "What's New?" idea on this page into a class history of the year. Compile each week's summary statements into a separate document. At the end of each month, print the document, add student illustrations (either original drawings or clip art from a computer program), and place it in a class album. A great project to reminisce over at the end of the year!

Julie Eick Granchelli

Computer Log

For

_____

(Class Name)

Date	Student Name	Software Used	Time FROM	TO

Note To Teacher: Duplicate a supply of this log to be kept at the computer station. Preprogram the log with student names for scheduling purposes. Or leave it blank, instructing students to fill it in as a record of their computer usage.

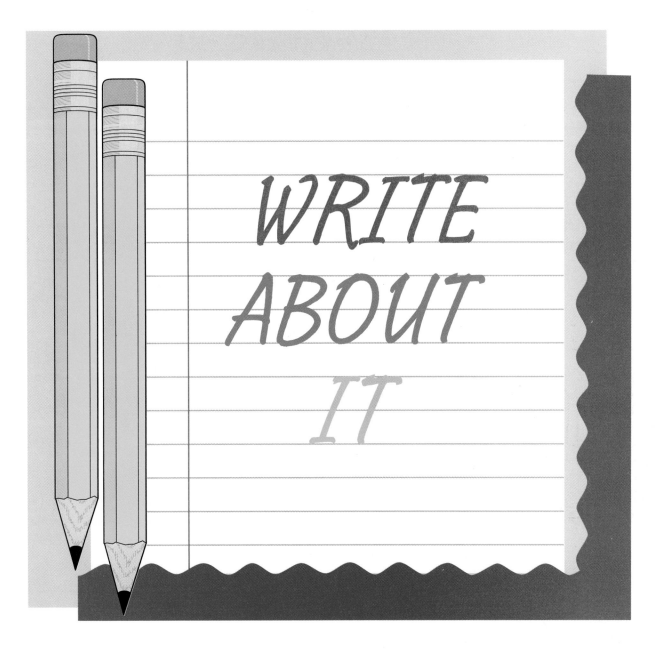

WRITE ABOUT IT

Write About It

Descriptive Paragraphs Using Calendars

At the beginning of a new year, recycle those scenic photographs from old calendars and use them for this descriptive-writing activity. After secretly selecting a laminated photograph, each student uses adjectives and sensory words to write a descriptive paragraph about her photo. I post the photos on a bulletin board, and each student takes a turn reading her edited paragraph. Meanwhile the audience listens carefully in order to match each paragraph to its corresponding photograph. Whoever matches the most paragraphs to pictures wins a prize!

Kathy Galford—Gr. 5, Greenbrier Intermediate, Chesapeake, VA

Night Writes

When winter nights start getting us down, my students begin their Night-Writes folders. I provide each student with a black or dark blue, three-clasp folder containing a page of directions and five sheets of yellow tablet paper. A large, yellow star on the outside of the folder provides space for the title and an illustration, and each student receives several shiny, gummed stars to scatter on the cover. Students write on a different topic each night, and we share writings on a voluntary basis the following morning. Writing guidelines include: write from memory as well as from imagination; use descriptive words; pay attention to neatness, punctuation, spelling, and grammar; and write at least ten sentences or two full paragraphs. Topics, which are changed weekly, include the following:

- Special people in my life
- Special places I have been or would like to visit
- "Let's Pretend"—an original short story
- Animals I have had as pets
- Dreams for the future
- I wonder why…

Joellen M. Marx—Gr. 5, St. Therese School Of Deephaven, Wayzata, MN

Up With LEGOS®!

LEGOS® are wonderful learning tools for older children, too! My students enjoy building with LEGOS®. While making their creations, students draw simple step-by-step diagrams. Next they write accompanying directions, making sure their instructions are clear enough for a classmate to understand them. Partners then trade diagrams/directions and build each other's LEGOS® creations. Reading, writing, and following directions—all integrated in a fun and uniquely creative lesson!

Paige Brannon—Gr. 4, Sadie Saulter Elementary, Greenville, NC

Power Verbs

Challenge students to use power verbs, and their writing will improve. Accomplish this by having students compile and insert in their writing journals lists of verbs that relate to seasons, sports, home, school, work, etc. Make these lists even more accessible by displaying them on the ceiling. Simply write synonyms for overused verbs like *said* or *went* on paper slightly larger than a ceiling tile. Tuck the paper around the edges of the tile. Then, by just looking up, students have a handy, visible thesaurus.

Denise Amos—Gr. 4, Crestwood Elementary, Crestwood, KY

Tabloids As Learning Tools

Check out your local supermarket for a truly sensational writing resource: the tabloids! Although most tabloid articles are not appropriate for the classroom, selected ones can be fun and easy to use. (What kid wouldn't be drawn to an article about an alien living in a Kansas woman's mailbox?) Over the summer collect various tabloid newspapers. Cut out a class supply of articles, paste them onto construction paper, and laminate them. Since these articles are usually filled with descriptive language, have students highlight different language techniques. Then have students write sequels to the articles or rewrite them from other points of view. Students can also write persuasive papers telling why they do or do not believe the facts presented in an article. I've yet to see a student who doesn't perk up when I use this unusual learning resource!

Lynn L. Layman—Gr. 5, Greathouse Elementary, Midland, TX

"Lewie's Great Escape"

My students love to write stories about Lewie, our class's pet rabbit. To get students started, I take pictures of Lewie in such places as a teacher's mailbox, the gym, a bathroom sink, and on the principal's desk; then I post the photos in the classroom. Students use the photos as springboards for their stories, which they title "Lewie's Great Escape." I display the completed stories and the photos in a hallway for the enjoyment of the entire school. Adapt this fun writing activity for any classroom pet or even a stuffed animal.

Kathy Galford—Gr. 5, Greenbrier Intermediate School, Chesapeake, VA

Sweet Writing

Need a pick-me-up idea for teaching students how to write contrasting paragraphs? Try this activity which has been "fruitful" in my classroom! Bring a bag each of Starburst® fruit chews and Skittles® candies to class. As students pass around the bags, have them compare price, ingredients, flavors, texture, packaging, and other features as you list them on a chalkboard. Using this framework of details, students can develop contrasting paragraphs. As students are working on their paragraphs, distribute the candies and watch the writing juices flow!

Julie Plowman—Gr. 6, Adair-Casey Elementary, Adair, IA

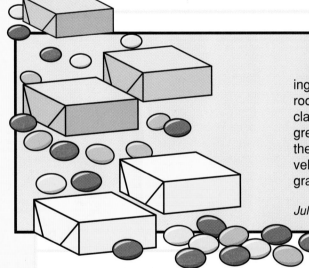

Cereal-Box Adventures

Liven up your adventure-writing lessons by using cereal boxes as springboards for topics. Ask students to bring in cereal boxes from home. Cut the top, bottom, and right side out of each box to create a perfect book jacket. Punch two holes in the left sides of the box and tie paper inside with yarn. Brainstorm with the students to create ideas for adventure stories about the cereals, the names of the cereals, or the characters on the boxes. Expect imaginative story titles like "My Life As A Crispix®" or "How Tony The Tiger® Lost His Stripes."

Angela Pickich—Gr. 4, Oak Park Elementary, Ocean Springs, MS

Editing Made Easy

To keep track of where each of my students is in the writing process, I developed a simple tracking system using the chalkboard, an animal-shaped notepad, and some magnetic tape. I wrote each child's name on a note, laminated it, and attached a piece of magnetic tape to the back. I then divided my chalkboard into four columns—first draft, edit, final draft, and completed work. Each student begins a writing assignment with his name under the first draft column and moves his marker as he progresses through the writing process. When the student reaches the editing phase, I call him up to conference individually. Now I no longer have a line of students at my desk waiting for help.

Jan Dempsey, Jefferson Elementary, West Allis, WI

Shrinking Stories

Even reluctant writers won't shrink back from this creative-writing activity! Take full-body photographs of four or five students at a time (so that each individual child's body is no taller than four inches when the photo is developed). Cut out each student's body from the photos; then give each child his cutout. Provide the class with plenty of old magazines (nature magazines are particularly good for this project). Instruct each student to cut out pictures of items that—when placed beside his body cutout—will make him look as if he's been shrunk, just like the kids in the movie *Honey, I Shrunk The Kids!* Have the student glue his photo and magazine cutout(s) on the front cover of a folded sheet of construction paper. Next brainstorm with students some problems they would have if they were actually as small as their photos. Have each child write a story about his shrunken life to bind inside his folded construction paper. Display the finished stories on a hallway bulletin board entitled "Honey, I Shrunk My Class!"

Susan Patee—Gr. 5, Farmington Hills, MI

What A Weekend!

You expect it every Monday morning—a flurry of hands belonging to students frantic to tell you about their weekends. Put that eagerness to good use by having each student write a brief, but descriptive, paragraph about her weekend activities every Monday morning. File these reports in individual student folders. At the end of the school year, have each student compile her weekend reports chronologically to make a personal "What A Weekend!" book. Students will easily notice how much their writing skills improved as the year progressed. Plus each child will have a wonderful keepsake to enjoy for years to come.

Lucy Willis, Manteo Elementary, Manteo, NC

An "Eggs-cellent" Description

Give descriptive writing a unique, seasonal workout with this "eggs-tra" fun activity! For homework, give each student a large cut-out egg to decorate with an original design. Have the student write an adjective-packed paragraph describing his egg.

The next day direct students to swap paragraphs and try to duplicate each other's designs, revising the descriptions as they work. After students turn in their revised paragraphs and eggs, give each child a duplicated sheet of blank eggs (see the illustration). Read aloud one child's description; then have students try to duplicate the described design by coloring in the first blank egg. Continue until each student's paragraph has been read. Post the original eggs and paragraphs in order on a bulletin board so students can compare them to the designs on their worksheets.

Ruth Pelican—Gr. 5, Shepard Hills School, Oak Creek, WI

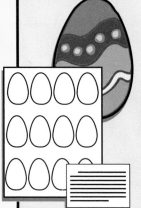

154

GETTING KIDS INTO BOOKS

Getting Kids Into Books

Passport To Literature

I want my students to choose and read a variety of books during the school year. To encourage an assortment of books, I give each student a Passport To Literature booklet at the beginning of the year. The passport consists of a cover and 16 minipages. The minipages include an informational page about the student, three student-choice pages, and 12 pages for recording different types of literature such as historical fiction, modern realistic fiction, biography, poetry, etc. On each minipage, the student writes the title of the book, its author, the dates he began and completed the book, and a rating of the book. To make the passport official, I photograph each student and glue the picture to the inside cover. After completing a book, the student takes his passport to the school media center for an official stamp. By the end of the year, each student has read at least 12 different kinds of books.

Janet Hornbostel—Gr. 5, Richmond School, St. Charles, IL

Novel Tablecloths

When reading a novel that doesn't have any chapter titles, my students create a novel tablecloth. First I cover a tabletop with white bulletin-board paper. Next I divide the paper into squares (one for each chapter of the book). After reading the first chapter, students divide into small groups and brainstorm possible chapter titles. I list their ideas on a chalkboard; then students vote for their favorite. The winning group writes its title at the top of the first square on the tablecloth, then illustrates a scene that best represents the chapter. It's a lot of fun to see our tabletop art develop as each chapter is read. By the end of the book, we have a colorful tablecloth representing the major events of our book.

Julie Plowman—Gr. 6, Adair-Casey Elementary, Adair, IA

Folded Book Reports

Introduce students to a new book report format with this unique project. Cut 12" x 18" white or lightly colored construction paper into 4" x 18" strips. Give each student two like-colored strips. Instruct the student to tape her strips together to make a 4" x 36" strip; then have her fold the strip accordion-style to create nine 4" x 4" sections. Instruct students to fill in the sections with the following information: the book's title, the author's name, the setting of the story, the main characters, the plot, and the student's evaluation of the book. If the information is written on a vertical strip, hang the report from a bulletin board. If written on a horizontal strip, stand the report on a table.

Betty Adams—Gr. 5, Staunton Elementary, Staunton, IN

Character Card Collections

While reading *The Lion, The Witch And The Wardrobe*, I wanted my students to complete in-depth character studies. Since many students have sports card collections, I decided that creating trading cards would be a motivating way to get the students to zero in on each character. For a prewriting activity, we evaluated several different kinds of sports cards. We categorized the information found on the front and back of the cards and discussed similar information that could be written about each character. We also looked for other common items such as logos, borders, and sequences. The students began their collections the day after they began reading the novel. They added a card as each new character was introduced. I periodically provided class time for students to work on their collections. While working, the students would discuss their favorite and least favorite characters. This was an added bonus! Use this activity with any novel or short story.

Sandra L. Kiper—Gr. 5, Clarkson Elementary School, Clarkson, KY

Dear Jennette,
I agree with
your review of The
Night Crossing.

The
Night Crossing

'Tis The Season To Share A Good Book!

These holiday decorations will both brighten your classroom and enlighten your readers! Instruct each child to write a brief review and recommendation for three of her favorite books. Have the student copy the information for each book onto a different ornament cutout. After students have decorated their ornaments, have them hang the projects from a holiday tree. As you take down the tree in January, instruct each student to select one recommended book that she has not read before. Instruct her to read the book for her first book report of the new year. Afterwards, instruct each student to write a letter to the original reviewer discussing the book and why she agrees or disagrees with the original review.

Sally M. Dickinson—Gr. 5, Dietz Elementary, Tucson, AZ

Free-Book Friday

Use this idea to encourage reading and positive behavior at the same time! Cover a shoebox with brightly colored Con-Tact® paper; then cut a slit in the top of the box. Paste cut-out pictures of books from book-club flyers over the entire box. Each week feature one book that can be won in a raffle drawing. (Use bonus points to order books from the book club to be used for the raffle.) When a student displays positive behavior, give her a slip of paper to write her name on and deposit in the box. On Friday draw a name from the box and award that student with the featured book of the week. On Monday morning empty the box and display a new featured book!

Nancy H. Wendt—Gr. 5
Weare Middle School, Weare, NH

Secret-Reader Day

Add a bit of mystery to your reading program! During an Open House—when children are not present—encourage parents to sign up for 15-minute slots to read to your class each week. Have each parent read a chapter from a book you are presently reading to your class. Or let her read a book of her choice that can be completed within the allotted time. On weeks when no secret reader is scheduled, ask your principal, your superintendent, or another teacher to pinch-hit. Your students will love the suspense of not knowing whom the mystery reader is until he or she walks through the classroom door!

Dawn Tameo-Greening—Gr. 6
Peter Thacher Middle School
Attleboro, MA

Graffiti Wall

Put the writing on the wall with this motivating novel activity! Cover a bulletin board with red paper. Create a bricklike design on the paper using a black marker. Then use poster paints to paint the name of your current novel and its author on the board. As your class reads the novel, challenge students to write concepts or new vocabulary words from the novel on the graffiti wall using different-colored paints. Each time a student adds a word or concept to the wall, have him explain its meaning or relevance to the book.

Barbara Parker—Gr. 6, Fredericktown Intermediate/Junior High, Fredericktown, OH

	bravery	Number The Stars	
relocate		by Lois Lowry
Annemarie		
	Baltic Sea	lying
	synagogue	

Thumbprint Story Maps

For a fun art project that doubles as a book review, try thumbprint story maps. First have each student draw a squiggly line from one edge of a piece of art paper to the other. Next direct the student to use an ink pad to make thumbprints strategically across this route. As he reads the book, have the student decorate each thumbprint to represent a character or an important item from each chapter read. Your students are sure to give these novel summaries a big thumbs up!

Debbie Patrick—Gr. 5, Park Forest Elementary, State College, PA

Getting Kids Into Books

Newbery Contest

At the end of the year—before reading motivation totally wanes—I challenge my students to a Newbery reading contest. If the class reaches a shared goal of reading 100 Newbery books, I treat students to a pizza party. In addition, I reward the top three readers with individual prizes. This contest has my students spending every spare minute reading excellent literature!

Donna Evert—Grs. 4–5, Monroe Elementary, St. Paul, MN

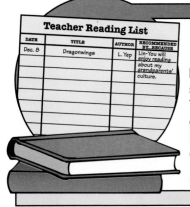

Teacher Reading List

Throughout the school year, I recommend that my students read certain novels or trade books that are related to our topics of study. I also recommend books to children who have special interests. To show my class how important I think it is to share literature, I post a Teacher Reading List. Students use the list to tell me what they think I should read. This gives me insight into my students' interests and keeps me updated on the current library hits. I make sure that the children see me reading books from the list. I also try to share my comments and thoughts with the student who recommended a particular book.

Jennifer Smithers—Gr. 5, A. S. Johnston Elementary, Irving, TX

A Big Book Of Reviews

Turn students' book reviews into a big book to share with your entire school. First ask each student to bring her favorite book to class. Have the student choose a favorite page from her book; then make a photocopy of that page. Next provide each pair of students with an 18" x 24" sheet of oaktag with a line dividing it in half drawn on it. Each student pastes her photocopy on one of the halves. Then she adds a review of her book, answering such questions as: "What is special about the page you selected? Why is this book your favorite? What is the book about?" The student also illustrates an event from the book. Combine all of the completed pages together into a big book. Display the book in the library so other students can use it as a source for reading suggestions.

Carmelle L. Lamothe—Gr. 4, Jewett School, Manchester, NH

Main-Character Photo Albums

Photographs promise to capture a moment forever—so why not capture the life of a favorite book character by creating a unique photo album? After a book has been read, have each student draw and color at least ten "photographs" that could have belonged to the main character. Have the student cut out each photo, mount it on construction paper (either singly or in groups), and write a caption beneath it. Provide the student with materials for making front and back covers. Have him staple his photo pages inside. Then have him write the title of his book on the front cover and illustrate it. Direct him to write his name on the back cover.

Anna Bordlee—Gr. 5, Boudreaux Elementary, Harvey, LA

A Definite Ten!

Organize your next book report assignment around the number ten. Have students list ten facts about the book, describe ten characters, detail ten important story events, or list ten reasons why the book was enjoyable. This activity will stretch your students' thinking as they dig deeply into their novels to find the ultimate ten!

Janet Moody—Gr. 4, Truman Elementary, Lafayette, LA

BUILDING CHARACTER

BUILDING CHARACTER

Helping children grow into kind, caring, and responsible people is a job that parents and teachers alike often find a challenge. Use these character-building activities from our subscribers to help your students learn to care for themselves and others.

Schoolwide Respect Program

To help our students have more respect for themselves and others, a faculty committee at our school sponsored a poster contest. The slogan of the winning poster—"If You Want Respect, Give Respect!"—was printed on colorful banners and displayed throughout the school. Following this contest, we held a Respect Assembly during which students read personal essays describing what respect meant to them. Staff members also charmed the students with a skit about respect performed to the tune of Aretha Franklin's famous hit, "Respect."

Following the assembly, each teacher was given a supply of red paper strips. When a student or staff member witnessed an act of respect, he described it on a paper strip, including the initiator's name, grade, and homeroom teacher. The red strips were collected and posted in the hallway in the shape of a giant arrow. Students were challenged to extend this "Respect-o-meter" down the hallways until it encircled the entire building. With this fun program, respect became a goal for our kids, not just a word!

Lisa Farnen—Gr. 4, Lafayette School, Shelton, CT

Tearing Down Walls

Try this activity that helps students become more aware of their attitudes. On a bulletin board, mount a large piece of brown background paper decorated to look like a stone wall. Add the title "We're Tearing Down The Walls." Have students discuss how they can become better school citizens, accept others more readily, and gain confidence in themselves. After this discussion, encourage each child to think about a personal "wall" or attitude problem that she might wish to change about herself. Duplicate a class supply of the reproducible on page 162. On a copy of the pattern, have each student describe her wall and ways she might change this negative attitude. (Instruct students who wish to remain anonymous to leave their names off the patterns.) Post the patterns on the bulletin-board wall.

Pamela McKedy, Heidelberg American Middle School
Heidelberg, Germany

Relationship Forms

Encourage friendship, communication, and problem solving with a simple system for handling classroom disagreements. Duplicate a supply of the form on page 162. Keep them in a basket on your desk. When two students have a conflict in the classroom, have each child fill out one of these forms before discussing the situation with you. After the forms have been completed, meet individually with each child to discuss the information on his form. With this easy method, the students have time to think through the problem and supply solutions before laying blame on a classmate. Solving the problem before involving the teacher is also a great confidence booster!

Susan Deprez
Substitute Teacher
Phoenix, AZ

Let's Discuss It!

Whenever a student in my class has a conflict, I tell him to "can it!" Throughout the year, my students write down any conflicts they have with their classmates and place these papers—unsigned—in an oatmeal can that has been covered with colorful paper. Each day I read aloud several papers; then we discuss possible options and solutions to the conflicts. The number of problems has steadily declined since my students now know that there are other ways to handle conflict.

Cindy Linton—Gr. 4
Tuppers Plains Elementary, Reedsville, OH

The "Quotes-Line"

All you need for this inspirational display is a length of string and some clothespins! Whenever I find an educational or life-affirming quote, I write it down and file it. Later I type each quote in large type on a computer, using a variety of fonts. I print the quotes on white paper, back them with colorful construction paper, and laminate them. Then I pin the quotes with clothespins to strings that stretch across the classroom. Students and parents, as well as school personnel, enjoy reading the quotes. I also encourage students to add their own original quotes to the line.

Christopher J. Stupak—Gr. 4
Litchfield Intermediate School, Litchfield, CT

Not to know is bad; not to wish to know is worse.

Nigerian proverb

A Bag Full Of Compliments

Heighten student self-esteem with this weeklong activity! On Monday, provide each student with a plastic, zippered bag containing five strips of paper. Instruct each student to write his name across the label of the bag. Then randomly distribute the bags among students each day of the week. Make sure that no one has his own bag or a bag he has already received. Encourage each student to write positive comments about the classmate whose name is on the bag on one paper strip. End the week on an exciting note by having students return the compliment bags to their owners.

Kimberly Only—Gr. 4
Sawgrass Elementary, Sunrise, FL

DAVID

David is a very good baseball player.

David can make me smile.

Senior Pen Pals

Cross-generational friendships are a great way for kids to learn understanding and acceptance. Nursing-home or retirement-center directors often look for special activities for their residents. I contacted one of these directors to find pen pals for my students. The center matched each child with a resident who wanted to participate. Each student soon received her first letter, beginning a correspondence that lasted all year. For holidays and other special occasions, students made cards for their pen pals. In the spring, we took a field trip to meet them. Practicing letter writing was only one benefit of this experience. The true reward was that students gained a better understanding of aging and a deeper appreciation for elderly folks.

Marilyn Davison—Grs. 4–5
River Oaks School, Monroe, LA

TEARING DOWN THE WALL

Do you have a *wall*—an attitude that you know you want to change? Describe that attitude on the lines below. Include at least three steps you can take to "tear down" (change) this negative attitude.

_____

_____

_____

_____

_____

_____

_____

_____

We Don't See Eye To Eye!

My name is _____.

Today's date: _____

I have a disagreement with _____

We disagree about _____

_____.

Here's what happened: _____

_____

_____

Two ways to solve this problem are:

1. _____

2. _____

Note To The Teacher: Use these patterns with "Tearing Down Walls" and "Relationship Forms" on page 160.

REPRODUCIBLES

A Poster All About...

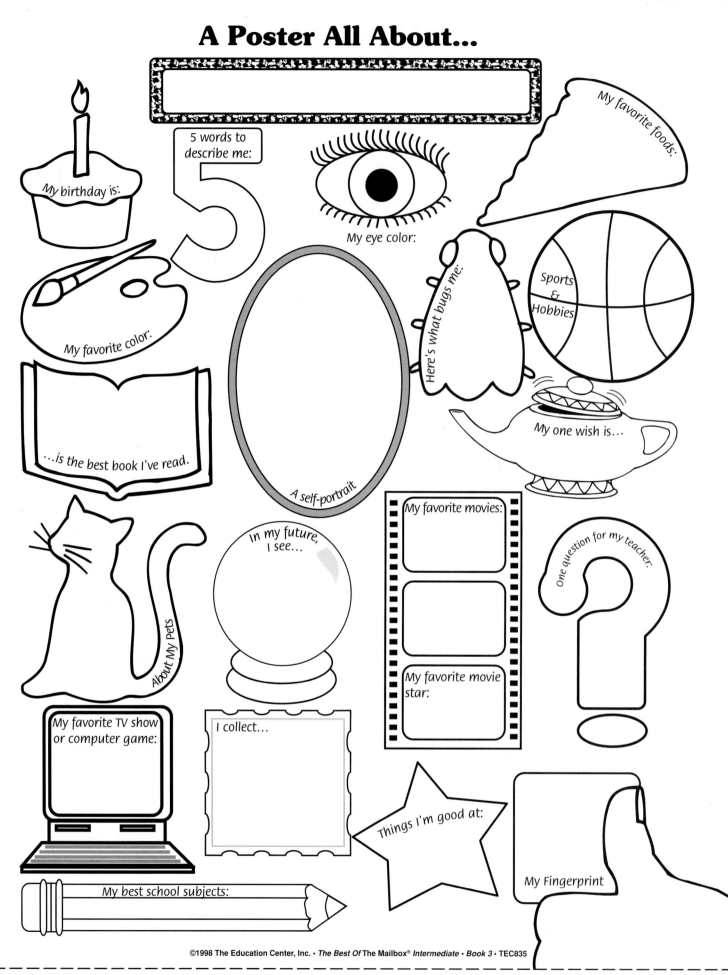

My birthday is:

5 words to describe me:

My eye color:

My favorite foods:

My favorite color:

Here's what bugs me:

Sports & Hobbies

My one wish is...

...is the best book I've read.

A self-portrait

In my future, I see...

My favorite movies:

My favorite movie star:

One question for my teacher:

About My Pets

My favorite TV show or computer game:

I collect...

Things I'm good at:

My Fingerprint

My best school subjects:

©1998 The Education Center, Inc. • *The Best Of The Mailbox® Intermediate • Book 3* • TEC835

Note To Teacher: Duplicate for each student. Have each student complete and color his poster; then have him mount it on construction paper after sharing it with the class. Display the posters on a bulletin board.

Got A Spot Of Free Time?

Monday	Tuesday	Wednesday	Thursday	Friday
Would you wear a *homburg* or eat it? Use a dictionary to find out.	Vowels are worth 53 cents each. Consonants are worth 27 cents. How much is your full name worth? Use a calculator to find out.	A *pangram* is a sentence that includes all the letters of the alphabet. Write a pangram. Remember: it must make sense!	"All that glitters is not gold." What do you think this proverb means? Write your answer.	Write five clues about any state. Give the clues to a friend to guess the state.
List seven favorite foods, seven favorite animals, and seven good things about you.	Draw a picture for a child to color. Write a one-sentence caption under the picture.	How many toes in your class? Multiply to find out.	Write the names of ten countries that are not in North America. Be sure spelling is correct.	You must teach a space alien ten sentences he/she will need to know to make it through the first day on earth. Write the sentences.
Make a list of at least 20 words that have to do with peace.	What would you do if you were awakened at your school desk and were told that you had been asleep for four weeks? Write your answer in a paragraph.	Write three questions you would like to find answers for next week.	Find out each of your classmates' favorite season of the year. Make a graph or chart to show your survey results.	List eight ways to cook without using electricity.
"A page is to a book as a piece is to a puzzle." Write five other analogies.	How many words can you write that contain the letter sequence ACH? To get you started: BEACH, ACHE.	Estimate how many paper clips are needed to go across your desk; then measure for yourself.	Name as many things as possible that scratch.	Write a task to put on the next free-time calendar!

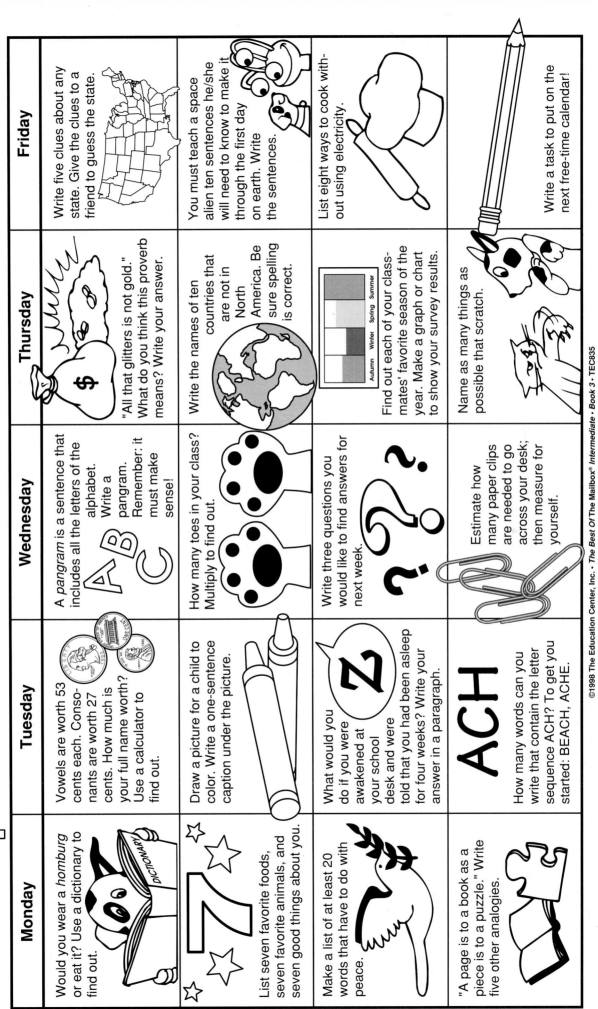

Note To Teacher: Have each student staple this page into a file folder. Completed work can be stored inside the folder.

The Un-Halloween Holiday

Guess this means we get the night off!

October has rolled around, and the mayor of your city has decided to do something different this year instead of celebrating Halloween. Ghosts, goblins, and other spooky creatures are out—but fun is in! The mayor wants your group's ideas on holding a different kind of celebration this October. Your group has just received this form from the mayor's office to complete with your ideas. Discuss ideas in your group; then have your recorder complete the form with your final decisions.

Name of new holiday: _____

What event, person, or other thing does your holiday honor or commemorate? _____
_____
_____

Instead of Halloween's orange and black, what colors will symbolize your new holiday? _____
_____ What does each color represent? _____
_____
_____

Will children still go door-to-door? _____ If yes, for what purpose? _____
_____

Will people still wear costumes? _____ If yes, what kind? _____

If no, how might people dress to celebrate your holiday? _____
_____
_____

Since jack-o'-lanterns won't be used, what new use will your holiday have for pumpkins? _____
_____
_____

How might people celebrating your holiday use all of the candy they usually give away on Halloween?
_____
_____

How might people be encouraged to decorate their homes during this holiday? _____
_____
_____

What other special activities will people enjoy during your holiday? _____
_____
_____

Why will a little kid—who's used to getting lots of candy on Halloween—like your holiday just as much?
_____
_____

Bonus Box: On the back of this form, write a letter to the editor of your local newspaper explaining to the citizens of your city why your holiday will be just as much fun as Halloween—maybe even more fun!

Tricky Treats

'Tis the season to load up on Halloween candy! That's exactly what Bryce wants to do. He's gone to Carl's Candy Court to buy treats for Halloween night. But because Bryce went shopping at the last minute, Carl has only three kinds of candy left: jawbreakers, lollipops, and chocolate bars.

Here's your challenge: Bryce wants to spend exactly $9.00 on exactly 100 pieces of candy. Use the chart below to try different solutions to this problem. If you need more space, draw another chart on the back of this page. Write your final solution in the blanks below the chart.

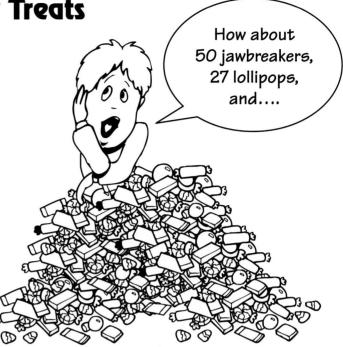

How about 50 jawbreakers, 27 lollipops, and....

	Jawbreakers two for 5¢		Lollipops 10¢ each		Chocolate Bars 20¢ each		Total	
	# of pieces	cost	# of pieces	cost	# of pieces	cost	# of pieces	cost
Trial #1								
Trial #2								
Trial #3								
Trial #4								
Trial #5								
Trial #6								
Trial #7								
Trial #8								

Final solution: Bryce should buy ____ jawbreakers, ____ lollipops, and ____ chocolate bars.

Bonus Box: Beth and Bob are shopping at Carl's Candy Court too. Beth wants to buy 100 pieces of candy for $7.00, while Bob wants to buy 100 pieces for $5.00. Draw a chart like the one above for each person; then try to find a solution to each of their problems. (Hint: Beth and Bob do not have to buy all three kinds of candy.)

A Pocketful Of Thankfulness

What's the best time of the year to be thankful? ANYTIME! Follow these directions to make a bulletin-board display that's full of thankfulness.

Directions:

1. On scrap paper, list words and phrases to describe something or someone you are thankful for.
2. On an index card, write a paragraph describing what or who you are thankful for. Include as many details as possible. **Do not** include the name of the object or person anywhere in the paragraph.
3. Glue the card in the box on the pocket; then decorate the pocket with markers or crayons.
4. Cut out the pocket. Staple it to a bulletin board, stapling only the sides and bottom so that the top of the pocket is open.
5. On a larger index card, draw a picture of the object or person you wrote about. Add a caption. Slip the picture into your pocket.
6. Read the paragraphs on your classmates' pockets. Guess what or who each paragraph is describing; then pull out the picture to check.

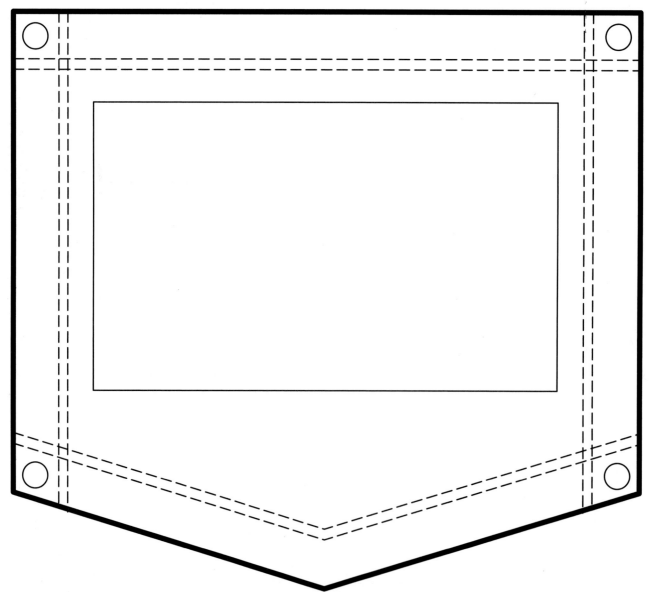

Note To Teacher: Use this reproducible to celebrate the Thanksgiving season or supplement a unit on descriptive writing. Duplicate the page on construction paper. Provide each student with scissors, crayons or markers, a 3" x 5" index card, a 4" x 6" index card, and glue. Post the pockets on a November bulletin board entitled "Pick A Pocket Of Thankfulness."

You Don't Say!

Below are quotes by famous people who were born in November. Choose a quote. On the back of this page, write a paragraph telling what you think the quote means. Use a dictionary to help you with any unfamiliar words in the quote.

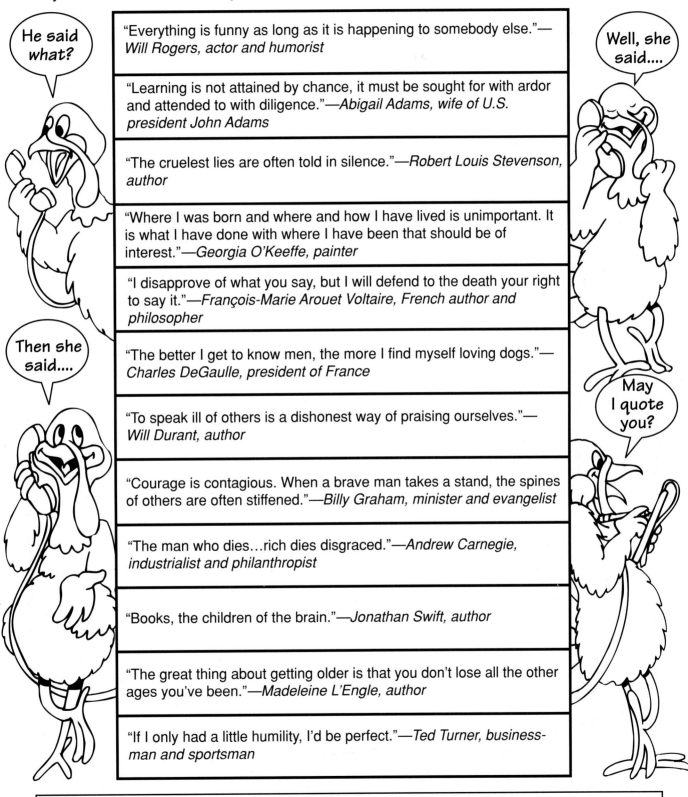

He said what?

Well, she said....

"Everything is funny as long as it is happening to somebody else."—*Will Rogers, actor and humorist*

"Learning is not attained by chance, it must be sought for with ardor and attended to with diligence."—*Abigail Adams, wife of U.S. president John Adams*

"The cruelest lies are often told in silence."—*Robert Louis Stevenson, author*

"Where I was born and where and how I have lived is unimportant. It is what I have done with where I have been that should be of interest."—*Georgia O'Keeffe, painter*

"I disapprove of what you say, but I will defend to the death your right to say it."—*François-Marie Arouet Voltaire, French author and philosopher*

Then she said....

"The better I get to know men, the more I find myself loving dogs."—*Charles DeGaulle, president of France*

"To speak ill of others is a dishonest way of praising ourselves."—*Will Durant, author*

"Courage is contagious. When a brave man takes a stand, the spines of others are often stiffened."—*Billy Graham, minister and evangelist*

"The man who dies...rich dies disgraced."—*Andrew Carnegie, industrialist and philanthropist*

"Books, the children of the brain."—*Jonathan Swift, author*

"The great thing about getting older is that you don't lose all the other ages you've been."—*Madeleine L'Engle, author*

"If I only had a little humility, I'd be perfect."—*Ted Turner, businessman and sportsman*

May I quote you?

Bonus Box: Research the person who is credited with the quote you chose. List five interesting facts about that person. Share your information with the rest of the class by making a small poster, giving a one-minute speech, or writing a short poem.

Challenge: fun puzzle

Holiday Acronyms

We use a lot of acronyms today to name organizations, products, and slogans. For example, the acronym UNICEF stands for *United Nations International Children's Education Fund.* Here are some other acronyms:

SCUBA: *Self-contained underwater breathing apparatus*
GASP: *Group Against Smoking In Public*
RIP: *Rest in peace*

For each holiday acronym below, create a name for an organization, a product, a phrase, or a slogan. Your answers may or may not be related to the holidays. Use the back if you need more space.

1. T.R.E.E. _____
2. G.I.F.T. _____
3. S.T.A.R. _____
4. W.R.A.P. _____
5. S.A.N.T.A. _____
6. L.I.G.H.T.S. _____
7. S.N.O.W. _____
8. G.I.V.E. _____
9. T.I.N.S.E.L. _____
10. B.E.L.L. _____

Challenge: equations, computation

Eights Are Great!

In honor of the eight days and eight candles of Hanukkah, solve these math problems featuring the number 8.

Part One: Add operation signs $(+, -, \times, \div)$ to make these equations true. Some equations may need parentheses. Answers vary.

EXAMPLE: 4 2 0 = 8   ANSWER: $4 \times 2 + 0 = 8$

1. 6 4 3 = 8   5. 7 5 5 1 = 8

2. 4 12 6 = 8   6. 8 8 3 6 = 8

3. 3 10 2 = 8   7. 12 6 24 5 = 8

4. 9 8 3 3 = 8   8. 40 20 4 25 = 8

Part Two: Arrange the specified number of 8s and add operation signs to equal the answer given. Hint: decimals or fractions may be part of the solution.

EXAMPLE: 3 8s = 11   EXAMPLE: 4 8s = 176
ANSWER: $88 \div 8 = 11$ ANSWER: $88 + 88 = 176$

9. 3 8s = 8 _____
10. 3 8s = 9 _____
11. 4 8s = 111 _____
12. 4 8s = 24 _____
13. 5 8s = 10 _____
14. 5 8s = 80 _____

I ♥ 8!

Merry Moolah!

A distant relative of yours, Uncle Bigbucks, has offered you a one-of-a-kind Christmas present. On the gift box below, he's put a magic square comprised of 64 boxes containing the numbers 1–64. This square is "magical" because each column and row of numbers adds up to 260! But there are many more ways that Uncle Bigbucks's square is magical. In fact, Uncle Bigbucks will give you and your partner a $100 bill for each way that you can find. Just follow the directions:

Directions: On the back of this page, list as many ways as you can find that the square is magical. Use a calculator to help you. Each time you find a way that the square is magical, draw a $100 bill (100) on the tree. How much merry moolah can you earn?

52	61	4	13	20	29	36	45
14	3	62	51	46	35	30	19
53	60	5	12	21	28	37	44
11	6	59	54	43	38	27	22
55	58	7	10	23	26	39	42
9	8	57	56	41	40	25	24
50	63	2	15	18	31	34	47
16	1	64	49	48	33	32	17

It's The Real Thing!

These ornaments are on display at Noel's Department Store. They are advertised as genuine Holly Jolly ornaments, which are very expensive collector's items. But someone has replaced many of the real Holly Jollies with second-rate counterfeits! Can you spot the phonies?

Directions: Use the clues to fill in the blanks at the bottom of the page. Rearrange the letters of the real ornaments to spell a word that is found on every Holly Jolly ornament box.

CLUES:

1. The only Holly Jolly ornaments that have specks are quadrilaterals.
2. If an oval Holly Jolly ornament has stripes, it should not also have a ribbon.
3. Holly Jolly ornaments that are polygons have no more than two different-shaped objects drawn in their interiors. They also don't contain letters.
4. The real Holly Jolly ornaments have either an even number of sides or are oval-shaped.

ANSWERS:

The real Holly Jolly ornaments are numbers _____.

The letters of the Holly Jolly ornaments are _____, which—when placed in correct order—spell _____.

Bonus Box: Using the clues, design another Holly Jolly ornament on the back of this page.

KWANZAA CARDS

Martin, Tanya, and Kalika are preparing Kwanzaa reports to share with the class. But they had a minor calamity! A gust of wind from an open window blew all of their note cards off the table, and now they're mixed up. Help the kids get organized by writing an *S, P,* or *C* on each card. Use this code to help you:

CODE

Martin is reporting on Kwanzaa principles. Put a **P** on each of Martin's cards.

Tanya is reporting on the symbols of Kwanzaa. Put an **S** on each of Tanya's cards.

Kalika is reporting on African clothing often worn during Kwanzaa. Put a **C** on each of Kalika's cards.

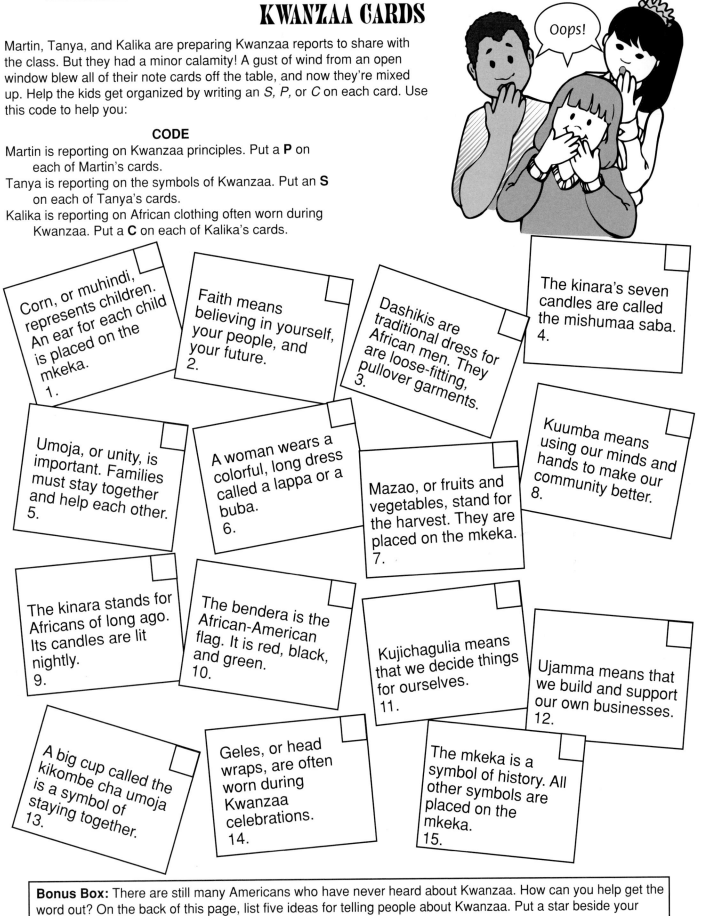

Corn, or muhindi, represents children. An ear for each child is placed on the mkeka.
1.

Faith means believing in yourself, your people, and your future.
2.

Dashikis are traditional dress for African men. They are loose-fitting, pullover garments.
3.

The kinara's seven candles are called the mishumaa saba.
4.

Umoja, or unity, is important. Families must stay together and help each other.
5.

A woman wears a colorful, long dress called a lappa or a buba.
6.

Mazao, or fruits and vegetables, stand for the harvest. They are placed on the mkeka.
7.

Kuumba means using our minds and hands to make our community better.
8.

The kinara stands for Africans of long ago. Its candles are lit nightly.
9.

The bendera is the African-American flag. It is red, black, and green.
10.

Kujichagulia means that we decide things for ourselves.
11.

Ujamma means that we build and support our own businesses.
12.

A big cup called the kikombe cha umoja is a symbol of staying together.
13.

Geles, or head wraps, are often worn during Kwanzaa celebrations.
14.

The mkeka is a symbol of history. All other symbols are placed on the mkeka.
15.

Bonus Box: There are still many Americans who have never heard about Kwanzaa. How can you help get the word out? On the back of this page, list five ideas for telling people about Kwanzaa. Put a star beside your favorite idea.

A "Peace-ful" Puzzle

Martin Luther King, Jr., spent his life promoting equality and peace. In honor of his birthday on January 15, here are 20 words that need some "peace." That is, each word needs to be completed by using only the letters in the word PEACE. You'll use some of the letters in every word, and you may repeat a letter in some answers. The first one has been done for you.

1. not awake   a s l e e p
2. one who builds with wood   __ __ r __ __ n t __ r
3. one of the seven continents   __ u r o __ __
4. songbird   __ __ n __ r y
5. a main dish baked in the oven   __ __ s s __ r o l __
6. a seasoning   s __ i __ __
7. part of a book   __ h __ __ t __ r
8. dairy food   __ h __ __ s __
9. mountaintop   __ __ __ k
10. a king's home   __ __ l __ __ __
11. to make ready   __ r __ __ __ r __
12. in short supply   s __ __ r __ __
13. hesitate   __ __ u s __
14. take apart   s __ __ __ r __ t __
15. sweet dessert   __ __ k __
16. hot chocolate   __ o __ o __
17. writing material   __ __ __ __ r
18. one who delivers a sermon   __ r __ __ __ h __ r
19. a body organ   s __ l __ __ n
20. to come into sight   __ __ __ __ __ r

Bonus Box: On the back of this page, list 10 words of three or more letters each using the letters in equality. (Don't repeat letters within a word.)

Name _____

A Fight For Freedom

Each event listed below is important to Afro-American History Month. Why? Because each played a part in granting African Americans their freedoms and right to vote. In the first column of blanks, write the numbers 1–12 to show the order in which you think the events occurred. Then use reference materials to find the actual year in which each event occurred. Write the year in the blank at the end of the sentence. When you are finished, write the actual order of events in the second column of blanks.

Predicted Order   **Actual Order**

_____   _____   1.   All women—black and white—were granted the right to vote. _____

_____   _____   2.   The 14th Amendment, which protected the rights of freed slaves after the Civil War, was ratified. _____

_____   _____   3.   The Civil War began. _____

_____   _____   4.   Rhode Island became the first state to abolish slavery. _____

_____   _____   5.   In *Brown v. Board of Education of Topeka, Kansas,* the Supreme Court ruled that segregated schools were no longer legal. _____

_____   _____   6.   The 13th Amendment was approved, making all slavery illegal. _____

_____   _____   7.   The U.S. Constitution was put into effect. It included a compromise on slavery which said the Congress would not stop the slave trade for 20 years. _____

_____   _____   8.   The 24th Amendment banned the use of poll taxes in federal elections. _____

_____   _____   9.   In the Emancipation Proclamation, Abraham Lincoln declared that all slaves in the Confederate states were free. _____

_____   _____   10.   In *Plessy v. Ferguson,* the Supreme Court ruled that blacks and whites could be segregated as long as the facilities were equal. _____

_____   _____   11.   The Voting Rights Act was passed, making it easier for blacks to register to vote. _____

_____   _____   12.   The 15th Amendment was ratified, giving black male citizens the right to vote. _____

Bonus: African Americans in our country have a history marked by a struggle for freedom. Pretend that you are an adult citizen of the United States. Which freedoms below are most important to you? Rank the freedoms, with 1 being the most important. After you rank the freedoms, design a button that illustrates your most important freedom in the circle. Cut out your button and wear it. Or tape it to your notebook or bookbag.

____ freedom to move about unrestricted
____ freedom of speech
____ freedom to vote for elected officials
____ freedom to visit my place of worship
____ freedom to read what I want to read
____ freedom to live where I want to live
____ freedom to apply for any job I would like to have

Math Valentines

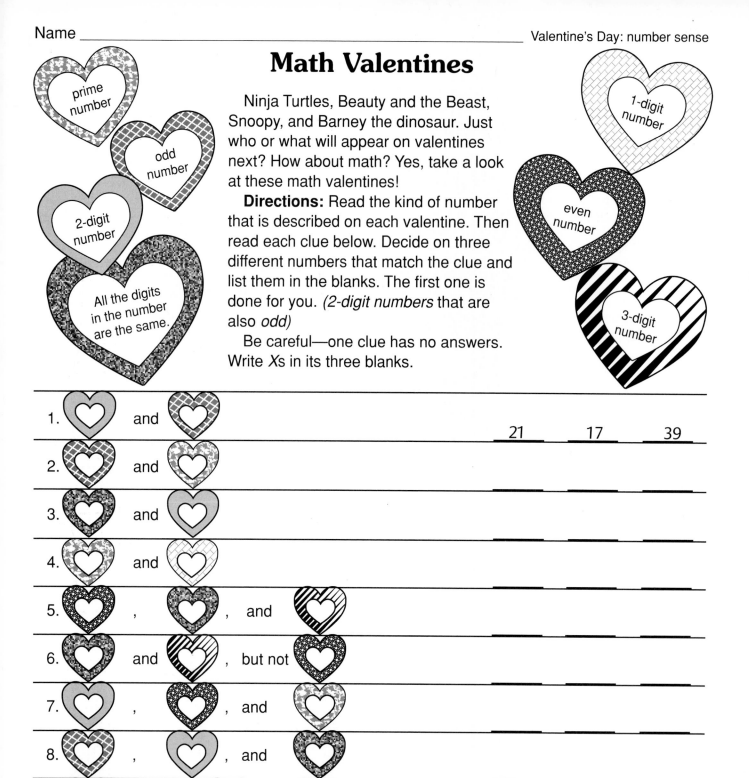

Ninja Turtles, Beauty and the Beast, Snoopy, and Barney the dinosaur. Just who or what will appear on valentines next? How about math? Yes, take a look at these math valentines!

Directions: Read the kind of number that is described on each valentine. Then read each clue below. Decide on three different numbers that match the clue and list them in the blanks. The first one is done for you. *(2-digit numbers* that are also *odd)*

Be careful—one clue has no answers. Write *X*s in its three blanks.

1. and   21   17   39

2. and

3. and

4. and

5. , , and

6. and , but not

7. , , and

8. , , and

9. , but not or

10. or , but not

11. , but not or

12. and , but not

Gimme An A!

It's only one week from Valentine's Day, and Mrs. Allbright is preparing cards to give to her students. The cards have all been signed and placed in sealed envelopes labeled with each student's name. Mrs. Allbright wants to arrange the envelopes in alphabetical order because the kids' valentine boxes are arranged that way in the classroom. Can you help her? Every student's name begins with A, so it's a little tricky. Write a 1 in the stamp of the first envelope; then finish numbering the envelopes in alphabetical order.

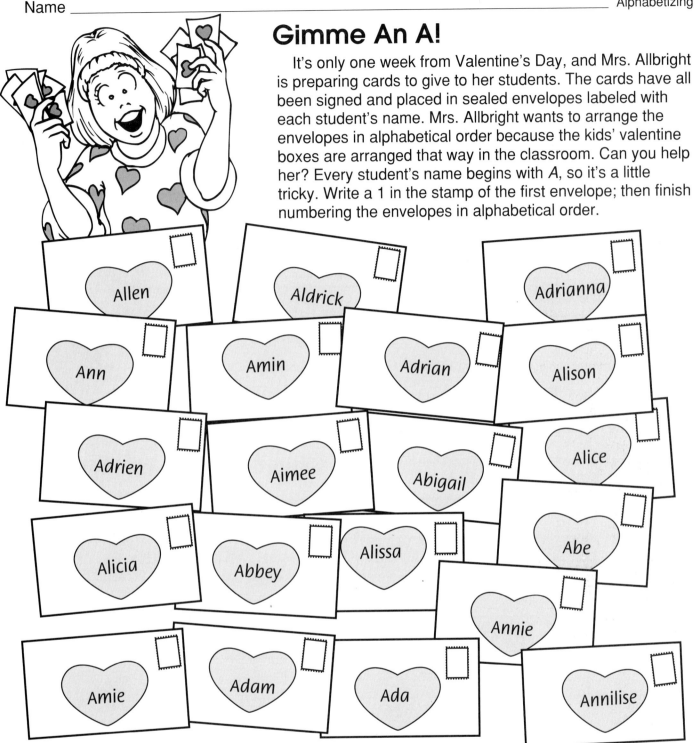

Allen
Aldrick
Adrianna
Ann
Amin
Adrian
Alison
Adrien
Aimee
Abigail
Alice
Alicia
Abbey
Alissa
Abe
Annie
Amie
Adam
Ada
Annilise

- A new student named Adansia joins Mrs. Allbright's class right before February 14. Between whose valentine boxes should Adansia's be placed? _____ and _____

- Another new student named Amber joins the class too. Between whose valentine boxes should Amber's be placed? _____ and _____

- List three more A names that could be placed after the last name on the list: _____,
_____, _____

Bonus Box: On the back of this page, list 10 to 20 first names that begin with the letter B. Then number them in alphabetical order.

Wheelin' And Dealin' With Leprechaun Lee

It's St. Patrick's Day, and who should knock on your front door but Leprechaun Lee. Lee is holding a huge pot of gold and a large bouquet of lucky four-leaf clovers. He is prepared to trade these for some human treasures he really wants: licorice, sunglasses, comic books, baseball cards, toothpicks, and squirt guns. Here are the trades Lee is willing to make in order to get these items from you:

ITEM	LEE'S TRADE	ITEM	LEE'S TRADE
5 pieces of licorice 1 comic book 3 baseball cards	3 clovers 4 clovers 5 clovers	10 toothpicks 1 squirt gun 1 pair of sunglasses	6 clovers 10 clovers 2 gold pieces

*Lee has offered to substitute 1 gold coin for every 7 clovers you collect from him.

Use the information in the chart above to answer the following questions:

1. Which of these items is worth the most to Lee? Circle your answer.
   - 20 pieces of licorice
   - 20 toothpicks
   - 9 baseball cards
   - 1 pair of sunglasses

2. Which is worth more to Lee: 10 squirt guns OR 8 pairs of sunglasses? Circle your answer.

You've decided that wheelin' and dealin' with Lee is a good idea. So you've let some of your friends in on the deal. Complete the chart as shown in the example.

Person Trading With Lee	Items To Trade	Lee's Payment In Clovers	Lee's Payment In Gold Coins
Rachel	30 toothpicks, 2 comic books, 10 pieces of licorice	18 + 8 + 6 = 32	4 coins 4 clovers left over
Clarence	2 squirt guns, 15 pieces of licorice, 30 toothpicks		
Amelia	1 pair of sunglasses, 5 comic books, 1 squirt gun		
May-Li	10 pieces of licorice, 15 toothpicks, 6 baseball cards		
Mickey	2 pairs of sunglasses, 4 squirt guns, 10 pieces of licorice		
Kirsten	2 comic books, 3 squirt guns, 20 pieces of licorice		
Rodney	7 comic books, 9 baseball cards, 1 squirt gun		
Tamira	12 baseball cards, 25 pieces of licorice, 40 toothpicks		

Bonus Box: Try to find three different combinations of treasures that could be traded for exactly 5 gold coins. Write your combinations on the back of this page.

Name _____

Recycling On The Brain!

To celebrate Earth Day, let's try some *mental* recycling. Think of one or two new uses for each of the following items. Write your ideas in the boxes.

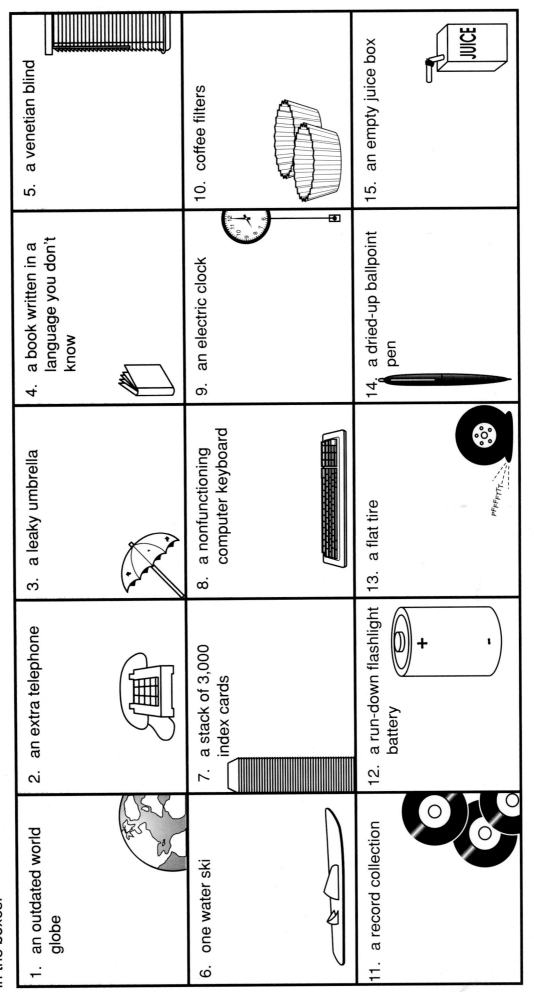

1. an outdated world globe
2. an extra telephone
3. a leaky umbrella
4. a book written in a language you don't know
5. a venetian blind
6. one water ski
7. a stack of 3,000 index cards
8. a nonfunctioning computer keyboard
9. an electric clock
10. coffee filters
11. a record collection
12. a run-down flashlight battery
13. a flat tire
14. a dried-up ballpoint pen
15. an empty juice box

Bonus Box: Choose your favorite new product from your suggestions above. On the back of this page, create a magazine ad promoting it.

©1998 The Education Center, Inc. • *The Best Of The Mailbox® Intermediate • Book 3 •* TEC835

179

I'd Rather...

April Fools' Day, or All Fools' Day, is celebrated the first day of April every year. On this day in many countries, it is tradition to play tricks on people.

The following sentences contain some tricky vocabulary words. See if you can avoid being fooled by agreeing to something you really don't mean. Read each sentence carefully; then write *yes* or *no* in the blank. Do <u>not</u> use a dictionary for this section. Good luck!

_____ 1. I'd rather be <u>bamboozled</u> by my friend than be told I was <u>astute</u>.

_____ 2. I'd rather have a <u>loquacious</u> class than one that is <u>tranquil</u>.

_____ 3. I'd rather be a <u>virtuoso</u> than a <u>novice</u> in art.

_____ 4. I'd rather be <u>aghast</u> than <u>audacious</u> in a new situation.

_____ 5. I'd rather be given an <u>arduous</u> assignment than one that is <u>effortless</u>.

_____ 6. I'd rather have a <u>rigid</u> teacher than one who is <u>benevolent</u>.

_____ 7. I'd rather live in a large <u>edifice</u> than a <u>vestibule</u>.

_____ 8. I'd rather have a <u>lackadaisical</u> worker in my group than one who is <u>diligent</u>.

> I've been told I'm susceptible to being hoodwinked. Is this a compliment or a put-down?

Now that you have decided on your responses, use a dictionary to find the correct definitions for the underlined words above. Write each word on the line in front of the correct definition below. When you have finished, look back over the sentences 1–8 above. Were you April Fooled?

_____ 1. easy to do

_____ 2. talking very much

_____ 3. doing or tending to do good

_____ 4. a person new at something

_____ 5. hard to do

_____ 6. having or showing a clever or sharp mind

_____ 7. showing little or no interest or spirit

_____ 8. feeling great shock or horror

_____ 9. strict; not changing

_____ 10. tricked or cheated

_____ 11. doing one's work in a careful and steady way

_____ 12. a person having great skill in one of the fine arts

_____ 13. bold or daring

_____ 14. calm or peaceful

_____ 15. a building, especially one that is large or looks important

_____ 16. a small hall through which a person enters a building or a room

Bonus Box: Find the meanings of the words in the speech bubble above; then answer the question, "Is this a compliment or a put-down?" Explain your answer on the back of this page.

MOMs Around The World

Mother's Day is celebrated the second Sunday in May. In honor of this occasion, take an imaginary trip around the world to find these special MOMs. Read each of the phrases below; then fill in the blanks with a location or geographical feature. Each answer in the group has either an *M* or an *O* as one of its letters. Use an atlas or other reference material to help you. The first one has been done for you. When you are finished, you will have completed a challenge that any mom would be proud of!

1. states that border Canada M I N N E S O T A _ _ _ _ _ O _ M _ _ _ _	**2.** countries located in Central America _ _ M _ _ _ _ _ O _ _ _ _ _ _ _ _ _ M _	**3.** Hawaiian Islands M _ _ _ _ O _ _ _ M _ _ _ _	**4.** mountain ranges in the world _ M _ _ _ _ _ _ _ O _ _ _ _ _ _ M _ _ _ _
5. U.S. capitals in the Midwest region _ _ _ M _ _ _ _ _ _ O _ _ _ _ _ _ M _ _ _
6. Caribbean islands M _ _ _ _ _ _ O _ _ M _ _ _ _ _ _	**7.** deserts (Hint: look in the United States, China, and South America) M _ _ _ _ _ O _ _ _ _ _ _ M _	**8.** large rivers that run through the United States M _ _ _ _ _ _ _ _ _ O _ _ _ _ _ M _ _ _ _ _ _	**9.** countries located in Northern Africa M _ _ _ _ _ _ _ _ O _ _ _ _ _ M _ _ _ _ _ _
10. states the Mississippi River borders M _ _ _ _ _ _ _ _ _ _ O _ _ M _ _ _ _ _ _ _
11. European countries M _ _ _ _ _ _ O _ _ _ _ M _ _ _ _	**12.** rivers in Africa _ M _ _ _ _ _ _ _ O _ _ M _ _ _	**13.** large cities in the state of Washington _ M _ _ _ _ _ _ _ O _ _ _ _ _ _ M _	**14.** countries in South America _ _ _ _ M _ _ O _ _ _ _ _ _ _ _ M _ _ _
15. bodies of water that the United States borders _ M _ _ _ O _ _ _ _ _ M _

Bonus Box: Using information about the state or country that you live in, create three MOMs of your own. Give them to another student to complete.

©1998 The Education Center, Inc. • *The Best Of The Mailbox® Intermediate • Book 3* • TEC835 • Key p. 192

Name _____ Teacher evaluation

About My Teacher, _____
(Teacher's Name)

Imagine that your teacher is moving hundreds of miles away this summer and is applying for a teaching position in a new community. The school board members in the new community have asked your teacher to provide references from several people. As a former student, you have been chosen to provide a reference. The school board would now like you to answer the following questions. Use the back of this sheet if you need more space.

1. What are your teacher's strengths? _____
    _____

2. In what area(s) would you like to see your teacher improve? _____
    _____

3. How does your teacher relate to students? _____
    _____

4. How does your teacher deal with misbehaving students? _____
    _____

5. In your opinion, what does your teacher like best about teaching? _____
    _____

6. What do you think your teacher likes least about teaching? _____
    _____

7. If your teacher were an animal, which animal would he/she be? Explain. _____
    _____
    _____

8. Describe your classroom's environment. (Is it organized, tidy, colorful, etc.?) _____
    _____
    _____

9. What was the most important thing your teacher taught you this year? _____
    _____

10. Describe one thing you'll always remember about being in this teacher's class. _____
    _____
    _____

Complete the following activities on another piece of paper. Fold your paper in half. Then complete question 11 on the top half and question 12 on the bottom half of the paper.

11. Draw a bird's-eye view (overhead) map of your classroom. Include student desks, the teacher's desk, the blackboard, and any other important pieces of furniture. Place a number 1 on your map to show the place where your teacher spends most of his/her time.

12. Draw a picture of your teacher doing something that he/she does very well.

Gabbing Gators

After all these weeks at school, thinking of something to write about can be as tough as an alligator's hide! Keep this page inside your writing journal or folder. When you need an idea to write about, grab a gator and write about the topic he or she suggests below. Color the gator after you've written about the topic.

Describe the perfect way to end a school year.

How was this year different from what you expected at the start of the year?

What are three things you've learned from your classmates this year?

What are three things you've learned about yourself this year?

If your classmates were asked to describe you, what do you hope they would say?

What was the most memorable news event of the school year? Why is it so memorable to you?

What's something you hope will never end?

If you could spend the first day of vacation with anyone in the world, who would you choose and why?

What kind of friend do you think you were this year? Explain your answer.

What are the three most important things you learned this year? Why do you think these things are so important?

Everyone makes mistakes. What one mistake do you not want to repeat next year?

What words of advice would you give the person who will be your teacher next year?

Page Designs

To make your written work interesting and eye-catching, use one of these layout designs for your final copy. The unlined sections show where to place your illustration(s).

Note To The Teacher: Duplicate a copy for each student to keep inside her writing folder.

A Costly Conversation

Marie and Marlene wrote the conversation below for Mr. Sawyer's English class. However, they left out a lot of the punctuation and received a grade of 54! Fortunately they were given a chance to correct their mistakes. Use what you know about punctuating quotes to help Marie and Marlene.

Directions: Rewrite the conversation on the lines below. Add capital letters, commas, and quotation marks where necessary. Each correctly used comma is worth 1 point, each correctly used pair of quotation marks is worth 2 points, and each correctly capitalized word is worth 3 points. See if you can boost Marie and Marlene's grade up to a perfect 100 points by finding the 46 points of needed corrections.

I can hardly believe that tomorrow is the last day of school Marie said sadly.

Marlene questioned aren't you excited about going to middle school?

Of course I am! responded Marie. I'm just a little nervous, that's all.

Why are you so nervous? asked Marlene.

Marie explained someone said that we'll get tons of homework in middle school!

Marlene commented I don't mind homework. I'm more worried about finding my way around that huge school!

I can help you with getting around said Marie. My sister has given me a tour of the entire school already.

Marlene exclaimed that would be great!

it's time to get to bed sighed Marie.

You're right replied Marlene. See you at school.

_____

_____

_____

_____

_____

_____

_____

_____

_____

_____

_____

_____

_____

_____

number of commas added _____ x 1 = _____

number of quotation mark pairs added _____ x 2 = _____   Total corrected points = _____

number of words capitalized _____ x 3 = _____

Bonus Box: On the back of this page, write a phone conversation that you would just LOVE to have with your favorite famous person. Ask a classmate to proofread your punctuation.

Name _____ Spelling contract

A Piece Of The Spelling Action

Don't forget to fit spelling into your schedule this week! Choose five activities to complete with this week's spelling list. Color a puzzle piece for each activity you complete. When you've colored every piece, turn in this contract to your teacher for a special treat!

ACTIVITIES:

1. Write an ad for your favorite soft drink, car, or restaurant using at least five of your spelling words.

2. Find five words on your list that have at least three things in common. Describe this group of words in a paragraph without naming the words. Give your paragraph to a friend. See if your friend can identify the five mystery words.

3. Create a cartoon strip using at least seven of your spelling words.

4. Choose five spelling words that you think are the most difficult. Make a learning aid to help you learn the spellings.

5. Write five alliterative sentences with your spelling words.

6. Use graph paper to make a word search puzzle including all of the spelling words. Give it to a friend to solve.

7. Write a "lost and found" ad for one of your spelling words. In the ad, describe the missing word so that someone else will recognize it immediately! Choose three other words and write ads for them.

8. Write the alphabet down the left side of your paper. Beside the letters, write the numbers 1–26 in order. Now predict which three words on the spelling list will have the greatest total when the values of the letters are added. Use a calculator to find out if your predictions are accurate.

9. Write a short story using as many spelling words as you can.

10. Create your own activity: _____

_____

_____

©1998 The Education Center, Inc. • *The Best Of* The Mailbox® *Intermediate* • Book 3 • TEC835
adapted from an idea by Jill Putnam—Gr. 6, Kainalu Elementary, Kailua, HI

Note To Teacher: Give each student a copy of the contract to store in a spelling folder. When a student colors every piece in the border and turns in the sheet to you, reward him with a "No Homework" coupon or other treat; then give him a new copy of the contract.

Hungry For A Hero!

George Washington, Michael Jordan, Harriet Tubman—heroes *have* to be famous, right?
Wrong! Ordinary people can do extraordinary things! Search through a local newspaper to find
information about a member of your community whom you think is heroic. Read the article to find
out *who* was involved, *what* happened, and *when* and *where* it happened. Then think about *why*
you believe this person is heroic. Record your information on the sandwich below; then color and
cut out your sandwich.

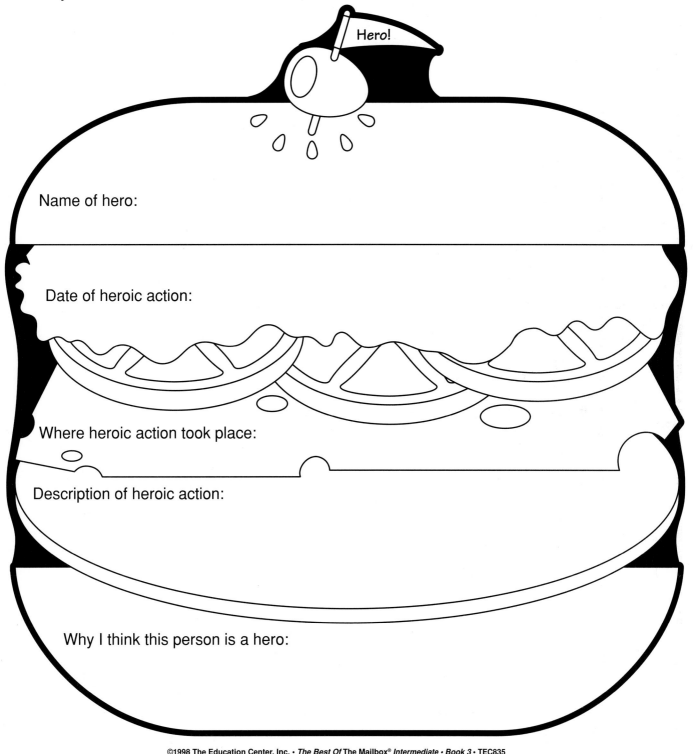

Hero!

Name of hero:

Date of heroic action:

Where heroic action took place:

Description of heroic action:

Why I think this person is a hero:

©1998 The Education Center, Inc. • *The Best Of* The Mailbox® *Intermediate • Book 3 •* TEC835

Note To The Teacher: Post the finished hero sandwiches on a bulletin board titled "A Taste Of Community Heroes."

Look What's Ahead!

Date: _____

Dear Parent,

Learning how to be responsible is an important part of becoming a successful student. Organizing time wisely and planning ahead are skills every student needs.

Your child needs to start preparing for the following assignment:

PROJECT	TEST
Description: _____	Subject: _____
_____	Date of test: _____
_____	What to study: _____
Due date: _____	_____
Additional comments: _____	_____
_____	_____
_____	_____
_____	_____
_____	_____

Please encourage your child to work on this project or study for this test daily and not wait until the last minute. Then please sign below, cut on the dotted line, and have your child return the signed portion to school.

Thank you for assisting me in helping your child learn to be a responsible student.

Signed: _____

- -

Cut on the dotted line and return the bottom portion only.

Student's Name: _____

Parent's Signature: _____

Note To The Teacher: Before duplicating, complete the appropriate section; then date the letter and sign your name where indicated. Give each child a copy to take home at least one week before a major test and even earlier for a major project.

Let's Pull Together!

_____
date

Dear _____,

    Would you please take a few minutes to answer the questions below? Your responses will help us prepare for our upcoming conference. I look forward to meeting with you on _____ _____.

    Please return this questionnaire before our scheduled conference day.

                  Thank you,

- What subject(s) does your child enjoy most?_____
  Why?_____
  _____
  _____

- What subject(s) seems difficult for your child?_____
  Why?_____
  _____
  _____

- About how much time does your child spend each night with homework and reading?
  _____

- Does your child participate in any after-school activities?_____
  If so, list them: _____
  _____

- Please list any concerns that you think we should address during our conference:
  _____
  _____
  _____
  _____

Note To Teacher: Send this questionnaire home about two weeks before scheduled conferences. Use parents' responses to prepare for your meeting.

Answer Keys

	A donor (red water)		B donor (blue water)		AB donor (purple water)		O donor (clear water)	
A receiver (red water)	color change? YES **(NO)**	**(SAFE)** or UNSAFE?	color change? **(YES)** NO	SAFE or **(UNSAFE?)**	color change? **(YES)** NO	SAFE or **(UNSAFE?)**	color change? YES **(NO)**	**(SAFE)** or UNSAFE?
B receiver (blue water)	color change? **(YES)** NO	SAFE or **(UNSAFE?)**	color change? YES **(NO)**	**(SAFE)** or UNSAFE?	color change? **(YES)** NO	SAFE or **(UNSAFE?)**	color change? YES **(NO)**	**(SAFE)** or UNSAFE?
AB receiver (purple water)	color change? YES **(NO)**	**(SAFE)** or UNSAFE?	color change? YES **(NO)**	**(SAFE)** or UNSAFE?	color change? YES **(NO)**	**(SAFE)** or UNSAFE?	color change? YES **(NO)**	**(SAFE)** or UNSAFE?
O receiver (clear water)	color change? **(YES)** NO	SAFE or **(UNSAFE?)**	color change? **(YES)** NO	SAFE or **(UNSAFE?)**	color change? **(YES)** NO	SAFE or **(UNSAFE?)**	color change? YES **(NO)**	**(SAFE)** or UNSAFE?

1. 206
2. 85
3. 13,000
4. 600
5. 300
6. 60,000
7. 106
8. 100,000
9. 40
10. 20
11. 22
12. 4
13. 9,000
14. 90
15. 500
16. 100
17. 100,000
18. 32

Page 77 (Bonus Box answers in bold.)

1. < **85.0**
2. < **18.6**
3. > **544.0**
4. < **7.44**
5. > **418.0**
6. < **4.04**
7. > **858.0**
8. < **4.04**
9. > **60.45**
10. > **87.23**
11. < **13.78**
12. > **65.3**
13. > **2,049.0**
14. < **256.5**
15. > **1,025.0**
16. < **124.62**
17. > **8,947.0**
18. > **281.16**
19. > **48,438.0**
20. < **4.55**

Page 89

1. 1/2
2. 1/2
3. 1/2
4. 1/2
5. 1/2
6. 2/4 or 1/2
7. 1/4
8. 1/2
9. 1/4
10. 1/4
11. 1/4
12. 2/4 or 1/2
13. 1/8
14. 1/8
15. 1/8
16. 1/16
17. 2/4 or 1/2
18. 3/4

Bonus Box: Answers will vary.
One solution:

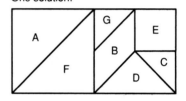

Page 78

	Divisible by...								
	2	3	4	5	6	8	9	10
16	✓		✓			✓		
258	✓	✓			✓			
13,795				✓				
6,076	✓		✓					
351		✓					✓	
9,088	✓		✓			✓		
51,234	✓	✓			✓			
180	✓	✓	✓	✓	✓		✓	✓
469,440	✓	✓	✓	✓	✓	✓	✓	✓
721								
31,968	✓	✓	✓		✓	✓	✓	
16,080	✓	✓	✓	✓	✓	✓		✓

Bonus Box: Total number of checks on chart = 45; 721 had no checks

Page 95

Possible answers include:
  A —active, angrily
  B —bashful, boisterously
  C —cautious, carefully
  D —dirty, diligently
  E —educated, easily
  F —frisky, feverishly
  G —gray, greedily
  H —hungry, happily
  I —impressive, informally
  J —jolly, joyfully
  K —keen, kindly
  L —limber, lazily
  M —marvelous, mischievously
  N —newborn, nicely
  O —old, outlandishly
  P —pretty, properly
  Q —quick, quietly
  R —red, remarkably
  S —stinky, slowly
  T —tame, timidly
  U —uncomfortable, urgently
  V —valuable, visibly
  W —white, wonderfully
  X —You're excused from this one!
  Y —young, yearningly
  Z —zany, zealously

Page 167

Bryce could buy 20 jawbreakers ($.50), 75 lollipops ($7.50), and 5 chocolate bars ($1.00). Or Bryce could buy 48 jawbreakers ($1.20), 26 lollipops ($2.60), and 26 chocolate bars ($5.20).

Answer to Bonus Box: Beth should buy 40 jawbreakers ($1.00) and 60 lollipops ($6.00). Bob should buy 68 jawbreakers ($1.70), 31 lollipops ($3.10), and 1 chocolate bar ($.20).

Answer Keys

Page 137

Possible answers:

1. There are rumors that the house is haunted. The Darrows have scared away anyone who rented the house.
2. Thomas is bothered and angry about it. Mr. Small is also disturbed. Mrs. Small likes the furniture arrangement. Thomas is distrustful of Mr. Pluto.
3. Thomas decides to investigate the hole under the porch and falls into the hidden passageway. He becomes frightened by a sound in the tunnel, drops his flashlight, and becomes disoriented.
4. Mr. Pluto chases Thomas in the woods. Even though Mr. Pluto is lame in one leg, he's able to run Thomas down and even pick him up.
5. The Small family finds the three triangles. Mr. Small decides that he and Thomas will have to stand watch during the night.
6. Mr. Small goes to confront Mr. Pluto because he thinks Mr. Pluto vandalized their kitchen. While looking for Mr. Pluto, he and Thomas find the secret cavern.
7. Mr. Pluto has become sick and weak. He's worried that the Darrows will take advantage of him and find the treasure now that he's sick.
8. Mayhew hears from Carr that a new family has moved into the house. He decides that he must make sure they leave his father alone and don't discover whatever his father is hiding from the Darrows.
9. They frighten and embarrass the Darrows so much that the Darrows will probably stop bothering Mr. Pluto.
10. Mr. Pluto is able to relax and stop worrying about the treasures. Thomas and Mr. Small will probably spend a lot of time in the cavern inventorying the treasures.

Page 170

Answers will vary. Students may group numbers in different ways and use different signs to get the same results. Remember: operations in ( ) are always done first. If an equation does not have ( ), multiply and divide from left to right; then add and subtract from left to right.

1. $6 \times 4 \div 3 = 8$
2. $4 \times 12 \div 6 = 8$
3. $3 + 10 \div 2 = 8$
4. $9 + 8 - 3 \times 3 = 8$
5. $7 \times 5 \div 5 + 1 = 8$
6. $(8 + 8) \times 3 \div 6 = 8$
7. $12 \times 6 \div 24 + 5 = 8$
8. $40 \times 20 \div (4 \times 25) = 8$
9. $8 \times 8 \div 8 = 8$
10. $8/8 + 8 = 9$
11. $888 \div 8 = 111$
12. $88 - (8 \times 8) = 24$
13. $8/8 + 8/8 + 8 = 10$
14. $88.8 - 8.8 = 80$

Page 171

There are hundreds of ways that Uncle Bigbucks's square is magical! Listed below are just a few examples:

- The four corner boxes plus the four middle boxes add up to 260.
- Any group of eight adjoining boxes (four boxes wide and two boxes high) adds up to 260. There are 35 such groups.
- Any group of eight adjoining boxes (two boxes wide and four boxes high) adds up to 260. There are 35 such groups.
- Any group of four adjoining boxes (two boxes x two boxes) adds up to 130. There are 49 such groups.
- Any group of eight boxes that form an octagon (for example: 14, 53, 6, 59, 12, 51, 4, and 61) adds up to 260. There are 25 such groups.
- In the first two columns of boxes, the sums of the side-by-side boxes are 113, 17, 113, 17, etc.
- In the second and third columns of boxes, the sums of the side-by-side boxes all equal 65.
- In the third and fourth columns of boxes, the sums of the side-by-side boxes are 17, 113, 17, 113, etc.
- In the fourth and fifth columns of boxes, the sums of the side-by-side boxes are 33, 97, 33, 97, etc.
- In the fifth and sixth columns of boxes, the sums of the side-by-side boxes are 49, 81, 49, 81, etc.
- In the sixth and seventh columns of boxes, the sums of the side-by-side boxes all equal 65.
- In the seventh and eighth columns of boxes, the sums of the side-by-side boxes are 81, 49, 81, 49, etc.

Page 113

1. Seven ways (see the chart):

TD (6)	PAT (1)	S (2)	FG (3)	
2	--	--	--	12
1	1	1	1	12
1	--	3	--	12
1	--	--	2	12
--	--	6	--	12
--	--	3	2	12
--	--	--	4	12

2. 56 passengers ÷ 7 = 8 vans
   56 passengers + 8 drivers = 64 people in all
3. 53
4. 13 (9 small triangles, 3 medium-sized triangles, and 1 large one)
5. 10 (AB, AC, AD, AE; BC, BD, BE; CD, CE, DE)
6. 15 (1¢, 5¢, 6¢, 10¢, 11¢, 15¢, 16¢, 25¢, 26¢, 30¢, 31¢, 35¢, 36¢, 40¢, 41¢)
7. 32 (8 x 2 = 16 sides; 16 x 4 = 64 pockets; 1/2 of 64 = 32 photos)
8. 45
9. 24 ways (see the chart):

3	2	1
0	0	14
0	1	12
0	2	10
0	3	8
0	4	6
0	5	4
0	6	2
0	7	0
1	5	1
1	4	3
1	3	5
1	2	7
1	1	9
1	0	11
2	4	0
2	3	2
2	2	4
2	1	6
2	0	8
3	2	1
3	1	3
3	0	5
4	1	0
4	0	2

10. There are 57 pennies in all. 57 ÷ 3 = 19. Remove one penny from the first stack and three pennies from the third stack. Add them to the middle stack.

Page 172

The real Holly Jolly ornaments are numbers 2, 4, 6, 7, 12, 14, 16, 21, and 25. The letters of the Holly Jolly ornaments are U, I, A, T, T, N, C, H, and E, which—when placed in correct order—spell AUTHENTIC.

Page 173

1. S
2. P
3. C
4. S
5. P
6. C
7. S
8. P
9. S
10. S
11. P
12. P
13. S
14. C
15. S

Answer Keys

Page 174

1. asleep
2. carpenter
3. Europe
4. canary
5. casserole
6. spice
7. chapter
8. cheese
9. peak
10. palace
11. prepare
12. scarce
13. pause
14. separate
15. cake
16. cocoa
17. paper
18. preacher
19. spleen
20. appear

Page 175

Actual Order

9	1. 1920
6	2. 1868
3	3. 1861
1	4. 1774
10	5. 1954
5	6. 1865
2	7. 1788
11	8. 1964
4	9. 1863
8	10. 1896
12	11. 1965
7	12. 1870

Page 180

Answers will vary for the *yes/no* section.

1. effortless
2. loquacious
3. benevolent
4. novice
5. arduous
6. astute
7. lackadaisical
8. aghast
9. rigid
10. bamboozled
11. diligent
12. virtuoso
13. audacious
14. tranquil
15. edifice
16. vestibule

Bonus Box: It is a put-down because it means that he's easily fooled or deceived.

Page 176

Answers will vary. Suggested answers:

1. 21, 17, 39 (any odd, two-digit number)
2. 3, 5, 7, 11, 13, 17 (any prime number, except 2)
3. 11, 22, 33 (44...99)
4. 2, 3, 5 (7)
5. 222, 444, 666, (888)
6. 111, 333, 555, (777, 999)
7. X X X
8. 11, 33, 55 (77, 99)
9. 1,111; 2,222; 3,333 (4,444...9,999 and larger numbers that are composed of the same digit)
10. 20, 76, 112 (any two-digit or three-digit even number)
11. 100, 102, 180 (any three-digit number that is even or a multiple of 5 would definitely not be prime; also cannot have all like digits)
12. 15, 21, 25, 27, 33, 35 (and other two-digit odd numbers that are not prime)

Page 177

1. Abbey
2. Abe
3. Abigail
4. Ada
5. Adam
6. Adrian
7. Adrianna
8. Adrien
9. Aimee
10. Aldrick
11. Alice
12. Alicia
13. Alison
14. Alissa
15. Allen
16. Amie
17. Amin
18. Ann
19. Annie
20. Annilise

- Adam and Adrian
- Allen and Amie
- Answers will vary.

Page 178

1. 9 baseball cards
2. 8 pairs of sunglasses

Clarence: 20 + 9 + 18 = 47	6 coins, 5 clovers left over
Amelia: 14 + 20 + 10 = 44	6 coins, 2 clovers left over
May-Li: 6 + 9 + 10 = 25	3 coins, 4 clovers left over
Mickey: 28 + 40 + 6 = 74	10 coins, 4 clovers left over
Kirsten: 8 + 30 + 12 = 50	7 coins, 1 clover left over
Rodney: 28 + 15 + 10 = 53	7 coins, 4 clovers left over
Tamira: 20 + 15 + 24 = 59	8 coins, 3 clovers left over

Bonus Box: Answers will vary. Some possibilities include:
3 baseball cards + 10 toothpicks + 1 squirt gun + 1 pair of sunglasses
3 squirt guns + 3 baseball cards
5 pieces of licorice + 1 comic book + 2 pairs of sunglasses

Page 185

"I can hardly believe that tomorrow is the last day of school," Marie said sadly.

Marlene questioned, "Aren't you excited about going to middle school?"

"Of course I am!" responded Marie. "I'm just a little nervous, that's all."

"Why are you so nervous?" asked Marlene.

Marie explained, "Someone said that we'll get tons of homework in middle school!"

Marlene commented, "I don't mind homework. I'm more worried about finding my way around that huge school!"

"I can help you with getting around," said Marie. "My sister has given me a tour of the entire school already."

Marlene exclaimed, "That would be great!"

"It's time to get to bed," sighed Marie.

"You're right," replied Marlene. "See you at school."

number of commas added __8__ x 1 = __8__
number of quotation-mark pairs added __13__ x 2 = __26__
number of words capitalized __4__ x 3 = __12__
Total corrected points = __46__

Page 181

1. Minnesota, Washington, Montana
2. Guatemala, Costa Rica, Panama
3. Maui, Oahu, Molokai
4. Andes Mountains, Rocky Mountains, Himalayas
5. Bismarck, Lincoln, Des Moines
6. Jamaica, Puerto Rico, Dominica
7. Mojave, Gobi, Atacama
8. Mississippi, Colorado, Missouri
9. Mali, Ethiopia, Morocco
10. Minnesota, Iowa, Missouri
11. Germany, Portugal, Romania
12. Limpopo, Congo, Zambezi
13. Olympia, Spokane, Tacoma
14. Surinam, Bolivia, Colombia
15. Lake Michigan, Atlantic Ocean, Gulf of Mexico